T0290621

Introduction to Public History

ABOUT THE SERIES

The American Association for State and Local History Book Series addresses issues critical to the field of state and local history through interpretive, intellectual, scholarly, and educational texts. To submit a proposal or manuscript to the series, please request proposal guidelines from AASLH headquarters: AASLH Editorial Board, 2021 21st Ave. South, Suite 320, Nashville, Tennessee 37212. Telephone: (615) 320-3203. Website: www.aaslh.org.

ABOUT THE ORGANIZATION

The American Association for State and Local History (AASLH) is a national history membership association headquartered in Nashville, Tennessee. AASLH provides leadership and support for its members who preserve and interpret state and local history in order to make the past more meaningful to all Americans. AASLH members are leaders in preserving, researching, and interpreting traces of the American past to connect the people, thoughts, and events of yesterday with the creative memories and abiding concerns of people, communities, and our nation today. In addition to sponsorship of this book series, AASLH publishes *History News* magazine, a newsletter, technical leaflets and reports, and other materials; confers prizes and awards in recognition of outstanding achievement in the field; supports a broad education program and other activities designed to help members work more effectively; and advocates on behalf of the discipline of history. To join AASLH, go to www.aaslh.org or contact Membership Services, AASLH, 2021 21st Ave. South, Suite 320, Nashville, TN 37212.

Introduction to Public History

Interpreting the Past, Engaging Audiences

Cherstin M. Lyon
*California State University,
San Bernardino*

Elizabeth M. Nix
University of Baltimore

Rebecca K. Shrum
*Indiana University-Purdue
University Indianapolis*

ROWMAN & LITTLEFIELD
Lanham • Boulder • New York • London

Executive Editor: Charles Harmon
Assistant Editor: Kathleen O'Brien
Senior Marketing Manager: Deborah Hudson
Interior Designer: Rhonda Baker
Cover Designer: Chloe Batch

Credits and acknowledgments for material borrowed from other sources, and reproduced with permission, appear on the appropriate page within the text.

Published by Rowman & Littlefield
A wholly owned subsidary of The Rowman & Littlefield Publishing Group, Inc.
4501 Forbes Boulevard, Suite 200, Lanham, Maryland 20706
www.rowman.com

Unit A, Whitacre Mews, 26-34 Stannary Street, London SE11 4AB, United Kingdom

British Library Cataloguing in Publication Information Available

Library of Congress Cataloging-in-Publication Data

Names: Lyon, Cherstin M., 1971– author. | Nix, Elizabeth M. (Elizabeth Morrow), 1964– author. | Shrum, Rebecca K. (Rebecca Kathleen), 1972– author.
Title: Introduction to public history : interpreting the past, engaging audiences / Cherstin M. Lyon, Elizabeth M. Nix, Rebecca K. Shrum.
Description: Lanham, MD : Rowman & Littlefield, [2017] | Includes index.
Identifiers: LCCN 2016051418 (print) | LCCN 2016053613 (ebook) | ISBN 9781442272217 (cloth : alk. paper) | ISBN 9781442272224 (pbk. : alk. paper) | ISBN 9781442272231 (electronic)
Subjects: LCSH: Public history. | Public history—Textbooks.
Classification: LCC D16.163 .L96 2017 (print) | LCC D16.163 (ebook) | DDC 900—dc23
LC record available at https://lccn.loc.gov/2016051418

♾™ The paper used in this publication meets the minimum requirements of American National Standard for Information Sciences—Permanence of Paper for Printed Library Materials, ANSI/NISO Z39.48-1992.

Printed in the United States of America

For Our Children

Gareth Imparato, Nicholas Imparato, Forrest H. Lyon,
Savannah M. Lyon, and Matthew Brady Shrum

Contents

Preface for Instructors

Welcome to *Introduction to Public History: Interpreting the Past, Engaging Audiences*. We wrote this book to provide public history educators with a foundational text that is short enough to adapt to a variety of situations, that will aid in assessment of student learning, and that can support more in-depth examinations of the questions that drive a variety of public history projects and venues. That said, we do not intend to provide a comprehensive, encyclopedic examination of every aspect of public history, nor cover every venue where nonacademic audiences encounter historical content. Given that the majority of students who take public history coursework do not become practicing public historians, we focus here on issues that arise at the kinds of venues that everyone encounters as consumers of the past.

This collaborative project began as a series of conversations between professors of public history at the annual meetings of the National Council on Public History (NCPH), the main professional organization supporting public history practitioners and teachers. One of those key conversations took place in Portland, Oregon, in 2010 at a working group organized by Cherstin Lyon and Rebecca Shrum, with Elizabeth Nix as a discussant, along with Donna DeBlasio, Jennifer Dickey, Catherine Lewis, Allison Marsh, and Phillip Payne. We continued to seek input from colleagues (both anonymously and known) and from students as we have developed this manuscript from the proposal stage, through an earlier draft, to the published version you have before you. Despite our efforts to meet diverse needs with a single volume, we know that each program, each instructor, and each group of students is unique. We encourage instructors to use this book in conjunction with the resources they have on their campuses and in their communities to develop activities and projects for their classes to serve as a genuine springboard into the field with as many local connections as possible.

Philosophy of the Book

The book as a whole aligns with the NCPH "Best Practices" for undergraduate students as a basic framework for introducing public history to undergraduate or graduate students.[1] Regardless of a student's standing, public history should first be rooted in the best practices of history and should be grounded in a solid understanding of historical content. Introductory courses are useful to orient students to the range of fields in which public history is practiced. Merely presenting the fields of practice, however, can look like a parade of career options to students, and also suggest that public history is a vocational choice rather than a distinct scholarly and intellectual enterprise with its own fundamental practices, premises, and lines of inquiry. Focusing on careers in this way can obscure how we all encounter and engage with public history and why it is important for everyone to understand what public history is and how it functions in our society.

This book is organized instead around the questions and ethical dilemmas that drive public history work so that students can understand the field's core values and practices. We leave the option open to orient students to their career opportunities as a way of considering next steps and to adapt to the special offerings of various institutions. Just as no one book can cover every place where history is practiced and do it well, no single university trains students for all specialty fields in public history. This book is designed to be flexible so that instructors can find ways to highlight their own strengths and to use the common questions as a way of exploring their own areas of expertise and to direct students to ask common questions of diverse fields of practice.

The authors of this volume are practicing public historians who teach history and public history to a mix of undergraduate and graduate students at universities. We approach the field from a framework that our colleague Cathy Stanton has described as "progressive public history." This type of public history has an activist identity and is, as Stanton wrote, often "concentrated in the areas of the profession that overlap most closely with the academy."[2] As scholars and practitioners, we engage with public history out of the conviction that it has the ability to make our world a more just and ethical society. Progressive public history can harness the innate sense people already have of themselves as historical interpreters, working with them to uncover liberatory tools in their lives, communities, and nations. Progressive public history can approach activism, but the public historian is always bound first and foremost to the ethics of the historical profession. Public history can be something more but is never less than an analysis based on sound historical evidence. By beginning with an overview of public history from a progressive model that places ethics and justice at the center of practice, we hope that students will be well positioned to ask critical questions in the future, either as consumers of public history or as practitioners themselves.

We believe that if students gain a strong foundation in the ethics and theories that ground the decisions that well-trained public historians make every day through reflective practice, they will be more confident in making informed decisions when the demands of working in the field do not necessarily correspond with textbook instructions. In consulting with practitioners, the overwhelming feedback we have received consistently over the past decade is that the classroom does not necessarily prepare you for the decisions that you must make when facilitating a wedding at a historic house, or navigating interpersonal relations with board members or community donors. When in doubt, we all retreat to our core values and guiding principles. This book is designed to support that framework of educating future public historians, as well as the future teachers and consumers of history.

Structure of the Book

Each chapter introduces a concept or common practice to students, highlighting key terms for student review and for instructor assessment of student learning. The body of each chapter introduces theories and basic conceptual building blocks intermixed with case studies to illustrate these points. Footnotes give credit to our sources, but also serve as breadcrumbs for instructors who might like to assign more in-depth reading for more advanced students and/or for the purposes of lecture development. Each chapter ends with suggestions for activities that we have tried with our own students.

Finally, each chapter contains suggestions for further study. This list is not a bibliography for the chapter, but a list of suggested readings, books, and websites that can deepen student exposure to the topic and support instructor development of supplemental readings to suit the level of their students and to design further assignments for the class. Above all else, we hope that instructors will find creative ways to adapt this book as a tool to enhance their own expertise and their own way of introducing students to the dynamic and creative field of public history.

We welcome your feedback and questions.

Cherstin M. Lyon, California State University, San Bernardino, clyon@csusb.edu
Elizabeth M. Nix, University of Baltimore, enix@ubalt.edu
Rebecca K. Shrum, Indiana University-Purdue University Indianapolis, rshrum@iupui.edu

Notes

1. National Council on Public History, "Best Practices in Public History: Public History for Undergraduate Students," available at: http://ncph.org/wp-content/uploads/2010/08/Undergrad-Best-Practice.pdf.
2. Cathy Stanton, *The Lowell Experiment: Public History in a Postindustrial City* (Amherst: University of Massachusetts Press, 2006), 15.

Introducing Public History

WHEN YOU THINK ABOUT learning history, do you imagine sitting in a classroom and reading a textbook? The book you now hold introduces a different approach to history that focuses on engagement. *Introduction to Public History: Interpreting the Past, Engaging Audiences* addresses history that people encounter outside the classroom and beyond the traditional history text. Its chapters guide you, the student, through an initial encounter with the field of public history, introducing you to underlying issues, theories, and core principles that ground the field. This book focuses on the big questions that underpin the how and, most importantly, the why of public history.

What Is Public History?

Public history is so diverse that even practitioners struggle to define it succinctly. In 1978, historian Robert Kelley, who founded one of the early graduate programs in public history, wrote, "Public history refers to the employment of historians and the historical method outside of academia."[1] If we agree that academia is a term used to describe institutions of higher learning like colleges and universities, then what is "outside of academia"? You can find public history at a museum, in a historic house, on a walking tour of a historic district, or on YouTube. Public historians can produce documentaries, historical markers, and smartphone apps. The field is broad enough to include more ephemeral venues as well: a community event, a theatrical performance, a folk-art demonstration. There are more forms of public history than we can name here, and new ones appear all the time, which is one of the things that makes the field vibrant and exciting.

But the question of venue—"inside the academy" vs. "everywhere else"—does not capture all of the differences between public history and traditional academic history. Before we look at those differences, however, we must recognize what all historians share with one another. This is what Kelley called, in his definition, the "historical method." All forms of history begin in the same place: with solid historical research based on a rigorous examination of available sources. All historians, regardless of where they work or who makes up their audience, rely on the systematic and critical examination of sources within their historical contexts to reveal stories of the past, to explain change and continuity over time, to consider contingency, and to reconcile competing versions of past events as preserved in a variety of historical sources. Through this process, we assign meaning to the past, taking a wide range of materials and using them to form a coherent argument about the meaning and significance of past events. These practices make up the **historical method**. Historians place their work within the context of what we already know and make efforts to contribute to that knowledge by using sources that have not been used before, by asking new questions of familiar sources, or by using sources in novel ways. The centrality of the historical method to public history is the reason you will find "Thinking Historically" as the next chapter in this textbook.

If public history and academic history share similar research methods and interpretive standards, what distinguishes them from one another? Some key concepts stand out for public history:

1. **Audience**. The audience is public, not academic. Public historians think differently about audience than they would when sharing their research in academic circles. The general public does not think about their own pasts or their relationship with the past the same way historians think about history. Understanding the audience means understanding what different publics expect and value when it comes to engaging in historical exploration. This textbook will introduce you to several different theoretical perspectives that help us work more effectively and ethically with public audiences.

2. **Collaboration**. Public historians practice two types of collaboration. First, they collaborate with the public. Public historians need to think beyond how they will best serve the public's needs as audiences or consumers of history, and to think carefully about how they will work with **stakeholders**—those who have a specific interest or a stake in the topics we study, the communities about which we write, or the institutions or places where we work. Stakeholders might include the people whose story a public history project will tell, board members at a public history institution,

funders, or politicians. Stakeholders are also potential members of the audience, but we distinguish them because of the specific relationships they have with the history being interpreted. Collaboration with the stakeholders whose history is being told is one of the defining features of public history work. The second form of essential collaboration requires work with professionals in other disciplines. Since public history involves skills that go beyond those of a historian, public historians collaborate with scholars and experts in other fields. Academic historians often work alone to produce a monograph; public historians work in teams to produce projects.

3. **Reflective Practice**. Public historians intentionally incorporate what they learn from the successes and failures of their professional experiences into future interpretive and engagement strategies. All historians have ethical responsibilities. We must represent primary sources fairly and accurately and acknowledge when we draw on the work of other scholars in our own work. Public historians have added ethical responsibilities that require many layers of reflective practice that will be discussed throughout the book.

Audience

Who Is the Public? What Is Their Relationship with "History" and "The Past"?

If one of the major defining characteristics of public history is a public audience, then who is this "public" and what is their relationship with history, or what some prefer to call "the past"? In 1994 and 1995, a group of historians conducted extensive phone interviews with 1,453 Americans in an attempt to explore how they understand their pasts and interact with history. In *The Presence of the Past: Popular Uses of History in American Life* (1998), historians Roy Rosenzweig and David Thelen interpreted the interviews and argued that Americans actively engaged with the past as they sought to understand the forces that had shaped the individual people that they were in the present and that would affect the people they wanted to become in the future. The survey respondents also expressed strong preferences for how they got information about the past. They trusted museums the most, with personal accounts from relatives following closely in second place, and firsthand accounts from someone who had been present at an event in third place. College professors, high school teachers, and nonfiction books still held some credence, but participants ranked movies and television programs as the least trustworthy (table 1.1). Americans also told the researchers they wanted to be able to assess what they learned from any source against their own previous knowledge and draw conclusions for themselves. Before Rosenzweig and Thelen, historians had not spent much energy analyzing their audience. While museum studies scholars and practitioners were already thinking deeply about audience reactions to exhibitions and museum visits, Rosenzweig and Thelen looked at people's relationship with the past in the totality of their lives. Their study remains our best source of information about the attitudes different populations have about their own relationship with history and the past, something that is not captured in visitor surveys about specific exhibitions.

Table 1.1. Trustworthiness of Sources of Information about the Past—By Racial/Ethnic Group

HOW TRUSTWORTHY DO YOU THINK ____ ARE AS A SOURCE OF INFORMATION ABOUT THE PAST?	RACIAL/ETHNIC GROUPS				
	NATIONAL SAMPLE	WHITE	AFRICAN AMERICAN	MEXICAN AMERICA	PINE RIDGE OGLALA SIOUX
Museums	8.4 (778)	8.5 (608)	8.1 (283)	8.6 (185)	7.1 (176)
Personal accounts from your grandparents or other relatives	8.0 (789)	8.0 (615)	8.4 (289)	8.2 (189)	8.8 (181)
Conversations with someone who was there	7.8 (790)	7.8 (611)	7.9 (290)	8.2 (188)	8.0 (177)
College history professors	7.3 (692)	7.4 (537)	7.0 (261)	8.3 (172)	7.1 (161)
High school history teachers	6.6 (771)	6.7 (594)	6.2 (293)	7.5 (189)	5.9 (178)
Nonfiction books	6.4 (747)	6.4 (583)	5.6 (278)	6.6 (181)	5.4 (169)
Movies or television programs about the past	5.0 (783)	4.9 (610)	5.2 (291)	6.0 (189)	4.2 (180)

Respondents were asked about seven "places where people might get information about the past." They rated the trustworthiness of each "as a source of information about the past using a 1 to 10 scale," with 1 meaning "not at all trustworthy" and 10 meaning "very trustworthy." This table reports the mean score the national sample and four racial/ethnic groups gave the sources of information in the far-left column. The number in parentheses indicate the number of respondents on which each mean is based.

Table 1.2. Most Important Pasts—By Racial/Ethnic Group

KNOWING ABOUT THE PAST OF WHICH OF THE FOLLOWING FOUR AREAS OR GROUPS IS MOST IMPORTANT TO YOU?	RACIAL/ETHNIC GROUPS				
	NATIONAL SAMPLE	WHITE	AFRICAN AMERICAN	MEXICAN AMERICAN	PINE RIDGE OGLALA SIOUX
The past of your family	66%	69%	59%	61%	50%
The past of your racial or ethnic group	8%	4%	26%	10%	38%
The past of the community in which you now live	4%	3%	4%	7%	7%
The past of the United States	22%	24%	11%	22%	5%
	100% N=796	100% N=616	100% N=297	100% N=191	100% N=176

Respondents were asked the following question: "Knowing about the past of which of the following four areas or groups is most important to you—the past of your family, the past of your racial or ethnic group, the past of the community in which you now live, or the past of the United States?" This table reports the percentage of respondents in the national sample and four racial/ethnic groups that chose each of the pasts in the far left column.

Tables 1.1 and 1.2 are from Roy Rosenzweig and David Thelen, *The Presence of the Past: Popular Uses of History in American Life* (New York: Columbia University Press, 1998) and are reproduced (with edited captions) with permission of the publisher from http://chnm.gmu.edu/survey/tables.html.

Experts in the science of learning have found that all humans learn within the contexts of their own experiences, just as the survey respondents from *The Presence of the Past* revealed. In their research on museum visitation, John Falk and Lynn Dierking found, "People make meaning through a constant process of relating past experiences to the present," connecting what is happening in the present to what has happened in the past.[2] It follows, then, that for public historians to engage their audiences in a meaningful experience, they must make history relevant to their lives. Understanding your audience should always come first, particularly if one primary goal is to facilitate this **contextualized learning**.

Diversity of Public Experiences

"The public" includes many different people with very different personal experiences. Diversity may come in the form of age, educational background, economic standing and class, religious diversity, different abilities, diversities of language, as well as cultural, racial, and ethnic diversities. Sometimes we can understand diversity of experience in terms of privilege or marginalization. For example, nondisabled people experience privilege every day whether they recognize it or not. A person with a disability might never see someone like themselves depicted in a public history venue. In fact, disability-rights advocates had to wage protests to add a statue of President Franklin D. Roosevelt sitting in a wheelchair to the FDR Memorial in Washington, DC, although his paralysis during his presidency is now widely known. *The Presence of the Past* revealed that Americans who had historically been marginalized, specifically African Americans, American Indians, Mexican Americans, and LGBTQ (Lesbian, Gay, Bisexual, Transgender, Queer) individuals, often understood themselves to be part of a specific "collective past." African Americans, for example, used their understanding of the black past to distance themselves from an "official" version of the past organized around a dominant narrative that erased the experiences of their families and communities (table 1.2).[3] Potential stakeholders and consumers of public history projects will approach the work through the lens of their own experiences; public history practitioners need to understand that phenomenon.

Because different segments of the public will approach history differently based on their own historically situated experiences, understanding your audiences is complex. You must look deeper when examining which publics you serve as a public historian in order to consider multiple layers of experience. For example, understanding basic demographic details of your audience may be a good start, but there are variations beyond typical profiles, such as age, economic levels, gender, race, ability, and ethnicity. It is easy to become complacent if we believe we have sufficiently considered more than one point of view. Our communities are always changing, and the needs and experiences of the public are always evolving. We must reexamine who our publics are and their historical and contemporary experiences in order to find ways for them to see themselves in the histories we interpret and represent.

Who Does the Public Trust?

Rosenzweig and Thelen found that the public trusts the history they learn about in museums more than any other source, for two very different reasons. First, people in the study concluded "museums arrived at their interpretations only after experts pooled their independent research."[4] In other words, historians and professionals in other fields had worked with one another to develop interpretations; one interpretation had not been able to control the museum's agenda. Second, museum exhibits allow members of the public to interact directly with "real" objects from the past, devoid of interpretative

Photograph 1.1.   Sandy Hanebrink poses by the wheelchair statue advocates added to the Franklin Delano Roosevelt Memorial in Washington, DC. Visitors want to see themselves reflected in public history interpretation. Courtesy of Sandy Hanebrink.

layers. This direct access provides an opportunity for the audience to test an exhibit against their previous knowledge about the subject matter and to make meaning of the past in terms of their own experiences and understanding. The public does not rely on, nor do they necessarily trust, academic historians to teach them history. They prefer to place their trust in the interpretations of the past that teams of experts present outside of classrooms, where they have unmediated access to the objects and pieces of the past to analyze and view for themselves. They prefer histories that can fit within their existing understanding of the past, and enjoy learning history in ways that inform their present and reaffirm their own identities.

Banking Education versus Problem-Posing Education

Another clear takeaway from Rosenzweig and Thelen's study is that rather than being told what to think, Americans prefer to participate in the intellectual process, asking questions and considering the possible answers in relation to their own experiences and new evidence. Rosenzweig and Thelen's findings can be understood further by applying Paulo Freire's **problem-posing model of education**.[5] Freire is the theorist who helped education specialists think about banking versus problem posing as educational models. **Banking** is a model where knowledge, or in our case history, is delivered as facts prepared by the experts to be accepted by the learner and regurgitated later as proof that learning happened. This model could easily be represented by a multiple-choice test that you might have taken in a high-school history class. That kind of history—the kind the public often associates with the formal classroom—is of little use to them and was ranked well below other more trusted ways to encounter the past. In contrast, people actively absorb information about the past if they can use it to shape their own identities in the present and for the future. Freire observed this process as he developed a critical pedagogy for adult literacy education. This approach invited the public to grapple with questions and engage in the process of historical inquiry based on problems to be solved rather than content to be memorized. Problem-posing education has a liberating effect on people.

Problem-posing education empowers participants to see themselves as actors in constructing history, and it emboldens the public to participate as citizens in the shaping of the futures of their communities, cities, and nations. Problem posing, according to Freire, is at the heart of critical pedagogical praxis, which he defines as "reflection and action upon the world in order to transform it."[6] By posing a problem to an audience and asking them to use their own experience and new knowledge to develop a solution, the teacher can encourage deep learning. When ordinary people are no longer the objects of education, but, Freire observed, are humanized through problem-posing education, they understand their own position in history. They can also see themselves as actors in the process of transformation. Freire wrote, "The banking method emphasizes permanence and becomes reactionary; problem-posing education—which accepts neither a 'well-behaved' present nor a predetermined future—roots itself in the dynamic present and becomes revolutionary."[7] Freire cautioned the expert "not to consider himself or herself the proprietor of history" or to become "the prisoner of a 'circle of certainty,'" in which he or she claims to know all of the answers for everyone.[8] Historians take pride in doing the reading, knowing the details, and supporting an argument with specific pieces of evidence. But public historians must welcome the expertise of their audiences, especially stakeholders whose experiences can add to a richer understanding of the past. Inviting the audience into a dialogue instead of a lecture encourages engagement and can become a source of empowerment and even liberation for the people public historians serve. When individuals are able to take control of their own history, when they engage in a dialogical relationship with their own education, they see the work that historical understanding can do in the world.

Problem-Posing Education as "Dialogic" History

When you invite the public to participate in a conversation using common questions and shared inquiry as your approach, when you recognize that the public comes to historical inquiry with knowledge, you can engage them in a dialogue with the evidence and with your own research. In the context of public history, this exchange leads us to what theorists call **dialogic history.** The idea arises from the study of literature and suggests that people enjoy reading novels because they contain conversations between characters, as well as a dialogue between the author and the reader. When we read a novel, we enter this intimate space where we become a part of the conversation, too. Falk and Dierking have found, "Learning is a dialogue between the individual and his or her environment through time. Learning can be conceptualized as a contextually driven effort to make meaning in order to survive and prosper within the world."[9] If we approach the presentation of history to the public in this way, by inviting them into a conversation between the documents and objects and people who lived in the past, and even with historians or exhibition designers posing questions, then the visitor can likewise become a part of the conversation through dialogic history.[10]

Many public history projects approach history as dialogic history. The Museum of Chinese in America (MOCA), founded in 1980 as the New York Chinatown History Project, transformed itself into a dialogue-driven museum by examining the ways in which various people actively created what we know as New York's Chinatown. This new focus required the intentional involvement of the past and present residents of Chinatown through a wide range of community-based approaches to collecting, researching, and interpreting the neighborhood's history. As John Kuo Wei Tchen explained, "We want to fashion a learning environment in which personal memory and testimony inform and are informed by historical context and scholarship." They began by rethinking the ways in which they involved the community in creating the content of the museum. MOCA conducted conversations with historians of Chinese American history, with Chinese Americans, with residents of the surrounding areas who are not Chinese, and with tourists. Those conversations brought new memories to light and raised new areas of study for the public historians. Including stakeholders in the research and collecting phase of the project added individual stories to the record, and what emerged was not one central narrative but a variety of points of view. Tchen also corrected historical trends that had erased Chinese Americans from history when he successfully pushed for the publication of Paul Chan Pang Siu's *The Chinese Laundryman: A Study in Social Isolation*, a dissertation that the University of Chicago Press had declined to publish years earlier. Including the public in the earliest phases of research all the way through the exhibition itself and promoting scholarship where members of the public could see themselves and their families created a more meaningful experience. The liberating effect that Freire wrote about was compounded when the museum conducted a series of community conversations where the public could discuss current immigration issues, demonstrating the power of actual dialogue in a museum setting to address issues that a community was grappling with in the present, as well as the past.[11]

Tchen discovered that it was not enough to invite the community to an exhibition opening or a gala and expect that they would then become regular attenders and donors; one exhibition on a subject dear to a visitor will not lead her to become invested in the museum long term. Tchen learned that audience development is about more than effective communication of a single message or one historical investigation. The goal for many institutions is to create lasting ties with the community by involving them in every step of the collection and interpretation process.

Free-Choice Learning

When the public either consumes history or engages in public history experiences, they do so by choice in informal educational settings. **Free-choice learning** (also known as informal learning) is a term used to identify modes of learning that take place outside a standard classroom setting, such as museums, zoos, and historic sites, as well as television or film. Unlike in a standard classroom setting, there are no exams to pass and no pressure to engage with and retain the material. Rather, adults and children alike might engage with what is being presented or ignore it entirely. The public is free to choose what they will spend more of their time on, and what they will skip altogether. In fact, one director of a small regional museum once noted that many visitors entered the museum just to use the toilets!

Nikolaj Frederik Severin Grundtvig incorporated this idea of informal learning into a practice that became a Danish tradition in the mid-nineteenth century. Realizing that formal education was not meeting the needs of the poor, and inspired by Enlightenment thinking, Grundtvig believed that education must relate to people's lives. Instead of placing expert teachers in front of a formal classroom where they would present knowledge to students—particularly adult learners who could not complete formal school, or graduates for whom a university education was not the next logical step—Grundtvig imagined an educational setting where students and teachers learned together in an environment based on communal living and shared inquiry. Without the need for tests or grades, in a place where class differences could be overcome, an atmosphere of mutual trust and respect would develop. The Grundtvig folk school model has inspired educational reform and even community organizing strategies far beyond the national boundaries of Denmark, well into the twentieth century. More recently, museum researcher John Falk has documented that most adults acquire new information through free-choice learning, an increasingly important way for young people to learn as well. If sparked by their own curiosity, adults who exercise control over their learning often continue their own exploration even after they leave the museum or walk away from the exhibition.[12] The original impetus for requiring history in public schools was to create good citizens for a strong democracy. Presumably the same goal holds for public history, even though the components may have changed. Still it is less important that visitors can remember the specific details of any one historical topic than that they engage in public history as a free choice, and as a result become lifelong learners.

Audiences can choose freely only if they encounter the material through a delivery method that works for them. The experience of Alaskan teenager Byron Nicholai demonstrates the importance of considering the audience when picking the delivery method. Nicholai, a teenage Yu'pik boy living in the remote village of Toksook Bay, Alaska, population 600, was the son of a single mother who had learned important cultural traditions, such as hunting and fishing, from his older cousins and uncles. When he was in sixth grade, his cousins passed on another legacy—drumming. Nicholai became fascinated by the history of his people, learning not only drumming patterns but also songs and dances. He wanted to share his historical knowledge with other teens, and his understanding of his audience led him to choose Facebook and YouTube as his delivery media. The CB/VHS radio had connected Native Alaskans for decades, but Nicholai's generation favored online platforms. Nicholai started posting videos of himself singing modern songs interlaced with words and phrases from his Yu'pik language.[13] Reflecting on his work, Nicholai told the *Alaska Dispatch News*, "Teens nowadays are so modern. They are starting to think the traditional ways are boring. So what if I mixed them. They would still be into the modern, but they would learn more about the traditional, too."[14] Soon he had 24,000 followers on Facebook, some from Alaska, some from other parts of the world. He went on tour around his state, discovering audiences of adoring fans who wanted to take selfies with him and who knew his Yu'pik songs word for word. By understanding his audience, this teenager has inspired young people to choose to learn the Yu'pik language and to embrace traditional cultural practices as relevant in their own modern lives.

Collaboration

Shared Authority with the Public

The public not only has choices about what they will learn and how they choose to relate to the past and to "history," but they also own their own histories. Respecting the public's ownership over their own history demands the recognition and practice of **shared authority**, a term Michael Frisch developed in his work as an oral historian.[15] As Frisch describes it, this shared authority is inherent in the work of oral and public history because public historians are not the sole interpreters: "the interpretive and meaning-making process is in fact shared by definition—it is inherent in the dialogic nature of an interview, and in how audiences receive and respond to exhibitions and public history interchanges in general."[16] Shared authority does not, however, require that public historians relinquish their expertise, but it does mean that public historians must be willing to do the work of collaboration, listening to and respecting diverse points of view, and seeking common ground whenever possible. Public historians share authority with stakeholders who seek to play a role in how the story of their people is being interpreted or how their money is being spent. We also share authority with the much wider audiences of our work. Although most of them will not play any role in the development or design of public history projects, they will still understand whatever we produce through the lens of their own worldviews, experiences, and understandings. When a stakeholder or audience member disagrees with a historical narrative, public historians should see that moment as an opportunity to engage in further dialogue and reflection rather than as a roadblock. There are also significant ways to share authority with public history consumers, for example, through evaluation of museum exhibits and civic engagement, which will be discussed in chapters 5 and 6.

Collaborating with Other Disciplines

Public historians collaborate frequently with non-historians across disciplines. Academic historical research typically gives preference to textual sources, like legal documents, letters, diaries, and maps. Academic historians, trained to use these kinds of sources, typically work alone. But public historians often consult a wide range of textual and non-textual sources, some of which may require interdisciplinary research techniques or collaboration with individuals trained as archaeologists, anthropologists, historical and landscape architects, art historians, and curators, just to name a few. Public historians also work with professionals who have the expertise to create public history installations, including designers, artists, installation experts, lighting professionals, web developers, and institutional directors. The collaborative nature of public history points to one way in which it functions as its own field of study and its own professional endeavor, requiring that public historians understand the needs and expectations of the other professionals they work with and that they more clearly and self-consciously explain their work and their standards to non-specialists. Therefore, public historians become masters of mediation and interpretation both of their professional standards and of history itself.

Sunnylands, the winter estate of Walter and Leonore Annenberg in Rancho Mirage, California, is an example of a site where public historians successfully collaborate across disciplines every day. The house is a mid-century modern landmark, containing an extensive art collection, and the grounds boast a professional golf course. The Annenberg Foundation Trust at Sunnylands offers guided tours of the historic estate and grounds. Through research on US and international political history, Sunnylands staff developed a script that university-student guides use to provide tours to the public fifteen times a day. This script tells the story of Walter and Leonore Annenberg and of their estate as a meeting place for current and past US presidents and world leaders. Now functioning as a high-end retreat center for world leaders, the complexity of the site requires more than a historical knowledge of the significance of the Annenbergs and their property. Sunnylands staff has collaborated with environmental resource specialists to model best practices in energy and water conservation in a desert environment, and with experts on hospitality to ensure the estate does not disappoint as a rarefied getaway for world leaders and high-profile guests. Experts in exhibit installation work with curators to display objects of interest in rotating exhibitions. Education specialists incorporate local high school students in scientific studies of the desert flora and fauna. The interdisciplinary efforts of the staff at Sunnylands and special contractors allow a diverse group of visitors to the estate, public center, and gardens to grasp the entire experience of Sunnylands, both its past and its present.

Photograph 1.2.   Experts in exhibition installation work with Director of Collections & Exhibitions Anne Rowe (far left) to prepare a new exhibition at the Sunnylands Center & Gardens in Rancho Mirage, California, 2014. Courtesy of The Annenberg Foundation Trust at Sunnylands.

Reflective Practice

Public history requires collaboration across disciplines and with the public, but this collaboration can make it difficult to identify, agree upon, and maintain focus on one or more project goals. The ability to find end goals that everyone involved in a public history project can embrace, and the ability to identify the problems that are central to a large project, takes experience. This is not a technical endeavor with a set of steps that can be followed exactly to guarantee success. Donald A. Schön, author of *The Reflective Practitioner*, explored how problem setting and problem solving work together in nonscientific settings where the end goals of collaborative projects are not predetermined and there is no preset problem that everyone can identify as the end goal. Schön wrote:

> Technical rationality depends on agreement about ends. When ends are fixed and clear, then the decision to act can present itself as an instrumental problem. But when the ends are confused and conflicting, there is as yet no "problem" to solve. A conflict of ends cannot be resolved by the use of techniques derived from applied research. It is rather through the non-technical process of framing a problematic situation that we may organize and clarify both the ends to be achieved and the possible means of achieving them.[17]

Public historians, like others, engage in reflective practice, drawing on what worked and what did not work from past experiences to "frame the problematic situation" to better understand how to approach the complexity and unpredictability of a new project.

Public historians cannot bring a team together effectively until they can identify the problems that will guide the team's work. In the real world of multiple experts and stakeholders working together, the process it takes to identify the problems that will guide everyone's work is messy. As Schön puts it, **setting problems** is the step before **problem solving**, in which a professional must "*name* the things to which we will attend and *frame* the context in which we will attend to them." The problem-setting phase includes, for example, the process of determining who the stakeholders are in any given project, determining what they believe the outcomes of the project should be, and the process of bringing all of the stakeholders to the table to bring their disparate visions together into a single set of clearly identified problems.[18]

As public historians begin their careers, many are still learning how to collaborate or to appreciate the value of collaboration. Developing an exhibition on the history of a historically oppressed group or preserving a nineteenth-century slaveholder's house on land understood as sacred to indigenous people without consulting those groups of stakeholders will likely result in an exhibition that leaves out these integral perspectives. According to Schön, the problems arise because inexperienced professionals pay more attention to problem solving than they do to problem setting. In other words, turning back to the example of the exhibition on the history of a historically oppressed group, a new public historian might immediately turn to what seems to her to be the problem at hand—primary and secondary source research about that historically oppressed group, so that she can begin developing that exhibition—instead of engaging in problem setting: bringing together stakeholders in the project to engage in dialogue with them to discover what they believe the key components of an interpretive exhibition might be. Consulting with stakeholders not only helps public historians maintain good community relations, but also, as you will read in chapter 3 in the case study of the *Baltimore '68 Project*, it helps us discover which questions we should be asking. Knowing how to gain access to the people and to earn their trust in order to understand and identify the goals that various stakeholders may have for any given project can be difficult and may develop only over time. Learning from those who have done this work in the past is vital, but so is evaluating the steps you undertook—or the steps that you should have taken—to identify or set the problems of the project and to solve them. Reflective practice requires that the practitioner not only set and solve the problem then at hand but, throughout the work, also reflect on what is working and not working as lessons for future projects. The chart on the next page suggests how this process might work.

Ethics are not determined by consulting a master book of rules. Quite often you select the most ethical response from a list of imperfect choices. If you develop the ability to think through ethical dilemmas in the safety of a classroom setting when the stakes are really quite low, you will be much better equipped to carry on similar discussions with colleagues in the future when together you face decisions in situations that you or your organization did not anticipate. We hope that this book will jumpstart conversations and debates focusing on common themes that bring public historians together in order to better understand

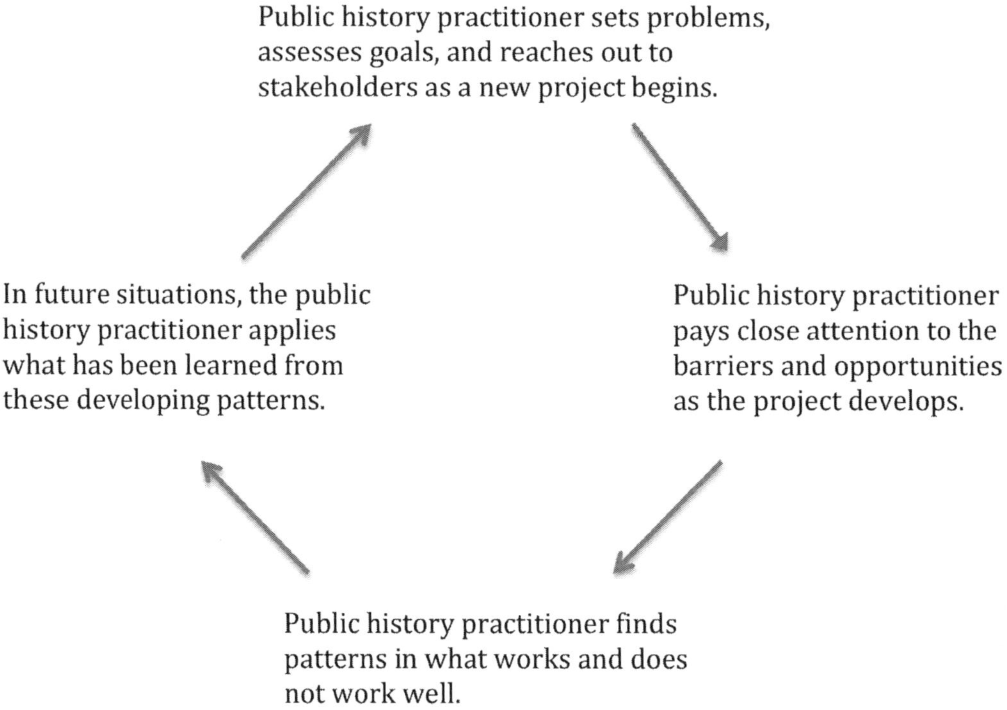

Public history practitioner sets problems, assesses goals, and reaches out to stakeholders as a new project begins.

In future situations, the public history practitioner applies what has been learned from these developing patterns.

Public history practitioner pays close attention to the barriers and opportunities as the project develops.

Public history practitioner finds patterns in what works and does not work well.

Figure 1.1. Reflective Practice in Public History. Adapted from David A. Kolb, *Experiential Learning: Experience as the Source of Learning and Development*, 2nd Ed. (Upper Saddle River, NJ: Pearson Education, 2015), 32.

the underlying theories that inform the field of public history and to inspire curiosity for further study. We also hope that those who find that public history becomes for you more than a passing interest will follow up with internships and hands-on projects that will allow you to see how the principles introduced in this text compare with the day-to-day demands of working in the field.

Notes

1. Robert Kelley, "Public History: Its Origins, Nature, and Prospects," *The Public Historian* 1, no. 1 (Fall 1978): 16. doi: 10.2307/3377666.
2. John Falk and Lynn Dierking, *Learning from Museums: Visitor Experiences and The Making of Meaning* (Lanham, MD: AltaMira Press, 2000), 61.
3. Roy Rosenzweig and David Thelen, *The Presence of the Past: Popular Uses of History in American Life* (New York: Columbia University Press, 1998), 149–162.
4. Rosenzweig and Thelen, *Presence of the Past*, 108.
5. Paulo Freire, *Pedagogy of the Oppressed*, 30th Anniversary Edition (New York: Continuum, 2006, 1968).
6. Freire, 51.
7. Freire, 84.
8. Freire, 39.

9. Falk and Dierking, *Learning from Museums*, 136.

10. For an explanation of the theoretical roots of "dialogic" as used in this case based on literary theorist Mikhail Bakhtin, particularly as used by Tony Bennett, see: Tony Bennett, "Exhibition, Difference and the Logic of Culture," in Ivan Karp, Corinne A. Kratz, Lynn Szwaja, and Tomas Ybarra-Frausto, eds., *Museum Frictions: Public Cultures/Global Transformations* (Durham and London: Duke University Press, 2006), 46–69; and Mary Hutchinson and Lea Collins, "Translations: Experiments in Dialogic Representation of Cultural Diversity in Three Museum Sound Installations," *Museum and Society* 7, no. 2 (2009): 92–109.

11. John Kuo Wei Tchen, "Creating a Dialogic Museum: The Chinatown History Museum Experiment," in *Museums and Communities: The Politics of Culture* (Washington, DC, and London: Smithsonian Institution Press, 1992), 285–326, quotation on 286; John Kuo Wei Tchen and Liz Ševčenko, "The 'Dialogic Museum' Revisited: A Collaborative Reflection," in Bill Adair, Benjamin Filene, and Laura Koloski, eds., *Letting Go? Sharing Historical Authority in a User-Generated World* (Philadelphia: Pew Center for Arts & Heritage, 2011), 83.

12. John H. Falk, "The Director's Cut: Toward an Improved Understanding of Learning from Museums," *Science Education* 88, no. S1 (July 2004): S83–S96; and Falk, "Free-Choice Environmental Learning: Framing the Discussion," *Environmental Education Research* 11, no. 3 (2005): 265–280.

13. You can see Nicholai's work on his Facebook page "I Sing, You Dance."

14. Byron Nicholai, "I Sing, You Dance," *Alaska Dispatch News*, April 9, 2016, http://www.adn.com/multimedia/video/video-byron-nicholai-i-sing-you-dance/2015/05/07/. See also *The Atlantic*, August 4, 2015; *Salon*, February 12, 2016.

15. Michael Frisch, *A Shared Authority: Essays on the Craft and Meaning of Oral and Public History* (Albany: SUNY Press, 1990).

16. Michael Frisch, "From *A Shared Authority* to the Digital Kitchen, and Back," in Adair, Filene, and Koloski, eds., *Letting Go?*, 127.

17. Donald A. Schön, *The Reflective Practitioner* (London: Ashgate, 1991), 41.

18. Schön, *The Reflective Practitioner*, 40. One of the most insightful descriptions showcasing the traditional work of the historian working with primary sources as reflective practice is found in Sam Wineburg, *Historical Thinking and Other Unnatural Acts: Charting the Future of Teaching the Past* (Philadelphia: Temple University Press, 2001), 17–22. Rebecca Conard identified reflective practice as one of the core elements of public history practice in "Public History as Reflective Practice: An Introduction," *The Public Historian* 28, no. 1 (Winter 2006): 9–13.

RESOURCES AND SUGGESTED ACTIVITIES

Professional Organizations

Learn about the organizations that represent public historians. Below are some of those organizations. Read their mission statements, determine who they represent, take a look at their publications, newsletters, blogs, and consider following them on social media.

- American Association for the History of Medicine
- American Association for State and Local History
- American Alliance of Museums
- American Historical Association
- California Council for the Promotion of History
- Institute for the Public Understanding of the Past
- National Association for Interpretation
- National Council on Public History
- National Trust for Historic Preservation
- Oral History Association
- Organization of American Historians
- Society of American Archivists

History Where You Live

Visit History Museums in Your Area

Where are the history museums in your area? Is there a historic house or building associated with the museum? Is it focused on national, state, or local history? Who is their main target audience? How do they engage the public with the material? What types of collections do they have? What seems to be their main historical narrative? Is the narrative reflective of the community living in the area? Why or why not?

Visit a Historic Site

Think about how that site is interpreted for the public. You might take a tour, or search for a podcast about the site, or read plaques at the site, or visit an interpretive center. Before going, you should take a look at James Loewen's "Ten Questions to Ask at a Historic Site" available in his book, *Lies Across America*, appendix B, or online at: http://sundown.afro.illinois.edu/content.php?file=liesacrossamerica-tenquestions.html.

Visit Your Local Public Library

Explore the special collections or local history collections if your library has them, or explore any exhibitions that might be on display interpreting the history of the area. Talk to a reference librarian to learn about other resources that might be available for people interested in local history.

Visit Your Local College Library

Colleges often have archives filled with primary and secondary materials that shed light on local history. Often alumni, professors, and politicians donate collections to their school's special collections. You may also find oral histories, institutional records, and ephemera.

Visit a Historical Society in Your Area

Most historical societies host guest lectures or special events in the community. Find out when they have an event or lecture or meeting and pay them a visit. Find out who they are, when they became organized as a historical society, and why. Ask about their collections or resources and about their organization. Who are their members, and who are their officers? What is their mission and how do they raise money? What are their most treasured assets and/or stories? Volunteer to write an article for their newsletter.

Get Creative!

Drive, bike, or take a bus around your city or town and look for monuments, statues, plaques, murals, or other markers of historical places. Explore a historical district, or a part of town that contains buildings and/or homes that are older than fifty years. Pay attention to movies in theaters that are based on historical subjects. Notice television or internet series that are based even loosely on historical subjects or in historical periods. Talk to family members, neighbors, friends, or acquaintances about how things have changed in your city, your neighborhood, or your region. What are their fondest memories of places that have changed the most or that are still exactly as they remember them?

Need some ideas? There are many ways to find historical points of interest online or on your mobile devices. Here are just a few ideas to get you started.

- Curatescape Projects, http://curatescape.org/projects/
- History Pin, http://www.historypin.org
- Next Exit History, http://nextexithistory.com
- National Trust for Historic Preservation, http://www.preservationnation.org

Thinking Critically about Representation and Local History

After touring your own area and visiting some sites, museums, and libraries, and thinking about public representations of history, pause and think about how your local community, your region, your country, or another country represents its own history through the most public forms of representation, such as advertising and tourism, monuments or place names, festivals or other means. Below are some ways you might frame this discussion, but there are many ways to think critically about historical representations of history that are all around us. Discuss historic representation in your community, on campus, and in your region. How does it compare with the demographics of your community, campus, or region? Which groups see themselves most heavily represented? Which groups are invisible? Discuss strategies to improve representation on campus or in the community.

1. How does your town, city, or community represent itself to visitors and/or tourists? Is that representation accurate? Does it preference one group over others? Is it idealized? Does it use or ignore history to sell authentic experiences of place to visitors? Why or why not? To answer this question, you might visit your town, city, or regional office of tourism. States all have official offices of tourism and provide excellent opportunities for analysis. For example, visit sites that cater to tourists visiting a city, state, or country. You might have to dig a little to see what type of history this site portrays, but the history or "heritage" of a place is always either an explicit or implicit selling point.

2. How often are people of diverse gender, cultural, racial, and ethnic groups represented on monuments, plaques, wayside exhibitions, official historic sites, museums, and the like in your town, city, or region? How does the percentage of any one group in historical representations compare with the demographics of the area? One 2014 study found, for example, that while there are fifty statues in New York City's Central Park, none of them represent real women (women who are not characters in fictional pieces of literature). Zero.[1] There are female fictional characters represented, including Alice in Wonderland, Juliet Capulet, and Mother Goose, but even these statues were created by men. By contrast, if you stroll through the park you might encounter Shakespeare, Beethoven, Simón Bolívar, Alexander Hamilton, or even the famous sled dog Balto. Nationally, within the United States fewer than 8 percent of public outdoor statues commemorating individuals are of women. Does it matter who we memorialize in sculptures in our public places? What does it tell us about which individual contributions in history publics value and what can you learn about efforts (or the lack thereof) to be more inclusive in public memorialization of historical figures in your country, your region, or your own community?

Note

1. Chloe Angyal, "Not One Woman Gets Her Own Pedestal among Central Park's Statues," September 5, 2014, http://blogs.reuters.com/great-debate/2014/09/05/real-women-belong-in-new-yorks-central-park.

RESOURCES FOR FURTHER STUDY

Cauvin, Thomas. *Public History: A Textbook of Practice.* London: Routledge, 2016.

Gardner, James B., and Peter S. LaPaglia, Eds. *Public History: Essays from the Field.* Malabar, FL: Krieger Publishing Company, 2004.

Kammen, Michael G. *Mystic Chords of Memory: The Transformation of Tradition in American Culture.* New York: Knopf, 1991.

Kean, Hilda and Paul Martin. *The Public History Reader.* London: Routledge, 2013.

Kyvig, David E. and Myron A. Marty. *Nearby History: Exploring the Past Around You.* Lanham, MD: AltaMira Press, 2010.

Lowenthal, David. *The Past Is a Foreign Country.* Cambridge: Cambridge University Press, 1985.

Meringolo, Denise. *Museums, Monuments, and National Parks: Toward a New Genealogy of Public History.* Amherst: University of Massachusetts Press, 2012.

National Council on Public History. "NCPH Code of Ethics and Professional Conduct," 2007. Available at http://ncph.org/about/governance-committees/.

Sayer, Faye. *Public History: A Practical Guide.* London: Bloomsbury Academic Press, 2015.

Townsend, Robert. *History's Babel: Scholarship, Professionalization, and the Historical Enterprise in the United States, 1880–1940.* Chicago: University of Chicago Press, 2013.

Wallace, Mike. *Mickey Mouse History and Other Essays on American Memory.* Philadelphia: Temple University Press, 1996.

CHAPTER 2

Thinking Historically

| KEY TERMS |

KEY TERMS	
history as a practice	change and continuity
historical thinking	turning point
secondary sources	using the past
historiography	through their eyes
research question	primary sources
historical categories of inquiry	sourcing heuristic
cause and effect	thesis

"When History Doesn't Matter"

IN 2016, PUBLIC HISTORIAN Anna Altschwager wrote a blog entry for the American Association of State and Local History titled, "When History Doesn't Matter."[1] A title like that is sure to raise eyebrows, particularly when published by an organization that is built around the importance of history. Altschwager explained that a colleague of hers had recently suggested she attend an entire conference with that title, because as the colleague suggested, "That's your thing!" After the initial shock, she realized her colleague might be right. Altschwager had come to the public history world from working for a natural history museum. She loved history and was committed to her work for the Ohio Village. How could history not be her thing? When did history not matter?

First, let us explain where Altschwager was working when she realized that, perhaps, history doesn't matter. Ohio Village is an open-air, living history museum outside Columbus, where visitors can walk the streets of a replicated nineteenth-century midwestern town and interact with staff dressed in period clothing.[2] The concept of the open-air museum is based on the historic preservation of original buildings or the creation of reconstructed buildings from a specific era that all function as an interpretive site where visitors are transported back in time. In a living history site, visitors can interact with costumed staff who play the part of people who lived and worked in the historical setting. The concept makes history accessible to the entire family, and living history sites often become popular vacation destinations. The 15-acre Ohio Village site was constructed in 1974 in preparation for the United States' Bicentennial celebration. The village interpreted life in the 1840s through replica buildings, only some of which were modeled after specific historic structures, where the public could stroll through the village, visit shops or houses, and watch one of two historic "base ball" teams play using nineteenth-century rules.[3]

In 2012, Ohio Village shifted its historical focus from the 1840s to the 1860s to commemorate the Sesquicentennial of the Civil War. From 2012 through 2015, Ohio Village interpreted each year of the Civil War, from 1862–1865. When that anniversary had passed, site director Altschwager and her team examined their mission to determine their next steps. Would they like to repeat the Civil War story in a continuous four-year loop? Should the site go back to its original 1840s programming? Or should they try something new? The staff at Ohio Village were free to explore these questions because the buildings, built in the 1970s, were not historic artifacts. Without structures tying their interpretation to a specific time period of significance, they were free to imagine the site in many different historical periods. They were, however, limited by budgetary concerns: moving the interpretive time period from 1840 to 1890 was possible without major reconstruction to the site, but moving the interpretive time period to the colonial era or 1920s would have required major reconstruction.

Under the leadership of Altschwager, the Ohio Village staff focused on determining what was at the heart of the work that this site did, what their "game" was. In the process of analyzing their work, the team made a monumental finding: the choice visitors made to come to the site "had nothing to do with learning a specific history." What Ohio Village did best was help visitors learn "*how history works, and how stories work.*" At the site, guests interacted with interpreters, heard stories about people from the past, explored objects that had been made in earlier times, and asked questions about the era. By interpreting the past through interaction, the site had introduced guests to the idea of **history as a practice**. The planning team concluded that the specific histories they were interpreting did not matter as much as the ways in which they used history as a tool to further their core values of "dynamism, dialog, connection, questioning, play and the keystone of relevancy."[4]

History as a Practice

What does it mean to think of history as a practice? Historians Nikki Mandell and Bobbie Malone undertook that question in their work *Thinking Like a Historian*. Mandell and Malone observed that "[h]istory is a *discipline*: a way of thinking that encourages students to analyze historical evidence, evaluate it, and then demonstrate their understanding of that evidence." When students, or the public at large, have the opportunity, as Mandell and Malone put it, to *do* history, it engages "their passion and enthusiasm for the past while applying the highest levels of critical thinking." "Such involved work," Mandell and Malone explain, "is well beyond simple memorization of factual material and prepares young people for the kinds of sharpened thinking necessary for a successful adult life."[5]

When we see history as a practice rather than a list to be memorized, historical thinking, or more broadly constructed, critical thinking, drives history as a creative endeavor. When historians draw audiences into the questions that inspire historical inquiry and invite them to participate in the act of *doing* history, suddenly history becomes vital. When people start *doing* history instead of simply learning history, they quickly realize that history is not a tidy narrative waiting for a student to memorize. Instead, historians construct history by analyzing remnants of the past that witnesses have left behind. The job of the historian is to discover and evaluate those sources in order to develop a responsible interpretation of the past.

Historical Methods

What are the historical methods that historians use? **Historical thinking** is the term that describes the reading, analysis, and writing that forms the foundation of the work that historians do. In the academy, historians are trained to begin with a question, one that arises from reading the **secondary sources** (work produced by other historians) on a particular topic. Historians read secondary sources both to understand the past but also to identify elements of past experiences that remain unexplored by historians. When historians write their results, they usually explain how they decided to conduct their research based on their secondary source reading. **Historiography**, or the history of how scholars have treated a subject over time, gives credit to the people who have published on the topic already and explains how you think your work will make a contribution to historical knowledge.

After identifying an area where further exploration is necessary, historians develop a **research question** to focus and guide their work, for example: "If President Truman believed that Japan was really ready to surrender to the Allies in 1945, why did he decide to drop the bomb?" or "How can we understand why the enslaved Africans who had successfully fled from their captors during the 1739 Stono Rebellion stopped to dance and drum so that whites were able to capture them—why didn't they keep running until they had reached safety in Florida?"

Developing a strong research question can be difficult, but it is likely the most important skill a historian can have. In their work, Mandell and Malone identified the process by which historians develop these questions that guide their work. They write, "historians' curiosity . . . tends to fall into recognizable patterns of inquiry. These patterns, or what might be called **historical categories of inquiry**, organize both the questions we ask of the past and the answers we construct."[6] These are the categories of historical inquiry Mandell and Malone established and how they described them:

- **Cause and effect** is perhaps the most familiar category of historical questioning and explanation. We ask questions about the causes and consequences of past events. Not surprisingly, our answers to these questions, our historical interpretations, take the forms of stories about causes and consequences.
- We also ask questions about what has changed and what has remained the same over time. Answers to questions about **change and continuity** connect events and give meaning to the chronological sequence of events.

- In some cases we wonder if the change was so dramatic that the topic of study was a historical **turning point**. By studying the historical record we are able to reach conclusions that some events or developments so dramatically changed a society's ideas, choices and ways of living that some paths of development could no longer be followed and others became more likely or possible.
- In other cases we look at the past as a guide to our present. We want to know about the particular course of events that shaped our present. Or, we are **using the past** to seek guidance in the forms of "lessons of history" that can help us grapple with current problems.
- We find it both necessary and fascinating to examine the ways in which people of different times, places and conditions made sense of their world. We consider how their experiences, needs and worldviews affected their actions and the course of events. We try to imagine the world **through their eyes**.[7]

Almost any historical event can be analyzed through several, if not all, of the categories of historical analysis. For example, the Stono Rebellion, which took place near Charleston, South Carolina, in 1739, can provide us with a window into the worldview of the enslaved Africans who rebelled against slavery in that colony. Using the through their eyes category, we can understand how what seemed like unusual behavior from the perspective of white observers made perfect sense in the context of the Kongolese culture from which they had likely come and in which some of them had likely served as soldiers. But the Stono Rebellion also represented a major turning point in South Carolina, after which enslaved Africans were subjected to a much stricter slave regime. Using the lens of cause and effect enables a historian to explore how Spanish offers of freedom for enslaved Africans, set against the backdrop of imperial competition between Spain and England in the New World, motivated Africans to attempt to flee South Carolina for Florida.[8]

We must recognize that the types of questions historians ask are shaped by the philosophies they hold true about the world. All of us are subject to this bias, and if the research project you undertake allows you to pick your own topic, then there is nothing wrong with pursuing a question that is of interest to you. But it is important to ask at the outset what might remain hidden by answering your research question. Historians all too often do their work without being explicit about their process. Explicitness about process can reveal these kinds of biases in the development of the research question. Being explicit about which categories of historical analysis you are using as a historian helps you determine which sources are most useful in your research, as well as what you should focus on in your writing. Moreover, identifying these categories helps your audience understand the meaning and significance of the work you have undertaken.

Once the research question has been established, the historian is ready to begin an analysis of the primary sources. **Primary sources** are the historical sources—documents, artifacts, visual materials—created during the period being studied. When historians evaluate evidence, one of the first things they encounter is conflicting information. Many times eyewitnesses leave vastly different accounts of the same event. How does a historian reconcile two or three conflicting reports? How can historians represent the points of view of the victors and vanquished at the same time in a single historical narrative of the past?

WHAT QUESTIONS DO WE ASK OF THE PAST?

THINKING LIKE A HISTORIAN

 CAUSE AND EFFECT	CHANGE AND CONTINUITY	TURNING POINTS	USING THE PAST	THROUGH THEIR EYES
What were the causes of past events? What were the effects? • Who or what made change happen? • Who supported change? • Who did not support change? • Which effects were intended? • Which effects were accidental? • How did events affect people's lives, community, and the world?	What has changed? What has remained the same? • Who has benefited from this change? And why? • Who has not benefited? And why?	How did past decisions or actions affect future choices? • How did decisions or actions narrow or eliminate choices for people? • How did decisions or actions significantly transform people's lives?	How does the past help us make sense of the present? • How is the past similar to the present? • How is the past different from the present? • What can we learn from the past?	How did people in the past view their world? • How did their worldview affect their choices and actions? • What values, skills and forms of knowledge did people need to succeed?

Figure 2.1.   What Questions Do We Ask of the Past? Thinking Like a Historian. From Nikki Mandell and Bobbie Malone, *Thinking Like A Historian: Rethinking History Instruction*. Courtesy of Nikki Mandell and the Wisconsin Historical Society.

How do our own biases or values shape the way we understand past events? How can we minimize our own ideas in order to better represent the past on its own terms? Answering these questions requires the skills of a historian.[9]

Studies have found that professional historians engage in the evaluation-of-evidence phase of historical thinking almost as second nature. Their particular ways of approaching a primary source are so ingrained that they have trouble teaching them to novices. In an effort to pin down the discrete steps in document interrogation, Sam Wineburg, an education professor at Stanford who majored in the history of religion as an undergraduate, asked professional historians to talk through their thought processes as they read a source. In his studies, Wineburg found a striking consistency in the practices of professional historians: before they even address the content of the primary source, they ask a number of questions about where it came from and the process by which it was created. To contextualize this exchange, to measure the credibility of the source and to make a judgment about it, historians regularly employ a **sourcing heuristic**, or a series of steps they walk through before they analyze the content of any document. Wineburg found that 98 percent of historians began with questions about the source before they began to read it because understanding who created the source is essential in uncovering its meaning.[10] Teachers have created a number of mnemonic devices to help history students remember to ask all these questions, and here we offer an original one that public historians can use to examine both texts and objects:

SOURCE

Series of steps
Origin
Use at the time it was created
Reality check
Context and Curiosity
Evidence

Origin:

Who is the author (in the case of a document)?
Who is the creator (in the case of an object)?
When was it made?
Where was it made?
How was it made?
Is this a unique document/object or is it one of many duplicates?

Use at the time it was created:

What was it intended to do?
Was it used in other ways?
Who was the audience (in the case of a document)?

Who were the users (in the case of an object)?
Was it common or rare?
Did the creator intend for it to last?

Reality check:

What are the limitations of this source?
What were the biases of its creator?
What questions about it can never be answered?
Would any community oppose its use in an exhibit?
What biases do you bring that might affect how you understand this source?

Context and Curiosity:

What *relevant* events were taking place at the time of this source's creation or use?
Is the source in keeping with your understanding of the historical context or does it surprise you? In other words, does it support or contradict what you already know about the subject you are studying?
Does this source represent a change or innovation?
What questions about it remain unanswered but answerable?
What further research might be necessary to fully understand the source?

Evidence:

How can you use this source as evidence in your current argument?
Do the answers to the other sets of questions establish its credibility to the point that you can include it with confidence?
If questions remain, do you have enough evidence to engage in responsible speculation?
What caveats about it do you need to include?

Historians use this process, or one like it, as they gather and evaluate sources, thinking through the answers to all of these questions as they examine every source, analyzing the evidence that may help them develop an argument that will provide an answer to the research question they have identified.

Novice and experienced historians alike constantly ask themselves, "How do I know when I have looked at enough evidence?" Sometimes, when there is not much evidence available, this question will not be an issue. But often, historians have assembled a tremendous amount of evidence—especially in this era of rapidly expanding digital resources—so much so that it can be difficult to know when they have enough to be able to make an argument. Mandell and Malone argue that the historian should consult "all reasonably available

Photograph 2.1.   A student examines a newspaper clipping in the Enoch Pratt Free Library's vertical file (Baltimore, Maryland). Photo by Audrey Hayes.

secondary and primary sources." When there is too much available evidence to consult, then historians look for the point at which the evidence they are gathering no longer tells them anything new about their subject—the point at which they have already encountered and included all of the different perspectives. When some evidence has not been consulted, the historian should acknowledge this in the final product. Historical work requires historians to study as much of the available evidence as possible as an ethical practice to represent the past as fully as possible.[11]

Once she has gathered the evidence, the historian begins writing in earnest. She has already been taking notes while reading sources and has developed ideas for the main argument that will answer the research question. Writing and research should happen simultaneously, although at the beginning of the process there is more research than writing out of necessity, with writing becoming the predominant activity later on. Along the way, the historian is developing an argument that will answer the research question. That argument is called the **thesis,** and it guides the writing by providing a frame and a point of reference for everything else in the final product.

Historical Thinking Matters

When the staff of Ohio Village declared that "history doesn't matter," they meant that the specific stories and the specific content of their message matter less than the dialogue that takes place when visitors engage with history. It is the process of thinking historically, asking questions about the past, and exploring how history relates to our lives that matters. The process of evaluating evidence to develop a historical argument is what really matters. Even though the Ohio Village buildings are modern, Ohio Village "is not an exception to a rule," Anna Altschwager wrote. "We just found an opportunity to articulate the work of public history in a new way." Altschwager is now the assistant director over guest experiences at Old World Wisconsin, where their buildings are all originals, but they have been relocated to the site. A farmhouse may have belonged to one family, but the outbuildings are from other farms, connected with the lives of different families. In this context, as with all historical interpretations, choices need to be made. Should they provide a seamless narrative organized around a single family's experience despite the fact that only one of the buildings belonged to that family, or should they use a variety of stories to provide a composite sketch of an immigrant farming community in history? If so, which stories do they choose and by what criteria? There is no single correct answer to these questions. Even when a site is "firmly grounded in a single event or family story," Altschwager said, "the dynamism of history (and therefore the opportunity for relevance, questioning, and connection) shines through when you decide that it is the *process* of history that is at the heart of your work."[12]

Why is this process so important? The tools of historical inquiry are inherently valuable for all citizens. The process of historical inquiry teaches people how to evaluate evidence, to think critically about conflicting pieces of evidence, and to ask questions that move beyond the most obvious facts. All of a sudden, history becomes a dynamic journey, a detective game, not just a series of facts to be memorized. The lessons learned based on historical inquiry at one site can easily be transferred to another time and place because the process is the same even when the subject changes.

Historical thinking is useful in everyday life. When people practice the skills of a historian, they are equipped to evaluate evidence they encounter every day, to seek out and understand sources that would seem to contradict that evidence, and to knit it all together to tell a coherent and meaningful story that helps them reach conclusions and make decisions. The work that historians do benefits us all. The more that historians speak explicitly about how they construct history, the more people will benefit from being able to use these skills in their own lives.

Notes

1. Anna Altschwager, "When History Doesn't Matter," AASLH Blogs, http://blogs.aaslh.org/when-history-doesnt-matter/.
2. The world's first open air museum was built in Sweden in 1891 and was quickly copied all over the world. There are several well-known open air museums in the United States, including Colonial Williamsburg, Old Sturbridge Village, Plymouth Colony, and Greenfield Village.
3. To learn more about Ohio Village, visit: https://www.ohiohistory.org/visit/ohio-village; and Lisa Abraham, "Ohio Village Jumps from Depicting 1860s to 1890s," *The Columbus Dispatch*, Wednesday, May 25, 2016, http://www.dispatch.com/content/stories/life_and_entertain ment/2016/05/26/1-ohio-village-jumps-from-depicting-1860s-to-1890s-a-period-similar -to-today.html.
4. Altschwager, "When History Doesn't Matter."
5. Nikki Mandell and Bobbie Malone, *Thinking Like a Historian: Rethinking History Instruction* (Madison: Wisconsin Historical Society Press, 2008), 1.
6. Mandell and Malone, *Thinking Like a Historian*, 7.
7. Mandell and Malone, *Thinking Like a Historian*, 8. Courtesy of Nikki Mandell and the Wisconsin Historical Society.
8. Mark M. Smith, ed. *Stono: Documenting and Interpreting a Southern Slave Revolt* (Columbia: University of South Carolina Press, 2005), 73. See also: Peter Charles Hoffer, *Cry Liberty: The Great Stono River Rebellion of 1739* (Oxford: Oxford University Press, 2010).
9. To see a historian at work analyzing a primary source, view "About an Inventory: A Conversation between Natalie Zemon Davis and Peter N. Miller," available at https://www.youtube.com/watch?v=hwiR3dz4Wg8.
10. Sam Wineburg, *Historical Thinking and Other Unnatural Acts: Charting the Future of Teaching the Past* (Philadelphia: Temple University Press, 2001), 76.
11. Mandell and Malone, *Thinking Like a Historian*, 7.
12. Anna Altschwager, e-mail to Cherstin Lyon, September 3, 2016.

RESOURCES AND SUGGESTED ACTIVITIES

A Midwife's Tale

This *American Experience* documentary produced by PBS introduces audiences to the research of Laurel Thatcher Ulrich into the diary and life of Martha Ballard. This documentary demonstrates how Ulrich pieced together the life of this eighteenth-century midwife through careful and creative investigation of documents that captured the world in which Ballard lived and explained the clues left behind in the mundane details of Ballard's diary.

Researching Local History

Based on the investigations you conducted on history in your communities, on your campus, and in your region, are there obvious groups who have been overlooked or who have been rendered invisible? What sources are available that might reveal more about this community? How could sources such as newspapers, city or county documents, census records, and oral histories be used to do historical research? What questions would you ask of your sources?

Visit a Special Collections Library at Your University or at an Area Library

Take a look at their manuscript collections. Look for a collection that pertains to a topic of interest to you. Read the finding aid and calendar. Request a box or two that might reveal substantive information about the topic or person. For example, if looking at a manuscript collection relating to an individual, their newspaper clippings or scrapbooks may be interesting, but a more revealing set of documents might be their correspondence folders. Based on your examination of the sources, what questions could you ask to further investigate the topic using the historical thinking skills described in this chapter? What secondary sources might help you establish context for understanding the manuscript collection better? Select one document to analyze using the sourcing heuristic described in the chapter. Present your analysis in class or in a short, written assignment.

RESOURCES FOR FURTHER STUDY

Brundage, Anthony. *Going to the Sources: A Guide to Historical Research and Writing*, 5th Edition. Malden, MA: Wiley-Blackwell, 2013.

Dobson, Miriam and Benjamin Ziemann, eds. *Reading Primary Sources: The Interpretation of Texts from Nineteenth- and Twentieth-Century History*. London: Routledge Press, 2009.

Kammen, Carol. *On Doing Local History*. Lanham, MD: Rowman & Littlefield, 2014.

Kyvig, David E., and Myron A. Marty. *Nearby History: Exploring the Past Around You*. Lanham, MD: Rowman & Littlefield, 2000.

Storey, William Kelleher. *Writing History: A Guide for Students*. New York: Oxford University Press, 1999.

CHAPTER 3

Interpreting the Past
Case Study: The Baltimore '68 Project

KEY TERMS	
community-based participatory research (CBPR)	Institutional Review Board (IRB)
experients	human subjects
shared authority	Belmont Report
banking versus problem posing	respect for persons
narrators	beneficence
dialogic	justice
subjectivity	informed consent
intersubjectivity	vulnerable populations
	cultural broker

HISTORICAL RESEARCH IS A complex process when you are working with existing sources. But what does historical research look like when the sources are scarce or when the popular memory of an event contains many conflicting versions? When interpreting contested recent history, the public historian should go back to the basics of historical thinking: develop a strong research question based on available sources and consider cause and effect, change and continuity, through their eyes, turning points, and using the past. But then the researcher might have to go one step further, creating sources to fill the documentary void. Many times, historians and public historians turn to oral history to fill in gaps of historical knowledge, and collecting individual recollections about events can simultaneously create a powerful record and engage the public in community-based participatory research. The challenge comes when popular memory diverges from the documentary record. When public historians commemorate a difficult period in the past or a tumultuous event where there were no clear winners, they must diplomatically deploy their analytical skills. The Baltimore '68 Project demonstrates the ways public historians can use the tools of the historian to construct an interpretation of a contested historical event, in this case the disturbances in Baltimore, Maryland, that followed the death of the Rev. Dr. Martin Luther King, Jr. in 1968. This project took on new resonance when the city erupted again in April 2015 after the death of Freddie Gray.

Urban Unrest in Baltimore

Like scores of cities across America, Baltimore experienced unrest after the assassination of Dr. Martin Luther King, Jr., the most prominent proponent of nonviolence in the civil rights movement. Arson and looting destroyed businesses, and six people were killed. Maryland's governor, Spiro Agnew, called in the National Guard and declared a curfew. In the decades following the events, "the riots" became an explanation for many changes in the post-industrial city. Historian C. Vann Woodward has noted that "the twilight zone that lies between living memory and written history is one of the favorite breeding places of mythology," and "the riots" in Baltimore were no exception.[1] In other words, because many historians do not interpret events from the very recent past, in the aftermath of some events, people develop their own stories in order to make sense out of what has happened. Some people in the region would remark, "Before the riots, I felt safe going downtown, but not any more." "Before the riots, people scrubbed their marble steps until they gleamed, but now people don't care about their city." "Before the riots, everybody had a job and got along, but now the city is so segregated and poor." There was surprisingly little public or scholarly examination of events that loomed so large in the public imagination, as if the entire city wanted to forget that April 1968 had ever happened.[2] However, as the city tried to move forward, "the riots" became the "elephant in the room," and some Baltimoreans felt that collective historical ignorance was holding the city back.

As the 40th anniversary of the 1968 unrest approached in 2008, Jessica Elfenbein, a history professor at the University of Baltimore, decided to break the silence in an effort to remove a stumbling block to future civic progress. She organized a steering committee of other academic historians, public historians, and professors in other disciplines. Never thinking that their work would have a direct correlation to future unrest in Baltimore, the steering committee examined the causes and effects of the events that transpired in 1968. In 2006, the university, with its expertise in law, business, local history, and public affairs, was uniquely positioned to successfully examine the unrest from many perspectives. But the professors did not conduct the research in isolation from the community that was most affected by the riots. They employed a variety of community-based participatory research strategies to conduct research in a manner that was inclusive of diverse perspectives, both academic and nonacademic.

Shared Authority

Community-based public history efforts become essential when institutions choose to interpret events that the public have lived through themselves. These particular stakeholders fall into a special category in public history we will call **experients**: community experts who have gained knowledge through their own lived experiences. Experients often have a variety of reactions in public history situations where they encounter historical constructions of events they know well: they are gratified that someone thinks that what they lived through merits historical examination, but they often perceive that the public historian is not getting it completely right. "That's not the way it was!" a veteran will insist during a tour of a WWII destroyer. "You've got it all wrong," a visitor will write on a comment card at the end of an exhibit about the Summer of Love. These particular types of interactions raise important questions for the public historian: Who owns history? The historian who has studied many facets of the period, contextualized events, and developed a coherent interpretation? Or the experient who has gained authentic knowledge from a particular point of view? Public historians conclude that neither of these groups holds exclusive rights to historical authority. Instead public history practice encourages collaboration between public history practitioners and experients in historical construction.

One of the most effective ways to involve experients in the construction of a program about the recent past is through the collection of oral history. In his 1990 classic *A Shared Authority*, Michael Frisch points out that oral histories can function as a "kind of searchlight throwing a beam of inquiry into an ordinarily unreachable corner of the attic of history."[3] As an example, researchers might interview the founders of shelters for domestic abuse victims, a network that goes largely undocumented because of fear for the safety of the people they try to serve.[4] The oral history may be the only sources available to a historian attempting to construct this history. Frisch writes that historians often incorporate this type of oral history into conventional academic productions, like exhibits or monographs. On the other end of the spectrum, Frisch suggests that oral history can function as "a short cut to a more direct, emotionally informed sense of 'the way it was.'"[5] The public historians who created the 9/11 Memorial Museum included an oral history component in their physical museum and website.[6] The 9/11 Oral History Project, which provides powerful witness testimony to an event that was extensively documented and which affected people in profound but different ways, will certainly prove valuable to future historians who may find it difficult to truly understand the scope of the fallout from the attack.

As they planned the Baltimore '68 Project, organizers recognized **shared authority** through the design of their research and outreach, and the outcomes proved both useful and accessible to broad audiences of the public. **Community-based participatory research (CBPR)** embodies the highest ideals of shared authority. CBPR is an approach where all stages of the research are done in collaboration with members of the community. The goal of this research is to ensure that the research benefits all of the partners. Trained historians, whether coming from a university, museum, library, or any public history institutional setting or government entity, will share responsibility for the planning, design, research, analysis, interpretation, and dissemination of the findings with their community partners. These partnerships are usually built over time, or are long term, based on mutual levels of trust and common sets of goals and values. The Baltimore '68 projects listed below contain elements you will encounter in the rest of this book (collecting, interpreting and exhibiting, engagement, and difficult encounters), and they are all framed within the rich and complicated framework of a CBPR project.

The Project

The Baltimore '68 interdisciplinary effort included the following components:

- An oral history project conducted by University of Baltimore students and Ameri-Corps volunteers, capturing the memories of a wide variety of community members.
- A community arts project led by Maryland Institute College of Art community arts student Christina Ralls, where people who had participated in the disturbances worked with people who had been victims to create a mosaic that is now on display at a YMCA.
- A community convening organized to commemorate the 40th anniversary of the unrest, where panelists discussed the events and community members could comment and provide their own oral histories.
- A series of community dialogues held at YMCAs around the region after the community convening.
- An online repository of photos, testimony, and documents, available at www.ubalt.edu/baltimore68.
- *Baltimore '68: Riots and Rebirth in an American City*, an anthology of scholarly articles and four edited oral histories.
- Special edition of *Passager*, a University of Baltimore literary magazine that solicits contributions from older residents of Baltimore.
- *One Particular Saturday*, a play Kimberley Lynne wrote using excerpts from the oral histories and performed by University of Baltimore students and high school students from Baltimore City public high schools. [7]

Some projects, particularly the oral history project, involved the collection of new and existing materials. Interpretation was done at various stages, particularly in collaboration with the public as interpreters of their own stories and their own memories during the recording of oral histories, the community arts project, and in the panel discussions and community dialogues. The results were exhibited in a variety of ways, including exhibitions of the art, online repositories of collected materials, publication of an anthology containing oral histories, and performance of a play. Each type of exhibition would reach a different type of audience, and all of the projects engaged audiences and participants in difficult encounters not as passive recipients of knowledge, but as participants who are both shaped by their encounters and who had the power to shape the results of the research through their participation (an example of the **problem-posing** approaches to education presented in the first chapter).

Following best practices in community-based participatory research, the Baltimore '68 Project was structured in ways that were mutually beneficial to all parties involved. This is not to say that every aspect of the project was perfect. Any project involving so many participants, based on shared authority, and conducted under the realistic constraints of finite budgets and deadlines has limitations; there were things that in an ideal setting could have been done better or differently. The Baltimore '68 Project, for example, collected the memories of many people who had lived through the events of 1968, but some of the Baltimoreans present forty years earlier had already died by 2006 when the project got underway. If the project had waited even longer—hoping for a more ideal set of conditions, perhaps—even more memories would have been lost. Moreover, in 2015, when unrest returned to Baltimore after the death of Freddie Gray, a twenty-five-year-old African American man who died in police custody, and the insights gained through the Baltimore '68 process suddenly became critically relevant to the city's present, it became clear that as long as a project is conducted ethically with respect for all involved, a completed project is better than an ideal project that never makes it out of the planning stages.

The historical knowledge and new sources created, collected, preserved, and archived as a result of the project revealed that the city had not been destroyed by the week of violence in 1968, as many in the community had assumed or had come to believe. Many areas of town had not been touched, and in the affected areas, businesses had reopened almost immediately. The unrest changed the way that people *perceived* Baltimore, however, illuminating but not causing problems of segregation, poverty, and disinvestment that had existed for decades.[8] The new information about 1968 opened up the possibility for new ways of perceiving the unrest in 2015, and the mechanisms were already in place to document the history of this current event without waiting first for forty years to pass.[9]

Photograph 3.1.   Oral history narrators put the finishing touches on the Baltimore '68 mosaic they designed under the guidance of community artist Christina Ralls. The mosaic is now on display at the 33rd Street YMCA in Baltimore. Courtesy of Christina Ralls.

Photograph 3.2.   Students from the University of Baltimore, Baltimore School for the Arts, and Baltimore City College High School perform *One Particular Saturday* at the Community Convening UB hosted in April 2008. Playwright Kimberley Lynne adapted the oral histories UB students had collected and invited the narrators themselves to the performance. Courtesy of Kimberley Lynne.

Overcoming Barriers by Establishing Trust

Baltimore '68 won awards from the National Council on Public History and the American Association of State and Local History, but the Baltimore community did not embrace it at its onset. Although the University of Baltimore (UB) sits in the heart of the city, UB has been perceived as a place where students drive in from the surrounding counties, take their classes, and leave via convenient highways that had been built as part of the push toward suburbanization after World War II that had caused many problems in city centers across the United States. UB's student population is currently more racially diverse than any other campus in the Maryland state system, but faculty and administration are disproportionately white in a predominantly black city. In an effort to make it clear that in Baltimore '68 public historians saw community members as participants in the construction of the historical narrative, organizers provided opportunities for collaboration, commentary, and criticism at every stage.

Oral History Project

For the purposes of this textbook, we will take a close look at just one of the aspects of the overall project: oral history. The UB history department's contribution to the project began with an unconventional oral history project. Because the city had so quickly stopped talking about the unrest after it had occurred, no one really knew what had happened. To fill that void, UB's public historians reviewed newspaper articles from 1968 and then asked the public to tell their own stories as **narrators**. Experients become narrators when they formally record oral history from their perspective. The choice of the term narrator is important. Given the interview format, they might be called *interviewees*, or in research terms they might be called *research subjects*. Some prefer the term *informants*, but that label—because of its association with police investigations—has negative connotations, especially on the streets of Baltimore. But in line with ethical principles of respecting the rights one has to his or her own history and the shared authority that exists when an interviewer facilitates, *narrator* emphasizes the agency one has in the telling of his or her own memories of the past.

Oral history is a valuable tool in conducting community-based participatory research because it creates "a source quite similar in character to published autobiography, but much wider in scope."[10] If autobiographies are limited to people who believe the stories of their lives are important enough to be told in published form, oral histories are often much more modest undertakings, capturing the stories of people from all walks of life whose stories might not otherwise be told, documented, or preserved. In fact, one of the first barriers in organizing an oral history project may be convincing people that their stories are important and that they do have something to contribute to the project. Once narrators begin telling their stories, aided by the interviewer, it is not unusual for them to be transformed by the process.

Oral history is not a simple recording of past events as told by the narrator; it is a **dialogic** experience, the results of which are shaped by the relationship between narrator and interviewee.[11] As Rebecca Sharpless has observed, an oral history is at its most basic level "two people sitting and talking about the past."[12] In the previous chapter, we explained that researchers should try to be objective even though we all bring our own attitudes, beliefs, preconceived notions, and personal interests to our research, leading to an inevitable amount of **subjectivity** in all research. In oral history, the combination of the interviewer's subjectivity and the narrator's subjectivity means that the two influence one another's behaviors and responses, leading to **intersubjectivity**. We can minimize the potential negative effects of intersubjectivity by remaining as neutral as possible in oral history interviews, but we also must be honest in understanding how the relationship between the narrator and interviewer influences the outcome. To remove some of the potential barriers between the public and the university, many Baltimore '68 interviewers were UB students who came from the communities who were to become a part of the study. The students' connections within the communities of interest became a clear asset to the project, and their personal relationships with the narrators provided a basis for greater trust.

Oral History Ethics

If oral history requires trust, it must then involve a level of vulnerability and a high level of ethics to protect participants, whom researchers ask to volunteer their time and give up their most private, personal memories for the benefit of historical research. From 1991 through January 2018, oral historians working in universities were required to submit their research proposals to their university **Institutional Review Boards (IRB)** for review to determine if the benefits of the proposed research would outweigh the potential risks to the participants in the projects. Federal rules changed in January 2017 (with January 2018 set as the time when the changes would be in force) removing oral history, journalism, and other historical methods from IRB purview. This change was made possible because the Oral History Association already holds oral historians to a high standard of ethical practice, exceeding in many cases the standards demanded by the IRB. Regardless of the fact that beginning in January 2018 oral history projects are not subject to IRB review, it is still important to understand the basic protections for humans who participate in research in order to better understand why it is important to think about the right that the public has to be treated ethically and with respect whenever public historians invite them to become active participants in the research and collection of stories and memories that are central to many public history projects.

To make their decisions about research projects, IRBs consult the **Belmont Report,** a document that summarizes the three most important guiding principles in conducting ethical research involving human subjects: **respect for persons**, **beneficence**, and **justice**. The National Commission for the Protection of Human Subjects of Biomedical and Behavioral Research wrote the Belmont Report in response to the ethical problems revealed by the Tuskegee Syphilis Study (1932–1972) in which researchers conducting a longitudinal study of the effects of syphilis withheld treatment from some patients in an effort to continue gaining information about the effects of syphilis when left untreated. The researchers' desire for continued collection of scientific data outweighed the right of the research subjects to a cure once it became common knowledge that syphilis could be cured with doses of penicillin. The ethical problems with the study were exacerbated by the fact that the research subjects were relatively uneducated, poor African American men in rural Alabama who believed they were receiving free healthcare. When the deception of the Tuskegee Syphilis Study was revealed, the public demanded strict oversight of any study that involved human subjects. The Belmont Report formalized the new guidelines by outlining the three principles.

First and foremost, respect for persons meant that participants were to provide **informed consent** before participating in any study. That means that researchers were required to disclose exactly what the purpose of the research was, the risks and benefits, and the expected outcomes; participants needed full disclosure in order to consent based on their understanding of the research. **Vulnerable populations** unable to give consent (children, prisoners, those with diminished mental capacities, and the like) were to have extra protections provided to ensure that a third party was advocating for their safety.

Beneficence means that the benefits of any research should outweigh the risks. In the case of a recent oral history project that collected interviews with participants in the armed conflict in Northern Ireland involving the Irish Republican Army (IRA) and loyalists, the desire for researchers to document the untold stories of this conflict placed the narrators at risk for criminal prosecution and possible violent retaliation. Northern Irish investigators succeeded in forcing the Boston College library to hand over some of the interviews in order to search for evidence that might be used in pursuing criminal charges against either the narrators themselves, or individuals they named in their oral histories, even though the project stipulated that their recordings would remain inaccessible until the narrators' deaths.[13] When beneficence is not respected, the present or future ability to collect oral histories can be seriously jeopardized.

Finally, justice requires that research is conducted in a way that is fair, nonexploitative, and with a fair distribution of benefits and risks to all participants. In practice, research should not be conducted with vulnerable populations such as prisoners, children in school, or other such populations just because they are confined or easy to access. Research subjects should not be coerced to participate with promises of extraordinary benefits or the threat of retaliation. And researchers should not have a conflict of interest—they should not profit disproportionately from the research and should remain objective enough to halt research if it becomes clear that the risks will outweigh the benefits despite precautions set up in the research design.

The university IRB approved the Baltimore '68 oral history project with some requests for modification. The components of the application included sample questions and the informed consent documents that the narrators signed demonstrating that they understood the purpose of the project and how their stories would be used and shared with the public. The IRB insisted that narrators be allowed to review the transcripts before they were posted on an open access website hosted by the university's Langsdale Library. This was done to reduce any risks that narrators might say something that they might later regret when their stories were made public and highly accessible through dissemination on a website.

The Oral History Association (OHA) promotes core principles and best practices in oral history and also works to protect the narrators who participate in oral history projects. The OHA was created in 1966 to bring together the many different individuals and institutions that all were using oral history as a tool of researching, collecting, and preserving the memories and stories of living individuals and of communities. In 1989, the OHA adopted a standard set of evaluation guidelines establishing core principles and best practices. These were updated in 2000 in what has been adopted by the OHA as the "Principles and Best Practices for Oral History" available through the OHA website. In the introduction to these principles and best practices, the OHA explains its purpose: "The Oral History Association encourages individuals and institutions involved with the creation and preservation of oral histories to uphold certain principles, professional and technical standards, and obligations. These include commitments to the narrators, to standards of scholarship for history and related disciplines, and to the preservation of the interviews and related materials for current and future users." The OHA formally recommends best practices that go beyond basic IRB rules of conduct involving human subjects.[14]

If projects follow the best practices established by the OHA thoroughly, the interests of participants will be protected and the project as a whole will uphold high standards of scholarship. Regardless of whether or not an institution or university requires that a project submit their research proposal to an IRB for approval, all projects should make every possible effort to uphold the highest standards of practice established by the OHA. The core principles include specifics such as who holds copyright for the narratives collected, what is the nature of the historical source that is created through the recorded interview, and the important role that preservation plays in any oral history project. Best practices require careful attention to planning in the pre-interview stage, including thorough research, intentional selection of potential narrators, and the importance of a pre-interview, providing narrators with sufficient information about the project to allow them to make an informed decision about their consent to participate. Best practices for the interview itself include using the best possible recording equipment, establishing an ethical relationship between narrator and interviewer that gives preference to the narrator as the authority and always involves documented informed consent, recording an in-depth conversation that is not satisfied with surface-level answers, and requiring scholars to use the best practices in historical inquiry that connect individual stories with larger patterns in history. Finally, researchers need to take great care after the interview is over to preserve the interview in ways that are clear to the narrator, including any potential uses of the interview in the near and distant future. The spirit of the original agreement for use of the interview should be upheld long after the interview has been completed, and interviewers should "strive for intellectual honesty" that guides their work in oral history and their professional standards as historians. Following the best practices will improve the quality of the project and protect the rights of the individuals we invite to participate.

Students as Researchers, Cultural Brokers, and Community Members

Students enrolled at the University of Baltimore made up the research teams that conducted the oral history interviews. Sixty students in the New South and Civil Rights class formed groups of three, with each student rotating between three roles: interviewer, recorder, and notetaker. The teams interviewed each narrator three times.[15] During the first visit, they discussed the narrator's life before 1968; the week after King's assassination was the topic of the second interview; and the third session invited narrators to discuss their impression of the way Baltimore had changed after the violence. The University of Baltimore student body is diverse in terms of race, age, and socioeconomic class, and the wide range of local networks that the students could tap into contributed to the ultimate success of the project. On their own, students found willing narrators who might not have responded favorably to a cold call from faculty at a university: a black National Guardsman who had served during the unrest, a white rent collector who continued his rounds during that week, and families who had lost everything in the violence, as well as people who admitted to looting. Thus, students played the role of **cultural brokers**—people who can become the bridge between two cultures and break down barriers in the process. Community members did not necessarily trust the university, but when a student who was also from the community approached a potential narrator, the distance between community and university was lessened, and both student interviewer and community narrator became community participants on a more equal footing. The close relationship between some interviewers and the narrators would trouble some oral historians, but organizers saw it as a way to hear from people who would not have otherwise come forward. To further complicate the oral history project, the questions revealed the fact-finding nature of the enterprise. Ordinarily, students would conduct extensive research before formulating questions for narrators, but since so little was known about the events, the transcripts of the interviews became the foundation of a basic understanding of events. Participants, acting as experts, actively constructed the history.

Photograph 3.3. Organizers of the 2008 Community Convening distributed these buttons to participants who had experienced the unrest of 1968, encouraging them to act as experts during the events. Courtesy of Elizabeth Nix.

Although they were novice interviewers, the students understood the gravity of their task. Narrators sensed that many students saw this assignment as more significant than the average class project. Four years after he was interviewed, one narrator wrote in an email, "My ability to discuss these events was directly relatable to the safety and care that I sensed from the interviewers. They were completely professional in their processes and questions; while being fully aware of the volatile nature of the subject and my personal feelings. Their work was a credit to their humanity."[16] After the *Baltimore Sun* published a front-page story about the oral history project on the 39th anniversary of the assassination, additional people came forward who were willing to tell their stories, demonstrating that UB had generated some trust in the community for taking on such a contested local subject where feelings were still quite raw.[17] The centrality of the oral histories to the larger project demonstrated the public historians' commitment to including a wide variety of perspectives in the interpretation of these events.

Terminology

In the course of the interviews, the narrators sparked a discussion of terminology, creating an area of investigation the public historians had not anticipated. In one of the earliest interviews, a student asked the Reverend Marion Bascom, an African American civil rights leader, about his experience in the "riots." Bascom told her, "I would rather call that experience, or those experiences 'disturbances' rather than 'riots'. . . . I call it 'disturbances' because in a real sense, there was during that time, so much hope—H-O-P-E—that things would change." Lee Baylin, a white newspaper reporter, also made a distinction: "I'm hesitant to call it 'riots'—I guess they were, but to me, from my viewpoint, they did not have the same sort of meanness and violence I associate with perhaps the Watts Riots or the Detroit Riots. I don't know . . . that 'unrest'? I haven't found a word for it." Homer Favor, who was a young man in a black neighborhood in 1968 and who went on to become an economics professor at Morgan State University, supported Baylin's definition: "'Riots' you go after people. You cut off the heads of pretty little young girls, you shoot and stab and cut anyone. We didn't do that. They just lashed out in despair. It was a 'disturbance.' I never called it a 'riot.'" Father Thomas Donnellan, a white priest on the borderline between white and black neighborhoods, called it a "major confrontation," while Father Richard Lawrence, another white priest, went so far to define it as "an extraordinarily civilized civil disobedience." Even Art Cohen, a white legal-aid lawyer who was hit in the head with a golf club when he was taking photographs of the crowds in East Baltimore, said that "riot" is not the right label: "The word that the Kerner Commission uses is 'civil disorder' or 'civil disturbance.' Some people say 'insurrection.' People use all kinds of different words. 'Riot' is a negative word and that's the reason I don't use it. I felt at that point people had such grief and sense of loss and anger that they had to express it somehow." Father Lawrence testified, "They weren't out to get white folks. If they wanted white folks there were plenty of rich white folks four blocks away. Nobody went after them. It wasn't about that. It was about getting somebody to notice."[18]

These impassioned responses, a form of collaboration, critique, and comment, early in the process led the public historians to eliminate the word "riot" in future interviews, but that shift did not sit well with all of the narrators. When Ruth Stewart heard her interviewer use the word "disturbances," the woman, who as a young black teenager looted stores in her neighborhood, interrupted her and insisted emphatically "They were 'riots.'" Judge Thomas Ward, a white resident of Bolton Hill who patrolled his neighborhood with a shotgun, took up the issue as well: "The [*Baltimore Sun*] and all the politically correct people never referred to it as the 'riots,' always a 'civil disturbance.' They were not 'civil disturbances.' They were 'riots.'" To some narrators, it only turned into a "riot" if the violence turned toward other people. Their refusal to use the word in reference to Baltimore in April 1968 emphasized their perception of the way the angry mobs successfully contained their violence. Other narrators who insisted just as vehemently that they were "riots" may have defined the word differently, but they may also have been making the same point. The energy behind the activities had reached the point of a "riot." The fact that the mob destroyed property and not people is testimony to the compassion of the participants and not the level of their anger. In 2015, *New York Times* reporters, struggling to label what had just occurred in Baltimore, consulted the Baltimore '68 organizers to see what the community had called the earlier events. Because they had pursued this line of investigation and compiled a cogent list of responses, the organizers were able to supply the reporters with a timely answer.[19] The research about the past became useful to the present.

Conflicting Versions of History and Memory

The oral histories were invaluable in understanding the events of the past, but they were not infallible. The variety of sources challenged public historians to reconcile conflicting versions of history in a way that did not alienate the community collaborators. For example, when the public historians were trying to establish a coherent timeline, they relied on the vivid memories of several narrators who described the beginning of the unrest. Barbara Gaines remembered very clearly, "When I heard about the assassination of MLK . . . I was on the 23 bus. All the way up all you could hear was screaming, breaking of glass, and when I got off at Hilton and Edmondson Avenue, at Sid and Joe's Liquor Store, all the liquor that was on the inside was on the outside." Rosalind Terrell remembered, "As information trickled down, that he had been killed, then the news media began to talk about, you kept hearing reports of rioting in this part of town, and rioting in that part of town. It was like a snowball." Herbert Hardrick told the interviewers that he was playing pool with friends in the 1300 block of Central Avenue when a man walked in and said, "'Y'all sitting around drinking and celebrating. They've killed our soul brother and leader. Get the sticks and let's go.' And at the time he said that, it was people down in Old Town Mall just tearing it up." These memories support an interpretation of the cause of the events that Barbara Gaines articulates succinctly: "Martin Luther King's goal was peace, and we flipped it. . . . We did the total opposite! Everything he stood for, everything he worked for went down the drain when they killed him." When the world's most visible advocate of nonviolence was mowed down, the most understandable response was violence. This remembered timeline supports a tidy, balanced narrative.

That timeline, however, is incorrect. While other cities including nearby Washington, DC, did erupt almost immediately after the media reported King's death on Thursday evening, April 4, police reports confirm that nothing violent happened in Baltimore that night. Things were still quiet on Saturday, April 6, when three hundred Baltimoreans attended a service honoring King. Only afterward, on that Saturday night, did several fires break out. Even then, the disturbances in Baltimore did not kick into high gear until Sunday morning, April 7. Nevertheless, some narrators remember that the uprising began immediately after the news of King's death reached Baltimore.[20] Faced with this conflicting information, some historians might completely dismiss the testimony of the narrators, echoing novelist David Mitchell's comment that "memories are their own descendants masquerading as the ancestors of the present."[21] But historians are obligated to examine this discrepancy and make sense of it. Why did these narrators come to recall the events this way if that is not how they actually unfolded? If the community believes that something happened in a certain way, most likely that interpretation explains a core truth about the community's understanding of itself. When black Baltimoreans remember that the city erupted immediately when citizens heard the news that Dr. King had been assassinated, that testimony emphasizes the profound hurt and sadness that the loss caused. That grief gets lost in the accounting of the violence and discord. By collapsing the timeline, narrators, perhaps unconsciously, emphasize the profound disappointment, sadness, and hopelessness that defined the event for them.

Public historians cannot ask the community to collaborate and then completely discount its contributions. But they must also stay true to the documentary record, using historical thinking skills to critically examine more traditional sources as well. The public historian can make all sources available so that individuals can draw their own conclusions, as Baltimore '68 did with their website. They can also offer an interpretation that honors and explains the *perception* of events as an essential layer of our understanding of the past.

Baltimore 2015

In April 2015, local Baltimore residents and social justice activists challenged Baltimore authorities when police took a local resident, Freddie Gray, into custody.[22] The video of his arrest went viral on the internet after Gray fell into a coma as a result of the injuries he sustained during his arrest. On April 19, 2015, Gray died of a spinal injury. Gray, along with Tamir Rice, Michael Brown, and Eric Garner, joined the list of unarmed African American citizens who died at the hands of police in recent years. Following Gray's coma and death, local residents wanted answers and accountability for what they felt represented an ongoing problem of police brutality and abuse of power. Activists from around the country joined Baltimoreans in the streets to bring national attention to Gray's death. Protests began on April 18 and continued for days. The representation of the activity in Baltimore by the television media highlighted the chaotic night that followed Gray's funeral after police in riot gear confronted high school students who had been stranded when their buses at a transit hub had been shut down, not the weeks of peaceful protest that bookended the violence.

A year after Gray's death, Baltimore, Maryland, served as the setting for the National Council on Public History's annual national conference. The majority of sessions, discussions, and poster presentations were connected by the theme "Challenging the

Exclusive Past." Although Baltimore had been selected three years in advance, with no way of knowing that the conference would follow just a year after Baltimore became the center of national attention once again (much as it had in 1968), the combined history and recent events made the city an ideal location for a conference organized around this theme. The conference's public plenary, "The Uprising in Focus: The Image, Experience, and History of Inequality in Baltimore," was held on Friday March 18, 2016 and was hosted at the Ebenezer AME Church. Elizabeth Nix, associate professor of history at the University of Baltimore and a member of the Baltimore '68 steering committee, moderated the plenary. The panelists included Devin Allen, a local photographer whose work on the Baltimore uprisings of 2015 was featured on the cover of *TIME* magazine. Allen, who had no professional experience prior to the uprisings, photographed the events from his perspective. Being a local, he knew the frustrations of the community and he experienced the abuse of power by authorities. Panelist J. M. Giordano, a local photojournalist and Al-Jazeera contributor, covered the 2015 uprisings. Panelist Paulo Gregory Harris, a local community member and director of the Ingoma Foundation, had been concerned about the contentious relationship between the community and the police force before the uprisings. The panel also featured Minister Devon Wilford-Said and Robert Birt, a philosophy professor, both narrators in the Baltimore '68 Project. Their testimonies provided the perspectives of complex historical memories. These crucial dialogues were indicative of the conference's themes, as they challenged privilege and exclusive narratives.

In 1968 and again in 2015, Baltimoreans found themselves unjustly represented by the mainstream media that ignored their narratives and experiences. Both events had different circumstances, yet the causes of civil unrest and discontent remained the same. The 1968 riots were triggered by the assassination of King, but the unrest had its foundations in the discrimination, poverty, and unemployment that plagued the African American community. The trigger for the 2015 uprising lay in Gray's death, but the history of discrimination and poverty in Baltimore affected the unrest as it had in 1968. Unlike the riots of 1968, the 2015 uprising became chronicled immediately. Platforms like Twitter provided an initial archive, but soon after the unrest, the website, http://www.baltimoreuprising2015.org/, became a digital repository and archive. The website aims to preserve the multiple perspectives of the complex narrative that occurred in April 2015.

Lessons from Baltimore '68

The projects designed to explore, document, and preserve the history of Baltimore's unrest in 1968 illustrate what historical thinking and historical research look like when conducted collaboratively with the public. Historical thinking and research are complicated even when a historian sits in quiet isolation in an archival reading room or library. But when historical research is dependent upon the cooperation of and collaboration with many members of the community who are not necessarily trained in historical thinking or research and who do not necessarily share or trust the goals of the project leaders, in this case university professors, the process can be much more complex, but the outcomes can be useful in unexpected ways.

How Are Topics Chosen?

In the previous chapter, you learned that historical questions and research topics are often selected after examining the secondary literature for holes, gaps, or opportunities to expand our understanding. In public settings, an upcoming anniversary or a new source of social unrest or conflict may raise new questions about historical events and prompt the desire for fresh interpretations and exhibitions, commemorations, or even in some cases celebrations of the past.

What Questions Do We Ask?

In science, we learn that we must have a clear set of questions, or even a single hypothesis to test with a carefully constructed research question. In social science, we control as many variables as possible so that we can determine the cause or the answer to our research question with the greatest possible degree of confidence. But history, particularly research using community-based research methods, is not like other forms of inquiry. The questions often emerge while doing the research, and it is not unusual for the terms to be defined by the community members we work with to record new sources through methods such as oral history or even a community dialogue session or panel discussion and town hall meeting. The community shaped the questions that were asked and the definition of terms in the Baltimore '68 Project, leading to some of its most significant discoveries.

Terminology

Shared authority over terminology is another aspect of ethics in community-based research. Anthropologists, for example, once treated native peoples as irrelevant in the reconstruction of the histories of their own people and cultures. It was not unusual for researchers to assign names and meanings to native traditions or identities. But practices have changed, and today we are reminded that it is most ethical to ask the people we study what they would like to be called, what their preferred terminology might be, and to consult the people who have the greatest stake in a subject in regards to what words they use and the ways in which they understand the meaning of common terminology. This is not to say that academics do not have a role to play in defining terms that are accurate and sometimes correcting the euphemisms of the past, just as the Baltimore '68 historians reconsidered their exclusive use of "riot."

Creating Sources: Oral History

When sources about past historic events are scant, and the perspectives of ordinary people were not recorded at the time allowing historians access to the primary sources they require to do their work, other methods are needed, such as the recording of oral histories. Oral histories can successfully be recorded by students with little previous experience, and become an important source for future historical research. Donald Ritchie notes that oral history's "interviewing techniques can be taught to students of all levels of ability," and that even young students can be especially effective interviewers because "older interviewees feel a special need to make young people understand the events of the past."[23]

Notes

1. C. Vann Woodward, *The Strange Career of Jim Crow*, 3rd ed. (Oxford: Oxford University Press, 1974), xvi.

2. Medrika Law-Womack had written her master's thesis on the events: "A City Afire: The Baltimore City Riot of 1968: Antecedents, Causes and Impacts" (MA thesis: Morgan State University, 2005). The year after the 40th anniversary saw the publication of Clay Risen's *A Nation on Fire: America in the Wake of the King Assassination* (Hoboken, NJ: Wiley, 2009).

3. Michael Frisch, *A Shared Authority: Essays on the Craft and Meaning of Oral and Public History* (Albany: State University of New York, 1990), 186.

4. For an example, see Celeste de Roche "The 'Somebody Else' Was Us," a Reader's Theater Presentation by the Feminist Oral History Project at the University of Maine Under the Auspices of the Women in the Curriculum Program, 1995, 1997, http://umaine.edu/womensgenderandsexualitystudies/files/2010/08/FOHP_Script.pdf.

5. Frisch, *A Shared Authority*, 187.

6. 9/11 Memorial, http://www.911memorial.org/oral-histories-0.

7. For a discussion of many of the elements of the Baltimore '68 Project, see *The Public Historian* 31, no. 4 (November 2009): 11–66.

8. For an example of another case in which a community's collective mis-remembering had shaped or been shaped by the community's identity and understanding of its own past, as well as an oral historian's theoretical framework that helps historians analyze why individuals and communities mis-remember rather than dismissing their faulty memories as unreliable, see: Alessandro Portelli, *The Death of Luigi Trastulli and Other Stories: Form and Meaning in Oral History* (New York: SUNY Press, 1991). See also: Portelli, "The Peculiarities of Oral History," *History Workshop Journal* 12, no. 1 (1981): 96–107.

9. For a discussion of whether or not it can ever be too soon to begin collecting and documenting the history of current events, see the archivists' discussions about efforts to collect and document history after the terror attacks on September 11, 2001. James B. Gardner, and Sarah M. Henry, "September 11 and the Mourning After: Reflections on Collecting and Interpreting History of Tragedy," *The Public Historian* 24, no. 3 (Summer 2002): 37–52.

10. Paul Thompson, "The Voice of the Past: Oral History," in *The Oral History Reader*, eds. Robert Perks and Alistair Thomson (New York: Routledge, 2006), 28.

11. Alesandro Portelli, "A Dialogical Relationship: An Approach to Oral History," (n.d.), http://www.swaraj.org/shikshantar/expressions_portelli.pdf.

12. Rebecca Sharpless, "The History of Oral History," in *History of Oral History: Foundations and Methodology*, eds. Thomas L. Charlton, Lois E. Myers, and Rebecca Sharpless (Lanham, MD: AltaMira Press, 2007), 28.

13. Ted Palys and John Lowman, "Defending Research Confidentiality 'To the Extent the Law Allows': Lessons from the Boston College Subpoenas," *Journal of Academic Ethics* 10, no. 4 (December 2012): 271–297; Ed Moloney, *Voices from the Grave: Two Men's War in Ireland* (New York: Public Affairs, 2010).

14. Available at: http://www.oralhistory.org/about/principles-and-practices/.

15. This method was developed by the Goucher College Holocaust survivors project.

16. Thomas Carney to Elizabeth Nix, e-mail communication, September 21, 2010.

17. Gadi Dechter, "In a First, UB Students Document the Deadly Convulsion 39 Years Ago," *Baltimore Sun*, April 4, 2007, A1.

18. For the full transcripts of narrators quoted here see: http://archives.ubalt.edu/bsr/oral-histo ries/index.html.

19. "Defining Baltimore: #Riot, #Uprising or #Disturbance?" Damien Cave, http://www.nytimes .com/live/confrontation-in-baltimore/riot-uprising-or-disturbance.

20. The collapse of the timeline recalls Alessandro Portelli's Italian narrators who conflate various events that actually occurred years apart. *The Order Has Been Carried Out: History, Memory, and Meaning in a Nazi Massacre in Rome* (New York: Palgrave Macmillan, 2007).

21. David Mitchell, *Ghostwritten* (New York: Random House, 2001), 318.

22. "Baltimore 2015" is based on Blanca Garcia-Barron, "State of the Field: National Council for Public History, Challenging the Exclusive Past," *History in the Making* 9 (2016): 173–180, http://historyinthemaking.csusb.edu/documents/2016FinalJournalpdf-HistoryintheMak ing1.pdf. Reprinted with permission.

23. Donald Ritchie, *Doing Oral History: A Practical Guide* (New York: Oxford University Press, 2003), 188.

SUGGESTED ACTIVITIES AND FURTHER RESOURCES

Conducting Oral Histories

Conducting oral histories does not require a tremendous budget. Most people have a way to record an interview digitally, whether on a phone, tablet, or some other handheld recording device. More expensive equipment can improve the quality of the sound, but even inexpensive equipment if used with care can record an interview suitable for transcription and archiving or even for dissemination online via an online repository or podcast.

Recommendations for Student Research Projects Using Oral History

What follows is a set of recommendations for collecting oral histories as a class project.[1] For more thorough guidelines, sample forms, and professional standards for oral history, faculty and students should consult the notes for this section before embarking on an oral history project.

Before the Interview

- Students and faculty members should be guided by the Principles and Standards of the Oral History Association in the preparation of any oral history project. This document is available at http://www.oralhistory.org/do-oral-history/oral-history-evaluation-guidelines/.
- Students should do significant background research into the subjects that the oral history interview will address. An interview can, of course, take an unexpected turn into unanticipated territory, but as much as possible students should be familiar with the ground the interview will cover so that they are better positioned to ask strong and well-informed follow-up questions, notice when a narrator's version departs from other accounts (and so know where and what to probe further), and just generally make the best use of the narrator's time and contribution. This background research can help identify potential interviewees, identify gaps in the historical record that oral histories can seek to fill, and assure the interviewees that the student researcher is taking the project—and by association, them—seriously.[5] As the Baltimore '68 oral history project revealed, the students' preparation assured the interviewees that they were committed to the project.
- Students should construct the list of questions to be asked during the interview after their background research is completed. The questions should be open-ended,

especially at the beginning of the interview. The first questions of an interview might simply be "Tell me about . . ." or "Describe . . ."[3] In reflecting on his experience as an oral history interviewer, Charles Morrissey notes that "often . . . I am passive during the first one quarter or one third of an interview, gradually becoming more active, concluding aggressively in the last quarter."[4] More specific questions usually follow the initial ones; these can be developed out of the background research and also a broad consideration of the types of people who might one day be engaging with the archived oral histories. This final consideration forces the interviewer to think beyond the scope of the project as he or she has envisioned it so as to consider who else might find this material beneficial. Oral historians are in the unique position of creating a primary source—a source from someone who lived through the time being studied—and should seek to make that source useful to as wide an audience as possible. For example, in a project collecting oral histories from former soldiers, the primary goal might be to record their wartime experiences, but interviewers might also ask the veterans questions about whether they had become involved in veterans' organizations after the war. Someone else might use that information in thinking about men's participation in voluntary organizations or in considering the long-term role participation in war has in shaping human identity.

- Students should decide which type(s) of recording technology (audio and/or video recording devices) will be the most appropriate and cost effective, and the least intrusive, during the interviews for the project. Students should then practice with the technology, in a setting that approximates as much as possible the one where the actual interviews will take place, until they are comfortable. Students should also practice interviewing. One way this could be achieved would be for students to do "mock" interviews with friends who are willing to be recorded. The students and faculty could then watch the interviews and discuss the strengths and weaknesses of the students' techniques. Another way to provide some "practice," suggested by Morrissey, is to begin the interviews with the people that you anticipate will have the least significant contributions to make to the project and move systematically toward those that you believe will make the strongest contribution. For a student collecting his or her first oral histories, both of the strategies could be used to improve their interviewing skills and build confidence.
- Projects based in universities can consult with their university's Institutional Review Board (IRB) to determine whether the project should pursue board review. Faculty mentors should also consider any additional legal issues that may pertain to the project under development.[5]
- Interviewees should sign a consent form that indicates their agreement to be interviewed for the project and includes their contact information.

During the Interview

- The interviewer should listen attentively, but also think about where the interview should go next in order to anticipate the next question or comment. The interviewer should not interrupt, and never correct, a narrator.

- The interviewer should take notes when the interviewee says something that the interviewer wants to follow up about later (including places and names that the interviewer wants to confirm the spelling of at the end of the interview). The interviewer, however, should not try to write down everything the interviewee says, but rather trust the recording device(s) chosen. The availability of mobile phones and tablets with recording capabilities has made it possible to record interviews on multiple devices, which should be standard practice. At the end of the interview, the interviewer should ask the interviewee if there is anything that has not been covered that needs to be included or any area of the interview that the interviewee would like to return to in order to make additional comments.

After the Interview

- Immediately following the collection of the oral history, the interviewee should sign a release form. As Sommer and Quinlan note, "the primary legal framework for oral history rests on the established legal premise that an oral history interview creates a copyrightable document as soon as the recorder is turned off at the end of an interview session." They also advise that the interviewer should explain to the interviewee "the purposes of the project as well as the expected disposition and dissemination of the materials" so that fully informed consent can be given.[6] Release forms should include anticipated future uses of the material, asking whether the narrator is willing to have their materials placed in an archive, posted on a website, quoted in publications, and/or any other uses that the project leaders envision.
- The project researchers might also have the interviewee sign another release form after he or she has read and approved the transcription.
- Once the oral histories have been collected, the student researchers should transform the recordings into a written format through transcription. Students should understand ahead of time that transcription is usually the most time-consuming part of an oral history project, with each hour of recording taking as many as six to eight hours to transcribe. Student projects should strive to include transcription in their project plans. Through the transcribing process, students will come to know their interviewees' stories much more intimately, and the students' ultimate findings will reflect this increased awareness and sensitivity. Furthermore, transcriptions are key to the ultimate usability of oral histories. Before beginning to transcribe the interviews, student researchers should read additional material that will aid them in understanding the difficult process of committing the spoken word to the page and help them understand the decisions that they will have to make as a part of that process.[7] Faculty may need to provide guidance at this stage as student researchers make decisions about which transcription methods to follow. If transcription is not to be a part of a student researcher's oral history project, the interviews should at the least be abstracted and indexed.
- Once the interviews have been transcribed, the transcriptions should be returned to the interviewees to ensure that the oral narratives have been accurately converted to print.
- Completed copies of the interviews (in their audio/video and transcribed formats) should be filed with appropriate repositories so that they can be used more widely.

Other Methods for Collecting Oral Histories

The preceding guidelines map out a traditional oral history project. In some cases, however, different methods for collecting oral histories need to be used, especially with interviewees who may have difficulty sharing their stories within the confines of the traditional oral history interview method. Below are some examples of ways that oral history interviews can be recorded in combination with other types of memory cues, such as walking or the use of art or meaningful objects.

Walking and Talking

Maggie O'Neill had been researching the lives of sex workers for years when she began conducting interviews with another group of vulnerable women, refugees and asylum seekers. She realized that the unique vulnerability of these women required a different approach. Going into a woman's home to conduct a traditional interview, sitting down with an expert conducting an interview with an informant or human subject, would not encourage asylum seeking women to develop trust or feel safe revealing the kind of information O'Neill sought. An alternative approach would be necessary. She developed two different strategies, each of which empowered the women as participants in shaping the research and resulted in a greater level of trust and a more satisfying and ethical outcome.

Women who were seeking asylum had often entered England as refugees and either existed on precarious documentation or had overstayed tourist visas and were vulnerable to deportation. This meant that the places where they lived, which were registered with authorities, were not necessarily the safe places many people associate with "home." Furthermore, a traditional interview that involved sitting in front of recording equipment with the interviewer asking questions and the narrator responding, despite the terminology that empowers the interviewee to tell his or her own story, still gives preference to the interviewer as an authority figure. Asylum seeking women were justifiably suspect of authority. When O'Neill took women on a walk and asked them to show her the places in their lives where they found community and where they felt safe, a different dynamic emerged. Women narrators took control over the route the interview took both literally and narratively.[8] Through the walking interviews, O'Neill discovered the public spaces that provided a sense of belonging and safety for vulnerable women.

Art, Objects, and Oral History

Another approach to working with refugee women is a project that encouraged women to express themselves through objects and art. Art has a fantastic way of "challenging the way we see the world," said O'Neill, "while at the same time challenging hegemony."[9] Even though her project was not "public history," she incorporated many of the techniques that bring public historians together with experts in other disciplines to engage the public in participatory research. She brought her expertise as a sociologist together with artists. Her first experiment was with sex workers. She shared the narratives of sex workers with a performance artist who created a dance piece. After that she started including artists in the entire process from research design, through the interviews, analysis, and interpretation, so that instead of O'Neill's expertise leading the art, art could inform O'Neill's work. Together they created art workshops where asylum seekers entered into a sensory space that contained textiles, objects, and photographs that had been provided by the asylum seekers to say something about their home and what belonging means to them. So instead of engaging participants in a cognitive or a dialogic way, which has its benefits of course, this project asked women to bring in an object that said something about themselves, where they are from, and what belonging looks like and how it feels. This approach created a multisensory experience that rapidly built trust and intimacy leading to the production of new knowledge that was both sensory and cognitive.[10]

Notes

1. This section is based upon Rebecca K. Shrum, "Oral History as a Model for Undergraduate Research," *Creative Inquiry in the Arts & Humanities: Models of Undergraduate Research*, eds. Naomi Yavneh Klos, Jenny Olin Shanahan, and Gregory Young (Washington, DC: The Council on Undergraduate Research, 2011), 59–66. Permission to use granted by the Council on Undergraduate Research (CUR), www.cur.org. Copyright ©2011 CUR. All Rights Reserved.
2. Charles Morrissey, "Oral History Interviews: From Inception to Closure, in *History of Oral History*, eds. Thomas L. Charlton, Lois E. Myers, and Rebecca Sharpless (Lanham, MD: AltaMira Press, 2007), 160–198.
3. Barbara W. Sommer and Mary Kay Quinlan, *The Oral History Manual* (Walnut Creek, CA: AltaMira Press, 2002), 59.
4. Morrissey, "Oral History Interviews," 177.
5. John Neuenschwander, *A Guide to Oral History and the Law* (New York: Oxford University Press, 2009).
6. Sommer and Quinlan, *The Oral History Manual*, 21–22.
7. See, for example: Elinor A. Mazé, "The Uneasy Page: Transcribing and Editing Oral History," in *Handbook of Oral History*, eds. Thomas L. Charlton, Lois E. Myers, and Rebecca Sharpless (Lanham, MD: AltaMira Press, 2006), 237–274.
8. For an analysis of oral history interviews as a narrative journey that can be accompanied by a spatial journey when walking or just discussing place, see: Jeanie Sinclair and Philip Reeder, "Sounds of the Sea: Making a Mixed Reality Oral History Application for the St. Ives Archive," *Museums and the Web*, April 7, 2012, http://www.museumsandtheweb.com/mw2012/papers/sounds_of_the_sea_making_a_mixed_reality_oral_.html.
9. Maggie O'Neill, Durham University, UK, Interview with Professor Nick Mai, January 19, 2015, available at: https://youtu.be/Nb7PNXb20L8. See also: Maggie O'Neill, *Asylum, Migration, and Community* (Bristol and Portland, OR: Policy Press, 2010); and Maggie O'Neill and Phil Hubbard, "Walking, Sensing, Belonging: Ethno-Mimesis as Performative Praxis," *Visual Studies* 25:1 (2010): 46–58.
10. Maggie O'Neill, Durham University, UK, Interview with Professor Nick Mai, January 19, 2015, available at: https://youtu.be/Nb7PNXb20L8.

RESOURCES FOR FURTHER STUDY

Berrebi, Marco, JR, Christian Caujolle, and Françoise Docquiert. *Women Are Heroes.* New York: Harry N. Abrams, 2012.

Blee, Kathleen. "Evidence, Empathy, and Ethics: Lessons from Oral Histories of the Klan," *Journal of American History* 80, no. 2 (1993): 596–606.

Boyd, Douglas A. "Designing an Oral History Project: Initial Questions to Ask Yourself," in *Oral History in the Digital Age*, edited by Doug Boyd, Steve Cohen, Brad Rakerd, and Dean Rehberger. Washington, DC: Institute of Museum and Library Services, 2012, http://ohda.matrix.msu.edu/2012/06/designing-an-oral-history-project/.

Elfenbein, Jessica, Thomas Hollowak, and Elizabeth Nix, eds. *Baltimore '68: Riots and Rebirth in an American City.* Philadelphia: Temple University Press, 2011.

"Great Questions from Story Corps," https://storycorps.org/great-questions/.

Kerr, Daniel. "'We Know What the Problem Is': Using Oral History to Develop a Collaborative Analysis of Homelessness from the Bottom Up," *Oral History Review* 30, no. 1 (2003): 27–45.

Klempner, Mark. "Navigating Life Review Interviews with Survivors of Trauma," *Oral History Review* 27, no. 2 (2000): 67–83.

O'Neill, Maggie. "Transnational Refugees: The Transformative Role of Art," *Forum: Qualitative Social Research* 9, no. 2 (2008), available at http://www.qualitative-research.net/index.php/fqs/article/viewArticle/403/873.

Portelli, Alessandro. "The Peculiarities of Oral History," *History Workshop* 12 (1981): 96–107.

Shopes, Linda. "Transcribing Oral History in the Digital Age," in *Oral History in the Digital Age*, edited by Doug Boyd, Steve Cohen, Brad Rakerd, and Dean Rehberger. Washington, DC: Institute of Museum and Library Services, 2012, http://ohda.matrix.msu.edu/2012/06/transcribing-oral-history-in-the-digital-age/.

Tebeau, Mark. "Listening to the City: Oral History and Place in the Digital Era," *Oral History Review* 40, no. 1 (Winter/Spring 2013): 25–35.

Wada, Anna and Nate Weisenberg. "Reservoir of Memories: A Student Oral History Project in Providence," in *Oral History in the Digital Age*, edited by Doug Boyd, Steve Cohen, Brad Rakerd, and Dean Rehberger. Washington, DC: Institute of Museum and Library Services, 2012, http://ohda.matrix.msu.edu/2012/07/reservoir-of-memories/.

Yow, Valerie. "'Do I Like Them Too Much?': Effects of the Oral History Interview on the Interviewer and Vice-Versa," *Oral History Review* 24, no. 1 (Summer, 1997): 55–79.

CHAPTER 4

Collecting History

KEY TERMS

collections	Freedom of Information Act (FOIA)
preservation	material culture
archives	Antiquities Act of 1906
built environment	Native American Graves Protection and
National Register of Historic Places	Repatriation Act (NAGPRA)
vernacular	repatriation
Gans-Huxtable debate	accession and deaccession
wonder rooms/cabinets of curiosity	

PROFESSIONALS WORKING IN museums, historic sites, libraries, archives, and historic preservation have to think about what to *collect*, *preserve*, or *archive*. While these terms can have multiple meanings, **collections** often refers to three-dimensional objects like those in museums; **preservation** refers to buildings, structures, and landscapes; and **archives** refers to two-dimensional paper records. While at times we will reference these distinctions in this chapter, we will also talk about "collections" as a term that encompasses all three kinds of items as we explore a common set of questions that public historians face as they seek to build and maintain a wide variety of collections. In this broader sense, collections can include textual documents, artifacts, and even landscapes, such as groves of trees or battlefields.

As an example of how diverse collections can be, consider the historic Reeder Citrus Ranch in Montclair, California. This site is most visible as a preserved historic house, but it is also an excellent representation of the small family-owned citrus ranches that dominated the inland regions of Southern California throughout the first half of the twentieth century. The collections that accompany the historic house include the outbuildings, farm equipment, furniture, and extensive paper collection of business records and documents, as well as the family's personal effects, photographs, and period appliances. The grounds, historic trees, and orchard round out the collection. Collections management challenges include

Photograph 4.1.   Historic Reeder Citrus Ranch, Montclair, California. Courtesy of the George C. and Hazel H. Reeder Heritage Foundation.

preservation of the house, the furniture, the paper records, as well as historically correct and industry-standard care for the citrus trees in the orchard. The diversity of the collections at Reeder Citrus Ranch is not unusual for small historic homes that also struggle with meager operating budgets, small staff, and a heavy reliance on volunteers. Even though most of this chapter deals with large collections and major institutions, it is important to keep in mind that the majority of places where public historians work share much more in common with the historic Reeder Citrus Ranch than with large national museums.

One of the fundamental realities of collecting is that it is impossible to hold on to everything. Knowing that we cannot save every document, material object, structure, or landscape requires that we must make choices about what we keep and what we do not. Before an item is collected, preserved, or archived someone has to believe the item is worth saving. Someone has to determine that the item or the lives it represents is of historical importance. Personal collections are a good place to start thinking about the decision-making process that goes into professional collecting. We all make decisions every day about what we will save, what we will toss, what we will collect, and what we no longer need. People who cannot make these choices may be classified as having a mental disorder and are featured on The Learning Channel's reality television program *Hoarding: Buried Alive*.

How do we decide what photos to erase from our phones? Do we create a physical archive of letters, cards, and images, or is everything safe in a digital format? Do we keep evidence of our daily lives, or only the extraordinary moments? What would historians be able to discern about our lives based solely on the scraps and artifacts we have collected and saved over our lives? How accurately would it reflect our lives? Who will be able to access that material a century from now? Where could interviews with family members, friends, neighbors, coworkers, or with ourselves fill in the gaps left by the material or digital record of ourselves? Carl Becker's 1931 American Historical Association Address, "Everyman His Own Historian," shows us that these questions are not new. Becker suggested that the skills that people use in their lives are the same skills as those of the historian. We all have imperfect memories. Becker asked his audience how they would ever remember how much coal they had delivered in the past to determine how much they would need in the future. Referencing scraps of paper, receipts, ledger books, and other forms of primary evidence, we can reconstruct a history of our own lives in ways that help us make meaning of the past in ways that are useful in the present.

Certain assumptions drive what we save personally and what professionals and society in general deem historically valuable. Should institutions keep objects that represent the ordinary daily lives of individuals, or only the extraordinary achievements of our society as a whole? Are the lives of illiterate workers, children, or prisoners worthy of historical inquiry, or do museums care more about the accomplishments of the rich and famous, the powerful and elite? If public historians have to choose what to collect and what will be lost to the dustbin of history, how are we to determine which is which?

Debating What to Keep from the Past

Debates about what deserves to be saved consume the field of historic preservation. Quite clearly it would be impossible, impractical, and even undesirable to preserve every old building or every aspect of the **built environment** (the man-made surroundings that serve human needs, including things like buildings, bridges, parks, cemeteries, and transportation infrastructure) just because it might be old. City planners and historic preservationists have to agree on clear criteria for what should be saved and what can be demolished to make room for new construction. But what is worth saving? The US federal government and many state governments have established criteria for having a property listed on the **National Register of Historic Places**. The property must be more than fifty years old and fit one or more of the following criteria: 1) associated with events that have made a significant contribution to the broad patterns of our history; or 2) associated with the lives of significant persons in our past; or 3) embody the distinctive characteristics of a type, period, or method of construction, or that represent the work of a master, or that possess high artistic values, or that represent a significant and distinguishable entity whose components may lack individual distinction; or 4) have yielded, or may be likely to yield, information important in history or prehistory.

Trends in historic preservation follow other trends in history. The National Register's criteria for listing properties gives preference to the work of a master architect or a building with high artistic value, and narrow interpretations of the definition of "significant" in their two criteria have limited preservation efforts for **vernacular**, or ordinary, architecture and landscapes in the past. Mansions associated with the rich and powerful stand for centuries, while sweatshops and tenements associated with the laboring classes are demolished for new development.

In 1975, urban sociologist Herbert J. Gans accused the Landmarks Preservation Commission of New York of bias in their decisions to preserve only the homes of the rich and the creations of famous architects. Preserving only the structures that represent the elite in society, according to Gans, "distorts the real past, exaggerates affluence and grandeur, and denigrates the present."[1] Ada Louise Huxtable responded both as an architectural critic and as a member of the editorial board of the *New York Times*. She wrote that it was not fair to accuse the commission of elitism for preserving examples of great architecture and that the commission also preserved examples of what she called vernacular structures. Gans pushed further that it was fine for private individuals to preserve whatever they liked, but as a public effort funded by tax dollars, the New York Preservation Commission should deliberately represent all boroughs of New York equally and should not allow preservation decisions to be made solely on the basis of experts who focus more on aesthetics than on representing a broad view of the city's history.

Dolores Hayden, a scholar of public history, called this exchange the **Gans-Huxtable debate**. In it Hayden identified even more significant questions neither Gans nor Huxtable had recognized: "He did not explore the problems of preserving and interpreting ghetto locations or bitter memories," and "she did not ask how to justify spending taxpayers' money without giving public access or interpretation."[2] Do we only want to preserve parts of the past that we can celebrate as a community or as a nation? Or do we want to preserve and be forced to reconcile evidence of slavery, of racially restrictive laws or segregation, and of the misery of sweatshop labor? If resources are limited, should those making preservation decisions make choices to represent the most exemplary samples of great architecture, or preserve structures that represent a broad spectrum of the city's history? Should pieces of history be available to the public and interpreted for public knowledge, or is it acceptable to spend public money to preserve spaces that will never be accessible to the public? Whose interests should be served as we work to preserve evidence of the past? While there are no definitive answers to these questions, looking back on past practices can help us better understand how these questions have been answered over time, and how these questions might be answered in the future.

From Private Collections to Public Display

Public access to historic structures preserved with public funds is a modern question, as historically there was no assumption that great examples of architecture, art, or material objects should be accessible. The world's greatest collections, for example, now housed at famous museums and accessible to the public for free or for a relatively reasonable fee were at first private collections. Before the fifteenth century, the word museum was used to describe groups of objects more so than the buildings that housed and exhibited the collections as we know them today. Collections that started as private enterprises were housed in rooms called "cabinets," which displayed "curiosities" of the natural world, science, or sometimes relics of history. Known in German as *Wunderkammer*, meaning **wonder rooms** or **cabinets of curiosity**, these early examples of display are considered the precursors to the modern museum. Rulers, aristocrats, and members of the merchant class delighted their friends and demonstrated their mastery over the natural world through the display of their own private collections.

Private collections, over time, have become absorbed into modern museums. In some cases, they provided the original basis for major institutions that now conserve and exhibit samples of their collections for public audiences. The British Museum in London, for example, started as the collection of Sir Hans Sloane and other notable collectors; the Chamber of Art and Curiosities in Austria at Ambras Castle was the collection of Ferdinand the II, archduke of Austria; and the Teylers Museum in Haarlem, Netherlands, was started by Pieter Teyler's private collection. Some current-day collections preserve the feel of these earlier collecting and display practices. The Museum Studies program at Baylor University in Waco, Texas, for example, as a part of their Mayborn Museum Complex, has an exhibit called *Strecker's Cabinets of Curiosities*. John K. Strecker was a self-educated librarian and naturalist who developed his own collection and museum between 1903 and 1933. The collection became the property of Baylor University, where museum staff keeps the association and feel of the original collector by maintaining it in the style of early natural history museums where the purpose was for visual entertainment and amazement rather than for public education.

Around the turn of the nineteenth century, private collections increasingly made way for more accessible collections of "national treasures." Public access to collections and the development of modern museums to serve and educate the populace also coincided with deliberate efforts to create self-consciously modern national identities. In some cases political leaders consolidated private collections of elite benefactors to create national museums. In other cases, new collections were developed, sometimes through archaeological excavations.

It might be surprising how relatively recently we developed modern concepts of collecting, preserving, and exhibiting fragments of the past for public audiences, particularly considering how common and widespread the practice is today. The remainder of this chapter considers three specific aspects of this modern trend toward public access by focusing on how collecting has become more systematic, representative, and ethical over time.

Systematic Collecting

The systematic retention and preservation of records is a very modern practice. The federal records of the United States came under the central control of the National Archives and Records Administration (NARA) only when this government entity was created through a congressional act in 1934. Before the creation of NARA, federal records were stored in nooks and crannies of government buildings with scanty indexing and no climate control or fire prevention.[3] In the absence of a centralized system, decisions regarding which federal records were worthy of preservation and which were trash were left to individuals who certainly had different opinions on the matter. In 1934, employees of the newly created NARA began surveying federal records across the country and transferring them to a central archive in Washington, DC. With new records being added continuously, the collections have become so extensive that many items are now kept in more than forty regional facilities nationwide, depending on the nature of the records. Even though NARA has a comprehensive and systematic plan for preserving federal records, there are limits in terms of storage capacity, staffing to process new collections, and priorities in terms of the lasting historical value of records, as well as privacy issues that regulate what is preserved long term and what is accessible to researchers and to the public.

The US federal government has intentionally increased transparency and accessibility of public records at many levels. Because of laws that demand public access and guarantee personal privacy, the public has the right to access almost any type of record or to learn the reason why they cannot. Municipal governments put the minutes of public meetings and associated documents online, and the National Archives has made it easier than ever to browse extraordinary documents from any device. You can search for the record group and location of original records from court proceedings, military service, immigration and naturalization processes, and miscellaneous records of all branches of the federal government. The accessibility of municipal records varies from city to city, depending on staffing and budget, but the overarching philosophy in America is that public records belong to the people.

In other countries, researchers find that records are not easy to access, and that record keeping and preservation is anything but systematic. In Egypt, for example, one needs a security clearance to access records housed at Egypt's National Archives.[4] Even in the case of the extraordinary accessibility of US federal records, it is useful to keep in mind how recently this became the norm. The 1966 **Freedom of Information Act (FOIA)**, for example, gives individuals the right to request access to federal records. Under this law, agencies must release any information that is requested unless the information is protected from disclosure by other laws, such as privacy laws. The law also requires that agencies automatically release certain information, especially frequently requested records, such as census records, military service records, and immigration records, vital to individuals doing genealogical research. Congress and the Supreme Court agree that FOIA has become a vital part of the nation's understanding of democracy, even though it is only a relatively recent legal protection.

Representative Collecting

History, some say, is written by the victors, from the perspective of those in power. Until the twentieth century, this certainly was the case. History was not a discrete professional endeavor and was largely written by the elite and powerful about the lives and conquests of other powerful elites. Over time, however, in response to world events such as World War I, the spread of political ideas that favored perspectives on everything from economics to political rights from the "bottom up," and increasing rights of diverse gender, cultural, racial, and ethnic groups worldwide, the study and practice of history has become more inclusive. Ideas have shifted about what constitutes "historically significant" collections, and the types of items that can be used to inform historical research have expanded from purely written records to **material culture** like housewares, textiles, crafts, and machinery.

Working Class History

When English historian E. P. Thompson published *The Making of the English Working Class* in 1963, he redefined how historians studied the lives of ordinary people. Since the early twentieth century, cutting-edge social historians had already begun expanding historical research beyond the elite to include labor unions, wages, and strikes. But E. P. Thompson worked creatively to reconstruct the lives of ordinary people from the bottom up in a completely new way, examining the lived experiences of the working class. Writing such a history became a challenge because standard historical collections did not keep the records of ordinary people. E. P. Thompson had to be creative, pulling from sources like popular songs or the reports of government spies investigating the working class, to piece together their lives. His insights depended on his access to collections that contained ordinary items that many institutions might not have deemed important.

Women's History

When a descendent of a pioneer family in Maine approached the Maine State Library in 1930 with a diary her great-great-grandmother had kept around 1800, the library had a decision to make. Martha Ballard, the diary's author, had been a churchgoing midwife, but she had not socialized with important people or made any scientific discoveries. She had merely recorded the daily details of her life and business on paper for five decades. Martha Ballard's diary did not record remarkable events, but the diary itself is remarkable in that it survived more than a century to find its way into the public record. It is also rare that women in the late eighteenth century left such an extensive written record. Most women growing up at the same time as Martha Ballard may have learned to read well enough to read the Bible, but writing was not seen as a necessary skill for women of her day. Even though Martha's handwriting is more crude than that of her husband's, her ability to write such a detailed record of her life and work is extraordinary for women of her time. The library chose to accept the diary, and when technology became available, they copied the fragile pages to microfilm. In the 1980s, when American historian Laurel Thatcher Ulrich started investigating the lives of women in the Early Republic, she found that there was not much in the written record that contained the voices of women. Like E. P. Thompson, and surely influenced by his work and the pioneering work of women historians, Ulrich developed innovative strategies to interpret what little evidence existed. She became absorbed in the diary that traditional scholars had dismissed as filled with trivia about delivering babies and tending gardens. But Ulrich systematically organized the information and revealed the inner workings of a community on the Maine frontier, highlighting the complex social and economic world the women inhabited. Her book, *A Midwife's Tale: The Life of Martha Ballard, Based on her Diary*, won the Pulitzer Prize, and Ulrich was chosen as a MacArthur Fellow. In the *American Experience* documentary that details the research that Ulrich had conducted on Ballard's life, Ulrich comments on the inherent bias that historians must overcome when researching the lives of those who left only sparse records or those who left no records at all. There is an inherent hierarchy of power and privilege in the fact that historians rely so heavily on written documents, particularly in times when the vast majority of the human populace could not write, and even those who did may not have left the type of records that were systematically or even haphazardly preserved from one generation to the next.

African American History

In 1947, the daughter of Civil War soldier Christian Fleetwood (1840–1914) donated her father's Medal of Honor to what was then known as the US National Museum, a part

Photograph 4.2. Christian Fleetwood (1840–1914). Courtesy of the Library of Congress Prints and Photographs Division.

of the Smithsonian. Because of their service during the Civil War, twenty-four African American soldiers had received the Medal of Honor. When Fleetwood's daughter approached the museum about this gift, according to Richard Kurin, she "not[ed] that this would be a first as the museum did not have or display any African American collections." Although the curator of historical collections at the Smithsonian, Theodore Belote, collected material from "men who served some capacity in government or the military," he rejected the Fleetwood medal, claiming that the museum did not have the space to display or store additional objects (a claim that Kurin notes was false). Belote's decision was overridden by the secretary of the Smithsonian who **accessioned** the item, or took it into the collection, but Belote displayed the medal in such a way that visitors would have no idea that its recipient had been an African American soldier. Fleetwood's daughter Edith pursued the matter further, and Belote was again overridden and the medal was displayed alongside the necessary and appropriate identifying information.

What does this mean? As we saw in chapter 1, the public owns their own histories and are sometimes the first to notice their exclusion from public narratives. If institutions are interested in being inclusive, they need to look at themselves first. Do they represent their communities in their own staffing? If not, what are they doing to gain an inclusive perspective? How can you see what is missing if you are blind to the gaps yourself? Being deliberate and using the principles we introduced in the first chapter requires effort. Inclusive collecting is an ongoing process. Fleetwood's Medal of Honor can be seen today at the National Museum of American History as part of the *Price of Freedom* exhibit, but it took his daughter's perseverance for it to be included in the collection originally.[5] The "master narrative" of

American history has become more inclusive over time, and therefore the collections and museums that represent American history have also become more inclusive, in part due to the efforts of the public to see themselves in the nation's history. Inclusive histories did not happen by accident. The grassroots efforts of individuals and communities for equality and justice precede institutional-level inclusion.

What about the larger story of African American history told on its own terms, in its entirety rather than just as an addition to an otherwise white national narrative? Demands for an official memorial recognizing the contributions of African Americans to American history came from African American veterans of the Civil War. They had not been allowed to parade with the Union troops down Pennsylvania Avenue when the war had been won in 1865, but they were included during the 50th anniversary of the war in 1915. Their inclusion, however, was severely limited by other forms of discrimination and segregation during the anniversary events. The "colored citizens' committee" that had organized for the event wrote to President Wilson informing him of their intention to build a memorial permanently recognizing African American achievements in Washington. Their efforts led to congressional approval of an act supporting the creation of such a memorial building in 1929. President Hoover appointed Mary Church Terrell (founder of the National Association of Colored Women and a cofounder of the NAACP), Mary McLeod Bethune (founder of the Bethune-Cookman College and the National Council of Negro Women), Paul Revere Williams (first African American fellow of the American Institute of Architects), and John R. Hawkins (president of Prudential Bank and the Association for the Study of Negro Life and History), along with eight other African American leaders, to a commission to build the memorial building. The act, however, was not funded, and the onset of the Great Depression diverted attention from the memorial and the building never came to fruition.

During the era of the civil rights movement, African American museums emerged in several major American cities, including the DuSable Museum of African American History in Chicago, the International Afro-American Museum in Detroit, the Anacostia Neighborhood Museum in Washington, DC, and the African American Museum of Philadelphia.[6] Between 1986 and 2001, individuals and groups initiated another push for construction of a national museum, working to achieve the bipartisan support they would need for renewed legislation approving construction of a national memorial museum resulting in passage of an act establishing the National Museum of African American History and Culture Plan for Action Presidential Commission to study and develop a plan to move forward with the museum. In 2003, the commission released its report, titled *The Time Has Come*, and delivered its findings to the president. The museum would finally be built as a part of the Smithsonian network of national museums on the mall despite many conversations and conflicting opinions during the early phases of development as to the proper location for such a museum. Directors not only had to plan a museum and fight for a suitable location, but they also had to raise a substantial portion of the funds from private donors, develop a museum plan, and develop a collection that would be housed in the museum and that would become a part of the interpretive exhibitions and support ongoing research. The museum opened to the public on September 24, 2016, with more than

36,000 artifacts in its collection, 101 years after African American veterans organized to demand formal recognition in the nation's capital.[7]

The collections at the National Museum of African American History and Culture did not simply appear by magic when the museum was finally built. Individuals, small organizations, regional museums, and private collectors had saved, preserved, and cared for these items for years, and sometimes for generations, before donating or loaning their items or collections to the museum. The collections pertain to the histories of families, civil rights, segregation, music, clothing, communities, education, literature and photography, military service, religious groups, and slavery. The collections will continue to grow as more people become aware of the museum, visit, and support its ongoing mission "to help all Americans remember, and by remembering, this institution will stimulate a dialogue about race and help to foster a spirit of reconciliation and healing."

LGBTQ History

Influenced by the new social history that looks at the lives of women, the working class, marginalized groups, and those whose lives did not generate plentiful written records, public historians have become more deliberate in their approach to collecting to make sure that a wider range of voices are included. The ONE archive located on the campus of the University of Southern California (USC) is an excellent example of a collection that was started by one individual who believed that the artifacts and records of gay and lesbian men and women were of historical value and needed to be preserved. This private collection of an individual has grown and expanded over time. "ONE National Gay and Lesbian Archives," according to the archives' website, "is the largest repository of lesbian, gay, bisexual, transgender, and queer (LGBTQ—lesbian, gay, bisexual, transgender, queer) materials in the world." Of course the collection did not begin this way.

Jim Kepner initiated what would become the largest collection of LGBTQ materials in the world when he purchased a single copy of Radclyffe Hall's book, *The Well of Loneliness*, in 1942. With this initial purchase, Kepner started a lifelong effort to collect material and advocate for greater awareness and visibility at first for gay men, but later to include an increasingly inclusive umbrella of LGBTQ lives. He was aided in his efforts by members of the Mattachine Society, an early homophile organization that had been founded in Los Angeles in 1951, by cofounders of ONE Inc., and through the publication of *ONE Magazine*, which quickly became the most widely distributed gay publication in the United States. The private collection that Kepner had developed over his life and career moved from his personal apartment to a storefront space in Hollywood. The collection moved to USC in 2000, and in 2010 it formally became a part of the USC library system. ONE Archives currently houses over two million archival feet, and the collection continues to expand. ONE's mission is "to collect, preserve, and make accessible LGBTQ historical materials while promoting new scholarship on and public awareness of queer histories."[8]

The history of the ONE Archives is instructive. When Kepner started his personal collection in 1942, the lives of gay men and lesbian women, not to mention those of bisexual, transgender, or queer people, were not regularly incorporated into the public record, and laws that persecuted LGBTQ individuals as criminals and psychologically abnormal pushed

Photograph 4.3. Descendants of Chokichi Nakano (the man at right in the exhibit photo in background) look through an exhibit based on the family's donations of documents. Mr. Nakano was a Block Manager at Manzanar during World War II. The exhibit is a Block Manager's office in a reconstructed barracks at Manzanar National Historic Site. Courtesy of Manzanar National Historic Site and the Nakano family.

Japanese Americans also organized grassroots efforts to preserve the memory of their unconstitutional incarceration during World War II in an effort to promote reconciliation and to prevent similar actions from happening to others. Their efforts led to many significant outcomes, only one of which was the preservation of sites of confinement like Manzanar, which after decades of struggle was designated a National Historic Site by Congress in 1992. The National Park Service is steward over the site's protection and interpretation, but Japanese Americans who were incarcerated during the war and their children and grandchildren remain deeply involved. Collections donated by families have been critical to ongoing efforts to expand and improve site interpretation.[1] For a fuller discussion of Manzanar National Historic Site, see chapter 7.

Note

1. Cherstin M. Lyon, "Portals and Praxis in Japanese American Public History," *Southern California Quarterly* 98, no. 3 (Fall 2016): 259–274.

any complete records of LGBTQ life into the shadows. Even more than in the case of il-literate or oppressed peoples, the histories of LGBTQ lives were deliberately hidden from public record. The trajectory from private collection to public repository can be explained as a function of a changing social and legal environment from one of criminal prosecution and marginalization to protections for individuals and increasing societal respect for the spectrum of personal identities and sexual orientations that fall under the broad queer umbrella.

Ethical Collecting

As collections have become more systematic and representative over time, and as the collections of private individuals made their way into national museums, professionals, community leaders, and government agencies have had to grapple with ethical questions that would regulate the relationship between the desires of collectors and the rights of the individuals whose histories those collections represent.

Native American History

When George Gustav Heye began collecting artifacts from indigenous peoples throughout the Western Hemisphere, he was able to grow his collection to more than 10,000 objects before any US laws regulated the way in which American Indian artifacts were acquired or who had the right to collect these items, specifically from federal land. The end of the nineteenth century saw a move to nationalize collections and promote the modernity of tribal nations. This emphasis came in combination with the displacement, murder, and confinement of native peoples to restricted lands. Lawmakers and anthropologists influenced by Social Darwinism (the crude, unscientific theory that humans, cultures, and societies are subject to the same Darwinian principles of natural selection as are plants and animals), and Manifest Destiny (the nineteenth-century belief held by white Americans that the United States was destined to expand throughout the territory of North America and perhaps even further and that this was both inevitable and justified), advanced the patently false idea that native peoples would soon disappear from the face of the earth. Believing that they were obtaining the last vestiges of a vanishing people, individuals and institutions collected, often through highly unethical means, the sacred and ordinary objects of indigenous people throughout the hemisphere, without considering the rights of the communities from which the objects were purchased or stolen.

The first US law regulating the collection of native objects came in the form of the **Antiquities Act of 1906**. Section three of the act pertains specifically to the collection of antiquities from federal lands, giving preference for "the examinations, excavations, and gatherings" of antiquities on federal land "for the benefit of reputable museums, universities, colleges, or other recognized scientific or educational institutions, with a view to increasing the knowledge of such objects, and that the gatherings shall be made for permanent preservation in public museums."[14] The law did not prevent looting of graves and sacred sites in practice, though, as enforcement remained a problem through the twentieth century and into the twenty-first. In 1979, Congress passed the Archaeological Resources Preservation Act, "to secure, for the present and future benefit of the American people, the protection of archaeological resources and sites which are on public lands and Indian lands, and to foster increased cooperation and exchange of information between governmental authorities, the professional archaeological community, and private individuals."[15] Nowhere in these laws regulating the excavation and collection of cultural items is there a recognition of the rights of American Indian people over their own sacred objects and graves.

In 1990, Congress finally enacted a law that responded to American Indian concerns that the graves and funerary objects (items that were buried or associated with the graves of people) of their own sovereign people were not being given the same respect that would be given to the graves of other people. Their graves were protected by law for their scientific qualities rather than as sacred objects that belonged to sovereign people. Congress passed the **Native American Graves Protection and Repatriation Act (NAGPRA)** in 1990, requiring that those institutions given preference in the 1906 Antiquities Act, and those institutions that benefit from federal funding, return items excavated after 1990 to the lineal descendants and culturally affiliated Indian tribes and Native Hawaiian organizations to whom the objects and human remains belong. NAGPRA also establishes procedures for tribal consultations regarding any inadvertent discoveries or planned excavations of American Indian cultural items or human remains on federal or tribal lands. The ethics of collecting and displaying Native American property and culturally sensitive items became an issue long before NAGPRA was signed into law. The law has many limitations. It does not apply to private collections or independent institutions. But it does set a legal precedent that identifies American Indians, not museums and universities, as the rightful owners of sacred objects.

Beyond the Boundaries of Law: Ethics and Indigenous Rights

Even though some attempts have been made to extend legal protection for indigenous people over their own sacred and cultural objects internationally, laws cannot fully regulate or enforce the ethical treatment of ownership. For example, auction houses in Paris have been in the news for their sale of sacred objects belonging to American Indian tribes. There was nothing in French law prohibiting the sale. Like the United States, France has a long history of imperial and colonial relations over territories where people lived on lands that were colonized by France. The colonial history France maintained over parts of Africa led to the private collections of indigenous artifacts from Africa, as well as other parts of the world. American Indian sacred pieces made their way into private hands, and these artifacts have made their way to the auction houses of Paris. In an effort to return these sacred objects to their rightful owners, representatives of the Annenberg Trust, directed by Gregory Annenberg Weingarten, quietly purchased sacred Hopi and San Carlos Apache objects in December 2013 and returned them to the tribes. The National Museum of the American Indian honored Weingarten in 2016 with its Repatriation award. The Annenberg purchase and **repatriation** of sacred American Indian objects has been praised widely as an excellent example of philanthropic altruism and ethics.

Deaccessioning: What Happens When Collections Need a New Home?

As we have noted already in this chapter, choices are constantly being made regarding what will be preserved, what will be collected, and what is no longer needed. This is particularly the case with personal collections. When a collector runs out of space, faces financial hardships, or dies, the disposition of their collection comes into question. What happens when a collection is no longer wanted, or no longer fits the needs or priorities of the individual or institution who owns or cares for the collection? Collections are not just created and preserved. Sometimes they are **deaccessioned**, a formal term for the process of removing an item or an entire collection from one person's or institution's holdings. What happens to the deaccessioned items can be routine, or it can be controversial. A typical path for de-accessioned items might be for an institution to return the items to the original owner or descendent of the original owner, or to donate the item(s) to an institution for whom the collection is a better fit. Controversy seems to follow the sale of items, particularly when a collection is divided up for auction.

Rago Arts and Auction House and the Eaton Japanese American Folk Art Collection

In early April 2015, news started to spread that Rago Arts and Auction would be selling the personal artwork and historical artifacts of Japanese Americans who had been incarcerated in American concentration camps during World War II. Japanese Americans had given these items to Allen H. Eaton, folk art expert, when he visited the camps near the end of the war. He opposed the incarceration of Japanese Americans and wanted to develop a collection of folk art that individuals had created while held in the War Relocation Authority (WRA) camps, so the world could see the resiliency of those who had been unjustly incarcerated during the war. He visited five camps and coordinated with photographers and curatorial assistants who worked at others to photograph Japanese Americans and collect samples of their artwork. As a result, Eaton amassed a collection of 450 pieces. His collections led to the publication in 1952 of his book, *Beauty Behind Barbed Wire: The Arts of the Japanese in Our War Relocation Camps*. He concluded that book with these words: "This evacuation, regardless of its military justification, was not only as is now generally acknowledged, a great wartime mistake, but it was the most complete betrayal, in one act, of civil liberties and democratic traditions in our history, and a clear violation of the constitutional rights of seventy thousand citizens."[9] Those who had donated items to his collection believed their work would be preserved, interpreted, and displayed in a traveling exhibition to tell their stories of civil rights violations, suffering, and resilience. They never imagined the pieces would be put up for auction.

Even though Eaton had intended the collection to be exhibited, and had used it for his own research, he never gave the collection to any institution, and when he died, it passed first to his daughter, then to a family friend, Thomas Ryan, and finally to Ryan's son, John Ryan. No longer interested in maintaining the collection, Ryan consigned the entire lot for auction with the Rago Arts and Auction House, seventy years after Eaton had assembled the materials. To facilitate the sale of so many items, the auction house divided the collection into twenty-four separate lots, jeopardizing its integrity. News of the impending auction came as a shock to thousands, who immediately began efforts to stop the sale.

For many descendants of Japanese Americans incarcerated in the camps, the very idea of auctioning this historical collection was a personal insult. Among the items were family photographs and nameplates created to personalize the entrances of family apartments amidst the indistinguishable monotony of hundreds of identical tarpaper barracks. The work of their parents and grandparents had never been intended for sale, and many families retained few possessions from the war years or before. One of the grave injustices of the government's wartime exclusion and incarceration of Japanese Americans was the subsequent loss of property and family treasures, in addition to life savings and prewar businesses and livelihoods. How could one man profit from the artifacts of a historical episode that had come about from the suffering and loss of so many? Many wondered how a collection that had been created through generous donations could now be sold for a profit. Many argued that these items, though in the care of John Ryan, were not his to sell. They belonged at the very least to the children, grandchildren, and great-grandchildren of those who created them. In a larger sense, the items also belonged to a broader public. The donors gave the items with the understanding that they would be preserved and displayed to help the public understand what had happened to Japanese Americans during the war. The public should have access to the collection as a whole, rather than having it split among institutions or, worse, divided up into many parts to disappear into private collectors' hands. Was it ethical to sell these historical artifacts at all? Shouldn't they just be donated to an appropriate museum?

The Heart Mountain Wyoming Foundation, representing one of the ten WRA camps where Japanese Americans were incarcerated during the war, began negotiations with Rago in an effort to stop the sale. They raised $50,000 to purchase the collection, but after the auction house refused their offer, they put the money into hiring a law firm to pursue legal action that would prevent the sale. Individuals from the Tule Lake Committee (representing another of the WRA camps) turned to social media to organize public protest. Under the title, "Japanese American History: NOT For Sale," 7,909 individuals, including well-known figures like George Takei, signed an online petition. George Takei also reached out to Rago personally in an effort to persuade the auction house not to go forward. An ad hoc committee of sixty-one scholars, journalists, attorneys, community leaders, activists, artists, and filmmakers sent a letter to stop the sale.[10] On April 15, 2015, Rago Arts announced that it had cancelled the auction, and that they would work with members of the Japanese American community "to see this property go where it will do the most good for history," which, according to a spokesperson for Rago Arts, had been their intention all along.[11] Since the pending auction had aroused so much attention, and the protest involved so many different groups of Japanese Americans, a Japanese American history consortium was created to negotiate next steps. Despite this joint effort, a single institution, the Japanese American National Museum (JANM), negotiated the purchase of the entire collection, for an undisclosed amount, much to the dismay of other members of the consortium who had hoped to be involved in the final negotiations.[12]

On the anniversary of the museum's acquisition of the collection, now formally the Allen Hendershott Eaton Collection of Japanese American Art and Artifacts, JANM released pre-conservation photos of the artifacts on Flickr, asking community members for any information they could provide about them.[13] JANM's decision to reach out to the community to learn more about the items in the collection was in part a response to the controversy over its acquisition and pressure from the Heart Mountain Foundation to allow them to exhibit work that came from Heart Mountain at the Heart Mountain Interpretive Center. JANM administrators asked for patience while conservation experts continued to work with the collection to assess the needs of each item and to catalogue the collection thoroughly.

The story of the Eaton collection, its creation, threatened sale, and preservation, raises many questions about the roles that collections and collecting play in the philosophy and practice of public history. Consider some particular items in the Rago auction: Are the nameplates that Japanese Americans created to distinguish their families' doors from those of their neighbors' art or are they historical artifacts? What about their family photos, or handcrafted chairs, or calligraphy they practiced in the camps? If these items are historical artifacts more so than pieces of art, does that mean that selling them becomes unethical? Can you sell art but not history? Or is the question more a matter of public access? Art often enters into private collections for the enjoyment of the owners and their guests. Are historical artifacts different? Should the collective art of Japanese Americans move from the private collection inherited by Ryan to public hands? Or should the nameplates, photos, calligraphy, and other artifacts have been returned to the closest relative available once the collection's original purpose was no longer valid?

Community-Based Collecting: Systematic, Representative, and Ethical

When the Smithsonian launched its *Latinos and Baseball: In the Barrios and the Big Leagues*, a multiyear community collecting initiative sponsored by the Latino Initiatives Pool and the National Museum of American History, they reached out to projects that were already in place across the country. One of those projects is housed at the John M. Pfau Library at California State University, San Bernardino, California (CSUSB). The Latino Baseball History Project started in 2004 when Terry Cannon, executive director of the Baseball Reliquary, and Cesar Caballero, who was then an associate library dean at California State University, Los Angeles, reached out to the community and asked them to share their memories, pictures, baseballs, uniforms, and other memorabilia from the rich history of Latinos in baseball in Los Angeles. Cesar Caballero, now dean of the John M. Pfau Library at CSUSB, remembered that the very first event was risky. They did not have a collection at all, but they hosted an event at the library and invited the public to attend. Caballero said people would ask him, "Where's the collection?" He would reply, "Well, we don't have one yet. That is why we've invited you. Do you have anything you would like to donate?"

The donations started rolling in with a baseball and glove, photographs of teams, and later, in the form of oral histories. Francisco Balderrama, a history professor at California State University, Los Angeles, created an oral history class around the history of Mexican

American baseball in 2005. Like they did in the Baltimore '68 Project, students came from the communities in which Latinos had carved out spaces for themselves to play ball when the big leagues and even many public parks were racially segregated. Students recorded the stories of baseball bringing community together after church on Sunday afternoons, and the community donated more items to the collections. In 2006 the resulting exhibition, *Mexican-American Baseball in Los Angeles: From the Barrios to the Big Leagues*, debuted at the John F. Kennedy Memorial Library at California State University, Los Angeles. It then traveled to other venues in Southern California. When Cesar Caballero took the dean's position at CSUSB, the project moved with him and the focus of the project expanded to include Latinos in Baseball in the Inland Empire of Southern California, and now the project reaches out to coordinate events with similar projects in Colorado, Kansas City, San Diego, and, since 2016, the Smithsonian. The project has supported many exhibitions, public events, reunions of ballplayers and their families, and the publication of the Mexican American Baseball series with Arcadia Press.

The Smithsonian's project, *Latinos and Baseball: In the Barrios and the Big Leagues*, focuses on the historic role that baseball has played as a social and cultural force in Latino communities across the United States. This national-level project was created in response to the growth of original research on the history of Latinos in baseball and the grassroots collections of organizations located within communities. Starting with an event hosted by the John M. Pfau Library at CSUSB, community-collecting events were held in Los Angeles; Kansas City, Missouri; and Syracuse, New York. The public was invited to donate items to their local area projects or to the Smithsonian, or in some cases they allowed their items to be digitized, allowing the family to keep the items and giving only copies to the collection.

The community-based project to collect, record, and share the history of Latinos in baseball is not only about baseball. As we saw with historical interpretations at Ohio Village in the second chapter, research on the history of baseball in communities that struggled in the face of race-based segregation and discrimination has shown that there is a lot more going on than just a ball game. Families gathered together to enjoy Sunday afternoon games, picnicking, chatting, cheering, and feeling the joy of what it meant to be a part of the community. Playing against teams from other communities fostered the development of friendships and political networks that supported labor organizing and civil rights work. Local restaurants and markets sponsored teams, placing their names proudly on uniforms as a way of advertising their businesses and their role in the community. Women played ball, representing their families and communities on teams like the San Bernardino Raiderettes. A ball game might be a good place for community organizers to encourage citizens to register to vote or to encourage immigrants to enroll in classes to work toward gaining citizenship. Communities were able to rally around the fun of sport, and at the same time develop strong ties that supported improvements in working conditions, political representation, and the enjoyment of their citizenship. Most important perhaps was the pride that came from sharing in a sport that could bring the whole community together.

The lessons learned from community-based collecting reinforce many guiding principles at the foundation of public history. Communities and families are the keepers of their own stories. When public historians invite them to bring their collections together, the results are a grassroots history that honors the communities that gave rise to the content. The ex-

Photograph 4.4.   San Bernardino Raiderettes of Our Lady of Guadalupe Church, Courtesy of the Latino Baseball History Archive, California State University of San Bernardino. The San Bernardino Raiderettes of Our Lady of Guadalupe Church posed for a team portrait in the 1950s. The Raiderettes competed against teams from various Inland Empire barrios. Church sponsorship was a crucial element in maintaining many Mexican baseball teams during this era. The Raiderettes include: first row, left to right: Virginia Villareal, Mary Lou Lopez, and Tillie Villegas; second row, left to right: Dolly Villegas, "Chris" Lopez, Lynn Vasquez, priest (coach, name unknown), Armida Neri-Miller, Juanita (surname unknown), and Angie Garcia.

hibitions, books, and events that are made possible from the collections create opportunities for individuals to see themselves in history, to see how their own experiences are important and are a part of a larger narrative.

Notes

1. Herbert J. Gans as quoted in Dolores Hayden, *The Power of Place: Urban Landscapes as Public History* (Cambridge, MA: MIT Press, 1995), 3.
2. Hayden, *Power of Place*, 5.
3. National Archives History, https://www.archives.gov/about/history/.

4. Judy Barsalou, "Post-Mubarak Egypt: History, Collective Memory and Memorialization," *Middle East Policy Council* 14, no. 2 (2012), http://www.mepc.org/journal/middle-east-policy -archives/post-mubarak-egypt-history-collective-memory-and-memorialization?print.

5. Richard Kurin, *The Smithsonian's History of America in 101 Objects* (New York: Penguin Press, 2013), 224–229.

6. Andrea A. Burns, *From Storefront to Monument: Tracing the Public History of the Black Museum Movement* (Amherst: The University of Massachusetts Press, 2013).

7. Robert L. Wilkins, "A Museum Much Delayed," *Washington Post*, March 23, 2003, B8; "Historical Origins," *Smithsonian Institution Archives*, http://siarchives.si.edu/history/national -museum-african-american-history-and-culture. For more information, see also: "About the Museum," https://nmaahc.si.edu/about/museum.

8. "History," ONE Archives at the USC Libraries, http://one.usc.edu/about/history/.

9. Allen H. Eaton, *Beauty Behind Barbed Wire: The Arts of the Japanese in Our War Relocation Camps*, foreword by Eleanor Roosevelt (New York: Harper & Brothers Publishers, 1952), 176. For more information, see: Brian Niiya, "Beauty Behind Barbed Wire," *Densho Encyclopedia*, http://encyclopedia.densho.org/Beauty_Behind_Barbed_Wire_(book)/.

10. Letter to David Rago, Suzanne Perrault, and Miriam Tucker of Rago Arts and Auction, April 13, 2015, reprinted as "Rago Arts Urged to Delay Auction of Camp Artifacts," *Rafu Shimpo*, April 14, 2015, http://www.rafu.com/2015/04/rago-arts-urged-to-delay-auction-of-camp -artifacts/.

11. Eve M. Kahn, "Contested Artifacts from Internment Camps Withdrawn from Auction," *ArtsBeat: New York Times*, April 16, 2015, http://artsbeat.blogs.nytimes.com/2015/04/16/ contested-artifacts-from-internment-camps-withdrawn-from-auction/?_r=0; Martha Nakagawa, "Vox Populi: Anger and Appeasement in Handling of the Rago Auction," *Rafu Shimpo*, July 9, 2015, http://www.rafu.com/2015/07/vox-populi-anger-and-appeasement -in-handling-of-the-rago-auction/.

12. Nakagawa, "Vox Populi: Anger and Appeasement."

13. Eaton Collection, https://www.flickr.com/photos/jamuseum/collections/72157667070222721/.

14. "American Antiquities Act," 16 USC 431-433, (1906), https://www.nps.gov/history/local -law/anti1906.htm.

15. Public Law 96–95; 16 USC 470aa-mm.

RESOURCES AND SUGGESTED ACTIVITIES

Community Collections

Find an example of a community, neighborhood, family, or other group that has developed a formal method of collecting and/or representing its history. You might find family associations, community groups, or neighborhoods that have collected documents, artifacts, oral histories, or preserved remnants of the past either in the built environment or open spaces. Evaluate these collections or representations in terms of authenticity, accessibility, and significance. What was the motivation for the collections or interpretation? Who is the audience? Who are the caretakers? What are their qualifications?

Community Collecting Events

In collaboration with a community partner, host a public event where individuals who have items related to the community partner's subject of interest and/or have firsthand memories to share come together to share their stories and either donate or allow photos/scans to be taken to add to the collection. Collect names and contact information for follow-up oral histories and collecting.

Plan a Community Collecting Event

One of the most important strategies for collecting that is used by organizations big and small is community-based collecting. If your local area, city, or university is anticipating an anniversary of an important historical event, organizing a community collecting event can serve multiple purposes.

1. Asking the community to gather and bring their photos, objects, memorabilia, and stories to a collecting event raises awareness that someone in the community is researching a topic that might be of interest to them. Reaching out to the community can provide opportunities for the community to shape the research questions early in the process.
2. If the collecting event is in anticipation of a larger event to come, such as an anniversary celebration or the opening of a new exhibition, the community outreach that takes place during the collecting phase can increase interest in the later events and provides an opportunity to expand your network of stakeholders. If one person donates a story, a photo, or an object that will be displayed as a part of a new exhibition, for example, he/she will be more likely to bring friends, relatives, and neighbors to the opening or associated events, increasing the audience.

3. Exhibitions need objects. Maybe you already have interesting stories about a period in your community's history or about an important event. Perhaps you have some photos, but they are all rather formal. Photos and stories are great for the narrative portion of any exhibition, but objects, as you will see in the next chapter, are extremely important too. Inviting the community to bring their objects and personal photos to donate or loan for an event can significantly enrich your collection and improve the quality of any exhibition to come.

4. Preservation of community stories, photos, and material culture either immediately following an event or before the generation most associated with an event have died is another reason to reach out to the community.

5. Interpretation of the meaning of events or of photos or objects already in a collection that may be missing information can be improved significantly with the input from community members. Either in person or online, organizations are reaching out to their communities to ask questions like, "Can you identify the individuals in this photo?" or "Does anyone know how this object was used?"

How to set up a community collecting event.

1. Why? First, make sure you have a clear purpose in mind. Why do you want to ask the community to come to an event and bring their personal items to share with you? What is your purpose? What are you trying to accomplish? You might have specific goals, such as we need photographs of various neighborhoods from the 1950s, before a certain development project started. Or we need common household items representative of a certain era in the community's history to accompany a photographic or oral history collection we already have. Or we want to collect ten oral histories representing individuals who played in the segregated baseball league in our community. The more specific the goals are, the clearer your purpose, the more successful the event will be and the easier it will be to know if you have accomplished what you set out to do at the event. Your guests will appreciate the clarity, too. They'll be better able to help you if you know what it is that you want and need.

2. Where? Make sure you know the best venue for the community collecting event. Should it be online to reach the broadest possible audience, or should it be in person? Where should it be held if in person? You want a venue that is large enough to be comfortable, but not so large that a small turnout will detract from the community feeling of the event.

3. When? Be aware that many people work during the week, many families have obligations during the weekends, and those who are elderly can experience difficulties getting around or driving after dark. Know your audience, and know who you are most interested in attracting, so that you do not schedule an event in direct conflict with the lives of the people you are trying to attract. Sometimes it helps to offer food or some formal event such as a panel discussion or lecture to attract people, or sometimes organizing the event around a reunion concept or community celebration will work best. Some sort of refreshment is always appreciated by those who give up their time to support your event.

4. Advertise broadly. You can get in touch with media outlets early with press releases, but do not forget about social media and, most important, your own personal networks. The more personal the invitation to attend a community collecting event, the more likely a person will attend. Let the community know how important their involvement is and how much it will shape ongoing research because the expected outcomes will increase the likelihood that they will attend.

5. Equipment and Staffing. Make sure you have adequate staffing and equipment to accept the objects that are offered either as loans or for digitization. Many families will want to keep their own original photographs, for example, but may not mind allowing you to scan them right then and there. A scanner and a laptop can be used to scan documents. A digital camera and stand can capture objects that are not flat or are too fragile to put in a scanner. Digital recording equipment can be useful to record oral histories. Take photographs of the event to document the day and the community involvement. These photos may come in handy later. Make sure your guests are aware that you are photographing the event.

6. Paperwork. Make sure you have the right paperwork to accept donations, loans, and digital copies, or to follow up with individuals who may just show up to see what is happening but who want to donate later. These will include a deed of gift form, informed consent, and a sign-in sheet to collect contact information.

7. Contact information. Collect the names and e-mail/mailing addresses of community members who attend, so you can add them to your list of contacts for future events. Also, be prepared to collect the contact information of anyone who came just to see what the event was all about but might have items at home to donate at a later time or might be willing to record an oral history interview for your project. No matter the reason, plan in advance and be ready to collect the names and contact information of your community participants, so you can continue to build on the networks created through the organization of your collecting event.

8. Be careful what you promise. Do not say you will be in touch if you do not plan to follow up with guests. Do not promise a grand exhibition if you only have a budget for the collecting event. If you need the community's help to follow through with any long-term plans, ask. There are people in the community who enjoy contributing to worthy projects if their roles are well defined, if the project already aligns with their personal interests, and if it seems that the larger goals of the project serve a greater good. Just make sure you can deliver on any promises you do make.

Evaluating Collections

Developing a collection should be aligned with the mission and core values of the organization. A strong mission statement clarifies every other aspect of an organization's operations. A museum's mission statement clarifies the topical or educational focus and defines the responsibility the museum maintains to its public audiences, researchers, and collections. Libraries add ongoing evaluations of the needs of their patrons. Archives focus especially on the ongoing collections. If the mission is clear, the collections plan should follow. For example, the mission of the Agua Caliente Cultural Museum Archives in Palm Springs, California, is

> to collect, preserve, and protect a variety of original documentary materials containing information of permanent historical value relating to the history of the Agua Caliente Band of Cahuilla Indians and Cahuilla culture in general. By collecting and preserving documents, artifacts, oral histories and preserving sacred places that reflect the life and activities of those who created such material, the Agua Caliente Cultural Museum Archives ensures that this material is available for successive generations to discover.

A look at the collections themselves at this institution will reveal what they consider to be items of "permanent historical value." Consider the mission statements of some of the institutions in your community or of some of our national museums. How well do they direct the work of the institution? How do they differ from one another?

One way to understand how collections work is to visit a museum, archive, historical society, or a similar place that maintains a collection of historical importance to see how they manage their collections. To understand how the collections strategy fits in with the overall goals and values of the institution, there are a series of questions one must ask. What is the mission statement and organizing values of the organization or institution? What are their preferred topics or areas of emphasis for their collections? In other words, how would they draw the line between things they might be interested in collecting and things they would not collect even if the item were of great historical or cultural value? Or by what criteria are potential collections judged or evaluated? What types of items/objects are already in the collections? How does the organization or institution organize their collections? Do they make them accessible to researchers and/or the public? If so, how? What do they do when they decide a collection or item is no longer needed or wanted? Or in other words, how do they handle the process of **accessioning** (formally making an item or collection a part of their overall collections, including permissions and cataloging and numbering the items to keep track of them in their inventory) and **deaccessioning** items or entire collections (the process of taking items or collections out of the inventory and determining what should be done with them, including legal obligations, ethical concerns, and practical questions concerning where these things should go next)? Are there any accreditation guidelines the institution follows? For example, is the organization or institution an accredited one, and if so, what are the standards of the accrediting organization?

Assessing a collection and the collections management plan of a museum, library, or archive can be approached similarly to writing an exhibition review or a critical book review or film review. You begin with an overview of the collection and institution you are reviewing, making sure you cover all of the major components of a complete/ideal collections management plan whether or not each item applies to the institution you are reviewing. A strong collections plan should include certain core principles: align collections with the overall goals and mission of the community, institution, or organization; plan for maintenance and continued conservation once the collection has been established; consult and collaborate with communities and stakeholders; and consider the educational strategy that will be used to interpret the collection.

Following the overview is your own assessment of the quality, scope, and significant ways in which the institution/collection aligns with or departs from an ideal collections management plan. Where are the significant assets of this collection/institution and where are the weaknesses. Finally you will end with recommendations. What would you recommend that the institution address moving forward in either highlighting strengths or addressing weaknesses?

RESOURCES FOR FURTHER STUDY

American Alliance of Museums. "Code of Ethics for Museums," available at http://www.aam-us
.org/resources/ethics-standards-and-best-practices/code-of-ethics.

Banks, Sarah, Andrea Armstrong, Kathleen Carter, Helen Graham, Peter Hayward, Alex Henry, Tessa Holland, Claire Holmes, Amelia Lee, Ann McNulty, Niamh Moore, Nigel Nayling, Ann Stokoe, and Aileen Strachan. "Everyday Ethics in Community-Based Participatory Research." *Contemporary Social Science* 8, no. 3 (2013): 263–277.

Boyd, Douglas A., and Mary A. Larson, Eds. *Oral History and Digital Humanities.* London: Palgrave Macmillian, 2014. http://www.digitaloralhistory.net.

Cook, Terry. "The Archive(s) Is a Foreign Country: Historians, Archives, and the Changing Archival Landscape." *The Canadian Historical Review* 90 no. 3 (September 2009): 497–534.

Fine-Dare, Kathleen S. *Grave Injustice: The American Indian Repatriation Movement and NAGPRA.* Lincoln: University of Nebraska Press, 2002.

Hamilton, Paula and Linda Shopes, Eds. *Oral History and Public Memories.* Philadelphia: Temple University Press, 2008.

Ishizuka, Karen. *Lost and Found: Reclaiming the Japanese American Incarceration.* Chicago: University of Illinois Press, 2006.

Jimerson, Randall C. "Embracing the Power of the Archives." *American Archivist* 69 (Spring/ Summer 2006): 19–32.

Linenthal, Edward. *Preserving Memory: The Struggle to Create America's Holocaust Museum.* New York: Penguin, 1995.

Russell, Molly. "Principles of Successful Civic Engagement in the National Park Service." US National Park Service Publications and Papers, Paper 99, 2011. http://digitalcommons.unl .edu/natlpark/99.

Tyler, Norman, Ted J. Ligibel, and Ilene R. Tyler. *Historic Preservation: An Introduction to Its History, Principles, and Practice.* New York: W. W. Norton, 2009.

Wallace, Michael. "Razor Ribbons, History Museums, and Civic Salvation," In *Mickey Mouse History and Other Essays on American Memory*, 33–54. Philadelphia: Temple University Press, 1996.

Interpreting and Exhibiting History

INTERPRETING AND EXHIBITING HISTORY can take place anywhere. Exhibitions can be permanent and formal, as is the case with displays at museums, or temporary and deliberately informal, as in a pop-up installation. People exhibit history online, in the streets, at historic sites, in museums, and in airports. Interpretations can be extremely serious, for topics such as the Holocaust, or deliberately playful, even bordering on the absurd. Consider the *London Bridge Experience* that begins with a history of London and the bridge, but ends with actors covered in fake blood chasing tourists through darkened, narrow passageways with chainsaws.[1]

Exhibitions can be text-based, as in a typical museum display; 100 percent visual, as in a banner exhibition; or completely audio, as in a podcast. Even though this chapter discusses interpreting and exhibiting history in museum exhibitions, the range of options for approaching the topic are immense. The chapters that follow will address a broader range of possibilities, but in this chapter we begin with basic principles, using the museum as a starting point. To introduce you to the kinds of interpretation and exhibition choices we will explore in this chapter, we begin with a walkthrough of the Museum of Memory and Human Rights in Santiago, Chile, a site that faced a challenge of interpreting a painful and controversial period in Chile's recent past.

Chile celebrated its bicentennial in 2010 along with other countries throughout Latin America. The country's proud history of democratic rule and civility had been broken in 1973 when the military violently deposed democratically elected socialist President Salvador Allende. The military dictatorial regime, led by General Augusto Pinochet, inflicted human rights abuses, including the arrest and torture of at least 31,000 Chileans; thousands were murdered and disappeared. Usually, on a significant anniversary, a nation would be expected to celebrate the high points of its past to promote its future. But Chilean President Michelle Bachalet knew her country's recent history would not allow that type of commemoration; she herself had been tortured under the dictatorship, so it was fitting when she inaugurated the bicentennial year by dedicating a museum designed to preserve the memory of human rights atrocities committed under the dictatorship that ruled the country from 1973 through 1990.[2]

The Museum of Memory and Human Rights, or *Museo de la Memoria y los Derechos Humanos*, opened January 10, 2010. Designed by Brazilian architect Mario Figueroa, the museum stands three stories tall over a recessed courtyard, flanked by a reflecting pond and surrounded by a thin screen of oxidized copper. The use of copper is deliberate, as it is the most important natural resource of Chile. The block-like geometric shape of the building hovers over the path that visitors use to enter the museum one story below the street level. Along the main ramp that descends under the museum, the entire text of the Universal Declaration of Human Rights hangs from the wall in bronze lettering.

When visitors enter the museum, they encounter a collage arranged in the shape of a map of the world. The individual pictures depict human rights abuses from around the globe. Below the map stand thirty plaques, representing truth commissions from Latin America, Europe, Africa, and Asia, including two that investigated the abuses under Pinochet in Chile.[3] If there is one message that is clear to all who enter the museum, it is that Chile is not alone. Other countries have not only suffered terrible human rights tragedies, but they have also faced their pasts. The museum's story may not be unique in the world, but it is a story that is shared by Chileans throughout the country. On the floor next to the truth commission exhibit lies a map of Chile showing the location and description of 160 memorials that preserve the memory of human rights abuses under Pinochet. Another map of Chile in the museum lobby shows the other places where the history of the military dictatorship is interpreted and/or memorialized through art installations or memorials to specific individuals, specific groups, or sites of imprisonment or torture.

The permanent exhibition, based on the reports of the National Commission on Truth and Reconciliation and the National Commission on Political Imprisonment and Torture, begins on the second floor. Visitors initially encounter evidence of the coup from Septem-

Photograph 5.1.   Exterior of the Museum of Memory and Human Rights, Santiago, Chile, August 2010. Photo by Cherstin M. Lyon.

ber 11, 1973. News reports flash on screens; a short documentary plays, showing scenes of the presidential palace being bombed from the air. Cubes across the floor encase computer terminals where visitors can choose the sources they want to consult in order to learn more about the coup as it unfolded and was reported on around the world.

Turning the corner, the exhibition shows how a junta formed immediately, suspended freedom of speech, and repressed dissidents. The portions of the exhibition that are based on the attempts to crush freedom of speech and the international outcry against the brutal dictatorial repression line the perimeter of the main exhibition, where light streams into the museum through the entirely glass walls, filtered by the skin of copper that envelops the outside of the building.

The light that illuminates the outer edge of the exhibition contrasts sharply with the darkness of the interior. The exhibits in this darker area show how more than 31,000 Chileans and foreign nationals were detained, often in secret locations, tortured, and in some instances killed; much to the horror of family members, some were disappeared in clandestine graves or disposed of in other nefarious ways. The walls of the interior section are painted black, the lighting is low, and visitors get a sense of the secrecy and shame that shrouds this portion of the national story. Only one large artifact makes the torture tangible. One metal bed frame with a large cell battery and electrical cords are a visible reminder of the barbaric torture techniques ostensibly used to gather information from the military's victims.

Photographs 5.2 and 5.3.   World maps and truth commissions from around the world with closeup of individual pictures that compose the world map collage. Photos by Cherstin M. Lyon.

Photograph 5.4. Map of Chile showing other memorial sites. Photo by Cherstin M. Lyon.

Throughout the museum, visitors can linger at flat panel interactive computer screens to investigate a subject further, examine artifacts and documents, or leaf through binders of documents that reveal how widespread the torture centers were throughout the country. It would be difficult for any single visitor to exhaust the research possibilities in the permanent exhibition alone.

There are two portions of the exhibition that stand out and are designed to be more affective or reflective in nature. On the second floor, after visitors have learned of the coup, the repressive regime, the torture and disappearance of civilians, and global efforts to break the silence and end the human rights atrocities, visitors come to a glass cube that extends like an observation deck overlooking the main floor. It is positioned directly across from the wall of more than a thousand pictures of individuals who were imprisoned, tortured, and then disappeared. The small room is surrounded by lights made to look like candles. Entering into the room for a moment of silent reflection is a powerful experience. The faces on the wall remind visitors of the unfinished nature of the story. Outside the museum, below the courtyard is an art installation by Alfredo Jaar, *La geometria de la conciencia* (*The Geometry of Conscience*), in which visitors enter a single room where silhouettes of generic faces stare back; the reflection of the visitors and the silhouettes are extended into infinity with the aid of mirrored sidewalls. The experience lasts three minutes, beginning with one minute of light in which visitors can see the silhouettes and themselves reflected together, one minute of absolute darkness, and a final minute like the first in light. The symbolic use of light and dark used in the museum carries over into this affective experience.

Photographs 5.5 and 5.6.   Light pours into the museum through the clear glass exterior walls, filtered through the thin copper sheath that surrounds the exterior of the building to illuminate the portions of the exhibition that interpret efforts to end the human rights atrocities committed by the military. The interior uses the darkness of black walls to accentuate the secrecy in which the military carried out the disappearances and torture of Chilean citizens. Photos by Cherstin M. Lyon.

Photograph 5.7.   Standing in this small room, visitors can reflect on the victims who were disappeared and spend a few minutes looking at the wall of photographs. Photo by Cherstin M. Lyon.

Exhibiting History

Every element of the *Museo de la Memoria y los Derechos Humanos* (Museum of Memory and Human Rights) is the result of deliberate and thoughtful choices made by a diverse team of professionals who designed it to convey specific messages to visitors. The use of light and darkness is particularly profound. The human rights atrocities are interpreted in areas set aside and marked by darkness, but even here, visitors encounter elements of human resiliency, such as dolls or other relics prisoners created with found objects while held in captivity. The light reveals efforts of Chileans and the international community to resist rules restricting access to information and efforts to bring evidence of human rights abuses to the public and to end the violence. The exhibition uses spatial organization, lighting, flow, color, video, and auditory elements to provoke a multisensory intellectual and emotional response. Interpreting and exhibiting history—like collecting—can reveal attitudes, beliefs, and ways of understanding our relationship with history.

The survey respondents in *The Presence of the Past* reported a strong draw to the collections of material culture in museums and at historic sites as a way to experience and understand the past. As Thelen and Rosenzweig reported, "the people who talked with us trusted history museums and historic sites because they transported visitors straight back to the times when people had used the artifacts on display or occupied the places where 'history' had been made." These visitors wanted to interact with **witnessing objects**: those objects that were there during the events and the times that the exhibition explains. Thelen and Rosenzweig found that by "approaching artifacts and sites on their own terms, visitors could cut through all the intervening stories, step around all the agendas that had been advanced in the meantime, and feel that they were experiencing a moment from the past almost as it had been originally experienced." The survey respondents rated museums as the most trustworthy of the places where they encountered history. This attitude toward witnessing objects underlines the responsibility of public historians—and all professionals who develop exhibits—to maintain this trust and to provide opportunities for the unmediated interaction between visitor and historical artifacts.[4]

Since most exhibitions have a specific educational goal, exhibits will provide more than these unmediated experiences. Principles for sound informal education should apply as museums develop their educational goals and plans for an exhibit. Adults and children should be invited to think through the interpretive process and to engage in a problem-posing model for education. As they plan exhibits and engagement strategies, public historians should focus on the involvement of the public: visitors of all ages and levels of ability should have the opportunity to engage with the display and interpretation at their own pace, following their own levels of interest. Despite the vast changes in the ways public historians have approached exhibits over time, both structurally and thematically, there are certain principles that apply to almost any well-constructed exhibition. Artifacts and images constitute the core components of most exhibits, and interpretive panels provide written context and meaning for them.

The "Big Idea"

Developing the content of an exhibition shares many elements with the core work of the historian described in chapter 2. In a public history setting, the institution may provide the public historian with a topic: "urban slavery in antebellum Columbia, South Carolina" or "the history of food production and consumption in post-1950 America." With that topic in mind, the public historian begins to do history: she reads the secondary literature and develops a research question. In a large institution, the historian is most likely working in collaboration with other staff members of the museum even at this early stage, while in a smaller setting he may be working alone. The analysis of primary sources enables the historian to develop a **thesis**, the main argument that will shape the narrative and that answers the research question. For example, in an exhibit about the development of factories in nineteenth-century America, the research question might have been, "Why were so many workers injured in late nineteenth-century American factories?" The thesis might be that "factories were not well regulated during this period, which put workers at significant risk." In academic research and writing, historians always seek to develop a new and innovative thesis; publishing journal articles and books usually requires an original contribution to the field. In exhibit development, however, historians do not always develop an original thesis—they may use the original work of other scholars to build a narrative with the unique set of documents and artifacts housed by their institution. This debt to the work of other historians is another way in which public historians work more collaboratively than traditional historians.

In exhibit design, the thesis you have developed—the argument you are making about the topic of the exhibit—is often referred to as the **big idea**, a written statement of what the exhibit will be about. While historians develop the thesis on their own, the exhibit team collaborates to develop the big idea. As Beverly Serrell has described it, the big idea is "one complete noncompound, active sentence that identifies a subject, an action (the verb), and a consequence ('so what?'). . . . A big idea is big because it has fundamental meaningfulness that is important to human nature. It is not trivial."[5]

What Does a Big Idea Look Like?
From Beverly Serrell's *Exhibit Labels: An Interpretive Approach*

Examples of big ideas that contain a clear subject, an active verb, and a "so what?" follow. As you read each one, what picture do you get in your mind of what you will see, do, and find out about in an exhibition with this big idea?

- Most of what we know about the universe comes from messages we read in light.
- A healthy swamp—an example of a threatened ecosystem—provides many surprising benefits to humans.
- Forensic scientists look for evidence of crimes against wildlife in order to enforce wildlife laws.
- The conditions for life on Earth in extreme environments help define the ways we search for life on other planets.
- Art depicting the California gold rush promoted a skewed romanticized vision of one of the nineteenth century's most important events.

As you can see in the examples above, the subject can be stated in one word (*swamps, scientists*) with adjectives (*healthy, forensic*), or more than one word (*most of what we know about the universe, the conditions for life on Earth, art depicting the California gold rush*).

The next three examples do not conform to the Serrell rigors of a big idea statement (subject-verb-so what?) but they do function just like a big idea in that they define or describe the content of the exhibition. By reading the title or the statement, you know what the exhibition will be about.

- *Manufacturing a Miracle: Brooklyn and the Story of Penicillin*
- Sharks are not what you think.
- What is it about dogs that strongly connects them to humans?

All of the examples above show the difference between a topic and a big idea. Topics—such as sharks, penicillin, forensic scientists, or Western art—are incomplete thoughts, whereas a big idea tells you *what about* sharks, *what about* forensic scientists, or *what kinds* of art.

Some people confuse topics, outputs, or objectives with big ideas. Topics and objectives will not help keep the exhibition focused.

These examples are *not* big ideas:

- This exhibit is about the settlement of the western United States.
- This exhibit will present the complex historical and scientific information surrounding the questionable authenticity of sculpture.
- Visitors will learn about molecular structure, chemical reactions, and the scientific process of analyzing unknown substances.
- Visitors will develop a sense of wonder about nature by exploring the secret world of animals.

The above are not big ideas because they don't say what the subject of the exhibition is or tell you what is going on. If "visitors" or "the exhibit" is the subject, you haven't got a big idea yet. If the visitors are doing something, it's probably an objective. If the exhibit is doing something, it's probably an output.[6]

Developing the "big idea" is not a simple process, but it is critical to exhibition development. The exhibition team should meet and seek to develop the big idea—have lots of butcher block paper or whiteboard space available—and they should not expect to accomplish this easily in one hour or even in one meeting. Including everyone on the team in developing the big idea makes the process more complex initially as many voices and agendas seek agreement, but involving all the stakeholders will translate into significant commitment to the project from everyone. Once established, the big idea should guide the work of the entire team throughout the rest of the process.

After analyzing the sources of the artifacts and documents, making sense of the content, and developing the "big idea," the exhibit team must determine the goals of the exhibition. Should the exhibit recover lost voices? Reclaim a past that has been lost to historical amnesia? Correct a wrong? Interpret a historical space? Celebrate an anniversary? An exhibit cannot simply present a collection of stories, as cabinets of curiosities once did; it must be laid out and interpreted in a way that honors historical thinking. It should not fall into the category that some would place all history, complaining that it is "just one damned thing after another," without a clear sense of why any of it matters in the first place. Here, the framework Nikki Mandell and Bobbie Malone developed, discussed in chapter 2, can be invaluable. Their categories of historical analysis—Cause and Effect, Change and Continuity, Turning Points, Using the Past, and Through Their Eyes—can be effectively deployed in exhibit development.

An exhibition team may choose to focus on only one of the categories for historical thinking as the primary goal, but using more than one category can help you build a powerful exhibition, too, as long as you remember that it cannot do everything. For example, let's go back to that exhibition about nineteenth-century American factories. Organizers might focus only on the category of cause and effect to help visitors understand the lack of regulation during this period, but the team could also choose to intersperse text panels and objects that help visitors see the factory "through the eyes" of its workers and their experiences. A final panel could consider lessons from this period that continue to be relevant in the political and economic sectors of our society today as Americans continue to "use the past" in shaping the present day. These categories of historical analysis make visible for the historian and the exhibition team the different ways they are engaging with the information; when clearly explained and understood, they can go a long way toward unifying the work of the entire team. As the exhibition develops, the public historian must choose artifacts, not for their aesthetic appeal or sentimental value, but because they contribute to the "big idea" and to an understanding of the historical categories of inquiry being used.

Developing the Big Idea at the *Voices of Lombard Street* Exhibit

In the *Voices of Lombard Street*, exhibit organizers at the Jewish Museum of Maryland developed their big idea by asking a cause-and-effect question: "What happened to Lombard Street?" A closer examination of their process shows how their institution developed an exhibit so complex and comprehensive that it has become part of their permanent exhibition. East Lombard had been central to Baltimore's Jewish community during most of the twentieth century. Baltimoreans remembered the fresh produce stands spilling onto bustling sidewalks, chickens hanging in kosher butcher shops, and families walking along it to nearby synagogues. They also remembered fires and looting that took place on the street during the urban disturbances that followed the assassination of Dr. Martin Luther King, Jr.

Today many visitors see the vacant lots and the one remaining Jewish deli along the street and often jump to the conclusion of cause and effect: most of the area must have

Photograph 5.8.   Vacant lots line Baltimore's Lombard Street in 2016. Photo by Elizabeth Nix.

been burned down during the violence of 1968. However, historian Deborah Weiner pulled together primary documents—photographs, oral histories, and newspaper clippings—to prove a different thesis. Although one business on the street burned to the ground during the unrest, the other businesses survived, taking out ads in the *Baltimore Sun* reminding customers that "We are open and ready to serve you."[7] A newspaper article a year after the disturbances called Lombard Street, "a tiny unchanged island, noisy and odorous, of ancient, old world foods, customs and conversations . . . a milling, pushing gaggle of shoppers talking to storekeepers in half a dozen languages over the noise of blaring automobile horns and squawking chickens."[8] Weiner used secondary sources like Thomas Sugrue's *Origin of the Urban Crisis* to place the experience of this particular shopping district into the context of American retail trends in the 1970s. She learned that a number of Jewish businesses closed after the 1960s because the parents had run the business to pay for schooling for their children. Their educated children did not want to take over a small business, so when the parents reached retirement age, they simply closed up shop. This generational change marked a turning point in Jewish history.

After reviewing the secondary literature, Weiner went back to the primary sources and discovered a street repair project that dealt the most lasting blow to the community. The City of Baltimore shut down Lombard Street in 1976 for resurfacing. Photographs show

Photograph 5.9.   Roadwork shut down Lombard Street in 1976. Photo Courtesy University of Maryland Libraries.

the road was impassable. Customers could not park for months, and the sidewalks were barely walkable. Government records indicate the project took longer than expected. An oral history underlines the impact of the project: "The way the city's busted up the street here, it looks like there's been a war and we've been bombed out."[9] City directories provide proof that by the end of 1978, twelve of twenty-eight stores had closed, and by 2015, only Attman's Delicatessen remained. Using primary and secondary sources, exhibit organizers developed the big idea of cause and effect: The 1968 unrest did not cause the demise of Lombard Street. Then they used artifacts and exhibit organization to walk their visitors through their evidence. Along the way, visitors learned about change and continuity in the shopping practices of Baltimore's Jewish community and experienced the history of the street through the eyes of past residents.

Writing Interpretive Text

After the secondary literature has been read, the primary sources analyzed, the goals of the exhibition are clear, the main historical category determined, and the big idea developed, the writing phase begins in earnest. Although we delimit them here for ease of explanation, these phases can and should overlap; historians are often in the writing phase from the very beginning of a project, keeping notes and ideas along the way, as well as developing potential big ideas to test against the secondary and primary sources very early on. Writing the interpretive content is a time-consuming but rewarding experience. You must take the complex and often intricate findings you developed in doing the primary and secondary source research for the project and create compelling and brief presentations of those ideas that provide context to artifacts, images, and documents.[10]

Developing the written content that will go into an exhibition means deciding on the information that will be presented at every level—from the title down to the captions that accompany individual artifacts. Exhibitions should include both an **exhibition title** panel and a **master label**. The exhibition title panel contains the title of the exhibition and should clearly state its topic and scope. For example, a popular exhibit at the Smithsonian's National Museum of American History is entitled, *Food: Transforming the American Table, 1950–2000.* The master label, which is the first thing that visitors will view as they enter the exhibit, should make it clear what the exhibit will cover. The master label often includes the exhibit's big idea, either exactly as the exhibit team developed it or in a form made more readable and understandable by visitors. Master labels should be 125 words or fewer. For example, that same Smithsonian exhibition's master label reads in part, "Between 1950–2000, new technologies and cultural changes transformed how and what we eat."

Within the exhibition, artifacts and images are grouped into sections. Visitors to the Food exhibit encounter sections that discuss "Shortcuts for Home Cooks," and "Snack Time," each with introductory text called the **section topic label**. These labels, which should run between seventy-five to one hundred words, introduce the visitor to the information presented within the section. An even smaller selection of objects can be grouped together in a **case or group label** of fifty to seventy-five words. The case or group label may be the only descriptive identification that these objects receive. In other words, there may not be labels interpreting each individual object, only the necessary information to identify the artifact, called the **object identification**. The object identification should include information that will explain to a visitor what the object is, who made it, and what it is made out of, as well as the object's accession number, which locates it within the museum's collection. If one object is of particular interest or adds an essential component to the big idea, it merits a **descriptive caption**, of twenty-five to fifty words each, in addition to the object identification.

The **interpretive labels** described above are not the only kind of information that should be made available to visitors to an exhibition. There should be several other types of text panels: **funder list**, **credit panel**, and **orientation label**. The funder list identifies and provides an opportunity for the institution to thank the organizations and individuals who provided financial support. It also assists visitors in evaluating the perspective offered by the exhibition. An exhibition on the historical significance of oil in the United States would likely look quite different if funded by an oil company versus an environmental activist group. The credit panel is also key to helping visitors understand the broader context of an exhibition. It has not been standard practice to include a credit panel at history museums. This may be in part because of the collaborative nature of exhibition development, but as historians embrace the idea that historical writing is an interpretation that is always filtered through the perspective of the historian, it should become more common for visitors to be able to see who the members of the exhibition team were and in what ways each person contributed to the exhibition's development. The orientation panel will help visitors understand the layout of the exhibition and give them the opportunity to focus in on certain areas that most interest them. In a large exhibition, this material can be helpfully repeated in a handout or smartphone app.

Writing the words for an exhibition represents a major accomplishment, but displaying those words is not as simple as selecting "print" from your computer. Designing interpretive panels requires careful attention to font, font size, and the color of both the letters and the background in order to increase the likelihood that visitors will actually read the interpretive labels. Certain practices make type easier for the eye to see, focus in on, and read. There may be times when you wish to break out of these guidelines, but do so sparingly, and only after considering whether it is worth the reduced readability of the labels.

It is preferable to use dark typeface on a light background. Capitalization should appear as it would in standard writing. Mixed capital and lowercase letter sentences are easier to read than sentences in all caps or all lowercase. Each line of an interpretive panel should aim for sixty or fewer characters (and characters means each element that occupies space in the line—letters, punctuations, and spaces), with ragged right margins. Finally, serif fonts—serifs are the projections that embellish letters in certain fonts, including this one—are preferred for readability over those fonts without serifs (called sans serif fonts). Compare, for example, the Times New Roman font (serif) with the Arial (sans serif) on your own computer.

Sarah Bartlett, senior exhibit developer for Split Rock Studios, reminds her clients when they hire her to design their exhibitions that there are some practical things she keeps in mind when writing interpretive text. It is important to remember that the rules for good interpretive text writing are different from the rules for writing a paper in your college courses. The audience reading the text will likely be standing up, distracted by other visitors, and experiencing a variety of visual and auditory stimuli. Visitors are not seated in a comfortable chair in a quiet room as they might be while reading a book. Visitors are also not compelled to read. This is an informal setting, and if one of the goals of the exhibition is to educate the audience, the visitor will need *to want* to engage in reading the text. Visitors will make the decision to read or not read the text of the exhibition within a matter of seconds. If you want to keep your visitor's attention, and engage your visitor in reading the text that you and your team have so carefully prepared, you will have to keep the interpretive text brief and engaging. Many exhibition designers have started using questions as titles to draw the reader in closer, and to encourage them to read on past the headlines. Alternatively, if a visitor prefers a quicker experience, the panel titles or headlines should provide enough information so that a visitor can still grasp the big idea. Having the big idea accessible right away, and an interesting and visually stimulating array of objects and artifacts, should generate enough interest that the visitor will slow down and read further. Finally, it is better to provide too little information with tips for those who are interested to learn more than to overwhelm your visitors with too much detail. Visitor studies at all types of museums have shown that the more overwhelming the text of an exhibition is, the more likely visitors are to refuse to read any of it at all.

The audio guide presents one solution for multiple problems: visitors not wanting to read the exhibition text, having both children and adults of different reading levels, and guests who speak diverse languages. The audio guide can offer guests the flexibility of listening to the interpretation at their own pace, in their own language, in a style geared toward adult interests or an approach suited for children. Audio guides also offer the visitor the ability to get detailed information about any part of the exhibition whether they can get up close or not. An especially popular site or exhibition may draw crowds, making reading difficult. Even in audio form, though, the principles of good exhibition writing should apply. Audio guides are first written scripts after all. Visitors will still reach a saturation point if too much detail is included, or if the audio guide asks them to stand in one place for too long.

An audio guide is an effort to make exhibits accessible to a wide range of visitors. This additional sensory experience might enhance the visit for a sighted person but would be essential to people who are blind. Audio guides also provide a logical plan that allows people who may not be able to use a map on a brochure to successfully navigate the exhibit. As you plan an exhibit, build in opportunities for your visitors to engage all the senses. Some museums implant motion-sensors in the walls that trigger speakers, allowing visitors to hear actors reading primary documents, shipboard sounds, or street noises as they walk through an exhibit. Other museums commission three-dimensional models of maps or artwork, so people with low vision can engage with what is otherwise an incomprehensible two-dimensional object. As you plan your wall labels and exhibit cases, consider people who use wheelchairs. Make sure they can see the text you have worked so hard to create. The Smithsonian has developed a comprehensive guide for accessible exhibit design that is available online.[11] As you design exhibits, remember that compliance with the Americans with Disabilities Act is not only the law, but accessible features often make the museum experience more appealing to all visitors. A ramp may help a father pushing a stroller, as well as a person with limited mobility. When we accommodate all ranges of abilities, public historians build multiple levels of content and a variety of experiences into exhibitions.

Whether one is interpreting a display textually, in an audio guide, or with live interpretation, it is important to provide layers and choices to visitors. Everyone should be able to grasp the big idea and understand the purpose of the exhibition regardless of how much detail they desire or how much time they have allowed to spend with the exhibition. Visitors are humans with other things going on in their lives. They may tire quickly due to physical limitations, or they may be enjoying a holiday with family or friends and your exhibition may not be the first or the last thing they will see in one day. Going back to our grounding in the theories of informal education and the liberating effects of engaging the public in problem-posing education, one of the goals that differentiates academic history from public history is that we want to inspire visitors and the public more broadly to learn more on their own: to be curious even after they leave the exhibition, to ask questions, and to engage in the historical process.

Interpreting Material Culture

At the core of many public history exhibits is **material culture**. These objects from specific times and places are some of the most powerful tools that museums and historic sites possess to communicate stories about the past. At the Smithsonian's National Air and Space Museum in Washington, DC, visitors crane their necks upward to see Charles Lindbergh's plane, *Spirit of St. Louis*, and the Apollo 11 command module, *Columbia*, among many others famous pieces of aviation history. Standing in the den of the much more modest Frances Willard House in Evanston, Illinois, visitors can picture the suffragist and temperance activist hard at work at the desk, surrounded by her extensive collection of books. These things—from an extraordinary spacecraft to an unremarkable desk and chair—make up what we call a society's material culture.

The material culture associated with famous events and people in American history are often compelling objects of interest to current-day museum goers. This interest is fueled by material culture's role as **lineage objects** that connect us to famous people from the nation's past or as witnesses to past events, called witnessing objects. Lineage objects are items of material culture that bring visitors closer to the famous men and women whose lives interest them. Frances Willard's desk, for example—or even more intimately, a pair of her earrings on display at the house—connect visitors to her daily life and routines.

When an object is collected because it was present at an important event, it becomes a tangible link to an important moment in American history. Being in the presence of witnessing objects enables modern day Americans to feel connected to these highpoints in the historical timeline. Henry Ford, the automaker whose product forever changed the American landscape, assembled in Dearborn, Michigan, an unusual collection of authentic preindustrial buildings and replicas of landmarks of American history, like Independence Hall. Most controversially, he acquired actual buildings that had played a role in America's business history like Thomas Edison's laboratory and the Wright brothers' shop. Ford removed these buildings from their original sites and assembled a collection in Greenfield Village, which opened in 1933. Over the course of the twentieth century, the museum continued to use Ford's criteria as they expanded their collection, acquiring large objects

Photograph 5.10. Material culture as "witness": President Barack Obama on the bus Rosa Parks rode that sparked the Montgomery Bus Boycott, on exhibit in *With Liberty and Justice For All*, at the Henry Ford Museum, Dearborn, Michigan. Official White House Photo by Pete Souza, April 18, 2012.

that played significant roles in American history. In April 2012, when President Obama visited the Henry Ford Museum, he took the opportunity to sit on the bus where Rosa Parks refused to give up her seat, the event that sparked the Montgomery Bus Boycott of 1955–1956. Seated on the bus, peering out one of its windows, President Obama physically occupied the space and could imagine seeing through the eyes of leaders and participants in America's civil rights movement.

For several generations, a gap existed between museum collections and professional historians. Early historians concentrated largely on politics, war, and economics, using written primary sources, mostly created by elites who had the time and resources to create this documentary record. With the rise of social history in the 1960s, historians began to uncover the stories of women and non-elites whose lives had to be explored by other means because they did not usually leave as rich a documentary record as the wealthy men did. Material culture began to play a much more significant role in the work of later generations of scholars. Historians who study material culture undertake creative and interdisciplinary work as they engage with historic archaeologists, curators and museum collections, and written sources that help us understand material culture (including probate records, store accounts, and catalogs).[12]

The ability of material culture to connect visitors to the lives of those who left little evidence in the written record has led museums to seek out new kinds of objects. Collections of everyday items can serve as valuable repositories of information about the lives of the ordinary men, women, and children who inhabited the past. In advance of the opening of the Smithsonian's National Museum of African American History and Culture, Lonnie Bunch, the museum's director, sought out material evidence from the middle passage—that horrific journey across the Atlantic that brought more than 12.5 million captive Africans to North and South America.[13] What he ultimately found was the wreck of the *São José Paquete de Africa*, headed to Brazil, which had sunk in December 1794 off the coast of Cape Town, South Africa. The men, women, and children who perished when the *São José* sank, estimated to be more than 200 lives lost in this single tragedy, had been forgotten until the ship's discovery in 2010. Despite the thousands of slave ship voyages, this wreckage was the first ever recovered from a ship that sank while carrying captive Africans to the Americas. What this find brings together is a material remnant frozen in time at a moment when it was a tool of the slave trade. The museum will display the iron ballasts that weighed down the ship for its voyage because human cargo was lighter than other material goods ships like these carried. This ship stands as a witness to that particular moment—to this particular piece of history. As such, as Lonnie Bunch tells it, the exhibition of the material remains of the *São José* will be displayed in a reverential "memorial space."[14]

But to stop there—to let objects only speak for themselves as witnesses to important moments in the American past or as lineage objects—greatly limits the interpretive potential of material culture. Even the objects most associated with famous events and people often began life as unremarkable material things. Of the objects we have already considered, we can also ask: Who made them? What kind of employment practices did these laborers work under? What does, for example, the Willard desk, placed in her home, tell us about notions of privacy or the gendered nature of work during her lifetime? What did these objects mean to the people who owned and used them? In what ways did these objects shape individual and collective identity? Material culture objects are embedded in multiple contexts—their production, their use, and their "afterlife" as objects of display—from which we can learn a great deal more than simply knowing about their association with past events and people.[15]

To more completely understand material culture, you must study the object itself, as well as interrogate a wide variety of other sources. These additional sources—documents, oral histories, other material goods—allow us to develop a more complete picture of the many meanings of material culture. Without these other avenues of information and understanding, the complex past meanings of the material world would remain largely obscured.

Historical archaeologist Paul Mullins has studied historically African American neighborhoods in Indianapolis, Indiana, where a frequently recovered item is the foil milk cap, an item used to close glass milk bottles in the early decades of the twentieth century. At first, researchers had set these aside because they appeared to reveal little more than the fact that the occupants of these homes drank milk. But as Mullins recounts, an elder of Indianapolis' African American community later told them how the city's Riverside Amusement Park, open only to whites, allowed African Americans admission one day each year. These foil milk caps were the required admission token, and African Americans in the city called it "Milk Cap Day." In the context of this oral testimony, these almost ephemeral pieces of material culture took on new layers of meaning for the residents in

Photograph 5.11. Early Twentieth Century Polk's Dairy Milk Caps (Indianapolis, Indiana). Photo courtesy of Paul Mullins.

whose yards they were recovered archaeologically and provided new interpretive possibilities in a museum exhibit today.[16]

The example of the Indianapolis foil milk caps shows how objects of the material world reflect the larger historical processes in which they are embedded, in this case racism and segregation in the mid-twentieth-century United States. Many scholars who study material culture argue that material culture objects do more than simply reflect these historical processes; they can also shape them. The home of a late nineteenth-century elite white American family, with its lavish material culture, for example, not only showcased their status, but it also helped to create it. That same family could not have claimed the same level of elite status had they lived in a small, plain cottage. Current-day museum goers can be challenged to think about how material culture reflected and shaped human identity in the past and at the same time be given opportunities to make connections to their own relationships with the material world.

Interpreting and Exhibiting History in the Digital Age

The digital revolution has had an impact on exhibit design. Many museums and historic sites offer companion websites where visitors can review exhibit materials and often dig deeper into certain elements. Some museums have added Quick Response (QR) codes to artifact displays that visitors can scan with their phones for more in-depth information. The Museum of disABILITY History has a brick and mortar presence in Buffalo, New York, but thousands of people also visit its virtual museum. This online exhibition allows users to explore artifacts in the museum's holdings from any computer and makes the museum experience accessible to people of all levels of ability.[17] Public history institutions can use a robust social media presence to provide information and engage in dialogue with visitors.

Digital technologies—especially smartphones—also enable displays to move outside the walls of a museum or the landscape of a historic site and can add a layer of interpretive content to a community, a city, or an entire state. There are many tools available for public historians who wish to engage in this kind of work. Historypin is a free, web-based tool that allows members to create map-based historical collections.[18] The collections include photographs, video, and audio clips, as well as text. Each piece of visual or audio material is called a "pin" and is pinned to the map. One Historypin project is "Mapping Emotions in Victorian London," which used crowdsourcing—in which volunteers contribute information to a project—to map the emotions described in works of fiction at specific locations throughout London.

Another such project, developed by public historians at the Center for Digital + Public History at Cleveland State University, is Curatescape, a mobile publishing platform for iOS and Android that enables projects to build branded, place-specific historical and cultural tours. Curatescape is built using the Omeka content management system.[19] Curatescape interprets places using geo-located tours comprised of a combination of archival and present-day images and film, text, oral history, and expert testimony. Cultural and historical organizations, as well as academic programs, license Curatescape for their projects. Curatescape provides the structure for the app and website and then each organization or program that licenses Curatescape "fills" the structure with information, photographs, videos, and audio files. One of the most compelling advantages of telling historical stories on a platform like Curatescape is the ease with which information can not only be entered and made available but also changed in light of new information or in response to user feedback. This represents a significant difference to physical exhibit displays, which often cannot be updated for many years because of institutional budget constraints.

Curatescape's name combines the words "curate" and "landscape," which are both key features of the product. Curation brings users good historical scholarship, written in compelling, user-friendly text, and engages them with audio and visual data as well. When a user selects a particular story at one of the Curatescape projects, what he or she encounters is a well-told narrative about a specific place rather than the all-too familiar, and often overwhelming, "data dump" of information that the internet commonly returns when one does a search on a specific historical actor, place, or event. Equally important is the project's emphasis on the landscape. Curatescape presents information structured around "tours" and "stories." Every Curatescape project offers users several tours to choose from, usually developed around a specific theme (e.g., music history and venues, sports, and arts and culture are some examples from Cleveland Historical) or a specific geographic area (e.g., Cuyahoga Valley and Coventry Village, also on Cleveland Historical). Each tour is comprised of individual stories that are linked to a specific map coordinate. The geo-location feature means that when Curatescape is being used on a smartphone, the app makes available on its map both the location of all of the sites for which there are stories and also the location of the user. The app connects to Google maps if the user wants to know how to get from his or her current location to one of the sites. By connecting every story to a specific geographic location, Curatescape continually reminds users of the importance of place in telling stories about the past. Rather than presenting historical information primarily as a set of ideas or through the biographies of principal actors, **place-based storytelling** emphasizes the significance of where the past unfolded and the importance of those places in our remembering of past events. Because Curatescape projects do not leave any kind of physical mark on the landscape, they also can provide information about places that are not normally open to the public, as well as sites that no longer physically exist. Curatescape engages public historians with new questions as the possibility for locations to interpret expands: What is the responsibility of public historians to inform and/or ask permission of places not normally open to the public or of sites that now exist on top of an older site being interpreted before including them in a Curatescape project? What kind of sites might not want to be advertised in such a way?

Developing technologies present challenges and opportunities for public historians. Increasingly visitors want to use their phones to interact with the museum environment or to discover history in the landscape around them. Public historians should recognize the ways that technology can build on visitor choice to deliver historical interpretation in real time to a curious and receptive public.

Collaborations and Stakeholders

Exhibits have a collaborative nature because institutions need to reach out beyond their walls—beyond their staff—to work with stakeholders in developing exhibitions. Public historians must identify who the potential stakeholders will be for an exhibit and engage with these groups from the very beginning. This collaborative work focuses on the process by which the exhibit is developed and understands that this process can be just as important as the final product in developing and maintaining meaningful relationships with stakeholders. **Stakeholders** are the communities or individuals (or, sometimes, their descendants) being represented by an exhibit. Other stakeholders might include an exhibit's funders, board members of the institution producing the exhibit, or politicians involved in the project. Disparate groups of stakeholders and museum staff may experience conflict as they work to develop the exhibit. Here public historians are well served by reflective practice, which will equip them over the course of their careers to learn from these experiences and to incorporate what they have learned into future projects.

There are numerous examples available in print (and many more that will never be printed) of public history professionals experiencing conflicts with their stakeholders.[20] Sometimes these conflicts can be resolved through careful listening, thoughtful negotiations, and a little give and take. Sometimes the conflicts require higher levels of mediation. Unfortunately, there are times when it seems the conflicts are irreconcilable. Those that are not handled well before they grow into major disagreements have killed projects and threatened funding of either exhibitions or entire institutions. One of the most well-known examples is the controversial, planned *Enola Gay* exhibition at the Smithsonian. World War II veterans challenged the staff of the Smithsonian and historians about the text that would accompany the refurbished plane that dropped the atomic bomb on Hiroshima, questioning especially the estimated number of lives that would have been saved by preempting an invasion. The Smithsonian eventually retreated from presenting an interpretive exhibition at all and in a label simply presented the fact that this witnessing artifact had dropped an atomic bomb. But in 2003, historians once again protested the exhibit plan, this time for not providing any historical interpretation at all.[21] They pointed to the **Standards for Museum Exhibits Dealing with Historical Subjects** that had been adopted by an impressive coalition of organizations representing historians and public historians: the Society for History in the Federal Government Executive Council; the National Council on Public History Executive Council; the Organization of American Historians' Executive Council; the American Historical Association Council; and the Medical Museums Association. The historic nature of the Enola Gay, they argued, must be interpreted, even if it is exhibited in an air and space museum setting.

Despite the high-profile nature of the Enola Gay controversy, and the fact that most museums will not attract the attention of the national press or Congress, every institution has a set of stakeholders they need to consider when planning their interpretation. Early consultation will save endless headaches and costly delays later in the project. This effort might include local political leaders if the project or museum receives any type of state or federal grants, board members if their reputations are public in nature and if they play a role in approving budgetary expenses, local community members who will either visit the exhibition or who will react badly if their needs are not considered, or individuals whose lives or the stories of their relatives may be the subject of the exhibition. Each set of stakeholders will likely have different basic values and priorities as they approach any given topic. Yet the best public history professionals adeptly address the most pressing concerns of these complex and sometimes contradictory opinions to produce an end product that will appeal to multiple, diverse audiences. Rather than thinking of stakeholders as potential roadblocks, we can embrace their diverse perspectives as an opportunity to make our work more relevant to a greater number of people.

Reflective Practice through Evaluation

The best way to prevent disasters in relations with stakeholders is to follow a process for evaluation that involves stakeholder input at every stage of the process. How can you be sure that you are not blindsided once you are too far into your interpretation and exhibition planning to effectively respond? Maintain contact with your stakeholders through a strong commitment to frequent and thorough evaluation.

It should be clear now that developing an exhibit requires a great deal of planning and attention to many different kinds of details. Most of the time, this work is done in large part by museum staff. But consultation with potential audiences is critical. Not only should stakeholders be involved in shaping an exhibition at the outset, but both stakeholders and the wider potential audiences should be given the opportunity to assess the strengths and weakness at several points during its development and deployment. This process is known as **evaluation**.

STANDARDS FOR MUSEUM EXHIBITS DEALING WITH HISTORICAL SUBJECTS (2001)[1]

In a democracy, a knowledge of history forms the context in which citizens make informed decisions. Historical knowledge also provides personal, family, and community links to the past. Historical understandings of other societies assist individuals in identifying commonalities in the human condition and in negotiating the differences that exist in our increasingly pluralistic world.

Museum exhibits play an important role in the transmission of historical knowledge. They are viewed by citizens of diverse ages, interests, and backgrounds, often in family groups. They sometimes celebrate common events, occasionally memorialize tragedies or injustices, and contain an interpretive element, even if it is not readily apparent. The process of selecting themes, photographs, objects, documents, and other components to be included in an exhibit implies interpretive judgments about cause and effect, perspective, significance, and meaning.

Historical exhibits may encourage the informed discussion of their content and the broader issues of historical significance that they raise. Attempts to suppress exhibits or to impose an uncritical point of view, however widely shared, are inimical to open and rational discussion.

In aiming to achieve exhibit goals, historians, museum curators, administrators, and members of museum boards should approach their task mindful of their public trust. To discharge their duties appropriately, they should observe the following standards:

1. Exhibits should be founded on scholarship, marked by intellectual integrity, and subjected to rigorous peer review. Evidence considered in preparing the exhibit may include objects, written documentation, oral histories, images, works of art, music, and folklore.
2. At the outset of the exhibit process, museums should identify stakeholders in any exhibit and may wish to involve their representatives in the planning process.
3. Museums and other institutions funded with public monies should be keenly aware of the diversity within communities and constituencies that they serve.
4. When an exhibit addresses a controversial subject, it should acknowledge the existence of competing points of view. The public should be able to see that history is a changing process of interpretation and reinterpretation, formed through gathering and reviewing evidence, drawing conclusions, and presenting the conclusions in text or exhibit format.
5. Museum administrators should defend exhibits produced according to these standards.

Note

1. "Standards for Museum Exhibits Dealing with Historical Subjects" (2001), available at: https://www.historians.org/jobs-and-professional-development/statements-and-standards-of-the-profession/standards-for-museum-exhibits-dealing-with-historical-subjects. Adopted by the Society for History in the Federal Government Executive Council, January 8, 1997; the National Council on Public History Executive Council, March 30, 2000; the Organization of American Historians Executive Council, April 2, 2000; the American Historical Association Council, January 4, 2001; and the Medical Museums Association, April 19, 2001.

Front-end evaluation happens before exhibit development is very far along; inviting comment while the exhibition is still in the planning and conceptualization stage means that feedback can be used in the design process. Asking for input from stakeholders too late in the planning process can result in costly setbacks or it can give stakeholders the impression that the request for input was insincere. By contrast, effective use of front-end evaluations can promote greater buy-in from community members and stakeholders and an increased likelihood that the exhibition will be well received.

A front-end evaluation allows community members, stakeholders, and content experts to provide input early in the exhibition development stage. The front-end evaluation materials should include a brief overview of the project, and an opportunity for evaluators to shape the exhibition plan. Exhibition organizers can use **focus groups**, surveys, informal consultations, informal interviews, community workshops, existing or previously conducted visitor surveys on similar topics or of comparable exhibitions, and literature reviews. Community workshops are especially valuable if the exhibition team is still looking for interpretive materials such as photographs or objects for display, or if they need community input for ethical interpretation of objects or cultural material. Focus groups allow the team to gather input from specific targeted audiences, such as community members, experts in the content area, advisory board members, donors, or other stakeholders. When it might not be practical to gather for face-to-face meetings or if the numbers are too extensive for individual interviews, surveys can provide meaningful information about potential audience expectations, areas of sensitivity, and issues that will require greater context or background information. No organization can easily absorb the cost of a cancelled exhibition or an angry protest, particularly if early outreach and deliberate civic engagement throughout the process could help raise problems when solutions are easier and less expensive to find.[22]

Formative evaluation happens during exhibition development and provides specific feedback on individual elements such as text, labels, graphics, or layout design. The team can present mock-ups of proposed exhibitions to small groups of potential visitors, community members, or content experts. Groups of fifteen to twenty are optimal for semi-structured interviews or workshop activities that draw out individual or collective responses to the planned exhibition. If they repeat questions in this stage similar to those that they used in the front-end evaluation, exhibition developers can check for improvement through the various stages of planning.

Remedial evaluation is used immediately after an exhibition or program opens to ensure that all parts of the exhibition are working. This form of evaluation allows the team to make refinements that might not have been visible at any other time. If unforeseen problems, questions, or errors arise after the public is invited in, there should be a plan to make changes as quickly as possible. Simple observation of visitor behavior, and feedback through comment books, forms, or surveys can highlight issues. The staff members on site are often the informal collectors of information. They might hear unsolicited responses from visitors or may have to field questions when something is unclear.

Finally, **summative evaluation** occurs near the conclusion of an exhibition or program. It allows the team to evaluate whether the exhibition achieved its goals and to discover whether or not the public was satisfied with the experience. Summative evaluation can ask who was drawn to the exhibition, how they used it, and what their overall impression was. It can provide feedback for future projects or suggest areas in need of further research. Funders often make summative evaluation a requirement of the grant; boards of trustees want to see it in the annual report. The team can conduct large-scale visitor surveys, structured observations of visitor behaviors in the exhibition (where did they linger, what did they read, which parts did they skip or skim lightly, and what was their overall demeanor), in-depth interviews, peer reviews, and, once again, focus groups or community workshops. Data from comment books, surveys, and visitor feedback forms can also prove useful at this stage.

Notes

1. For more information on the London Bridge Experience, visit: https://www.thelondonbridge experience.com/experience.
2. Portions of the description and analysis of the Chilean Museum of Memory and Human Rights were originally published as: Cherstin M. Lyon, "Museo de Memoria y Derechos Humanos and Parque por la paz Villa Grimaldi." [Museum of Memory and Human Rights and Peace Park at Villa Grimaldi] *Public Historian* 33, no. 2 (2011): 135–144. Reprinted with permission.
3. The two commissions that investigated atrocities under Pinochet were the National Commission for Truth and Reconciliation, or the "Rettig Commission," May 1990–February 1991; and the National Commission on Political Imprisonment and Torture, or the "Valech Commission," September 2003–June 2005.
4. Roy Rosenzweig and David Thelen, *The Presence of the Past: Popular Uses of History in American Life* (New York: Columbia University Press, 1998), 105–106.
5. Beverly Serrell, *Exhibit Labels: An Interpretive Approach* (Lanham, MD: Rowman & Littlefield, 2015), 7.
6. Serrell, *Exhibit Labels*, 9–10. Reprinted with permission of Rowman & Littlefield Publishers.
7. Quoted in Elizabeth Nix and Deborah Weiner, "Pivot in Perception: The Impact of the 1968 Riots on Three Business Districts" in *Baltimore '68: Riots and Rebirth in an American City*, eds. Jessica I. Elfenbein, Thomas L. Hollowak, and Elizabeth M. Nix (Philadelphia: Temple University Press, 2011), 186.
8. Quoted in Nix and Weiner, 186.
9. Quoted in Nix and Weiner, 187.
10. This section draws from the work of Beverly Serrell, *Exhibit Labels: An Interpretive Approach* (Lanham, MD: Rowman & Littlefield, 2015), 31–46, and an unpublished guide developed by Katherine C. Grier.
11. Janice Majewski, "Smithsonian Guidelines for Accessible Exhibition Design," http://access ible.si.edu/pdf/Smithsonian%20Guidelines%20for%20accessible%20design.pdf.
12. Historians may even find themselves trawling eBay, an excellent source of material culture, especially for those working on twentieth- and twenty-first-century projects. For material culture analyses using collections built in part from eBay, see Katherine C. Grier, *Pets in America: A History* (Chapel Hill: The University of North Carolina Press, 2006) and Rebecca Shrum, "Selling Mr. Coffee: Design, Gender, and the Branding of a Kitchen Appliance," *Winterthur Portfolio* 46 no. 4 (Winter 2012): 271–298.
13. David Eltis and David Richardson, *Atlas of the Transatlantic Slave Trade* (New Haven: Yale University Press, 2010), 15 (Map 9).

14. Roger Catlin, "Smithsonian to Receive Artifacts from Sunken 18th-Century Slave Ship," *Smithsonian Magazine*, May 31, 2015. http://www.smithsonianmag.com/smithsonian-insti tution/sunken-18th-century-slave-ship-found-south-africa-180955458/?no-ist.

15. Jennifer L. Anderson, *Mahogany: The Costs of Luxury in Early America* (Cambridge: Harvard University Press, 2012) is a recent example of work that brings these insights together on multiple levels.

16. Paul R. Mullins, "Racializing the Commonplace Landscape: An Archaeology of Urban Renewal Along the Color Line," *World Archaeology* 38, no. 1: 60–71.

17. http://museumofdisability.org/virtual-museum/.

18. Historypin is not available on mobile platforms at the time of this writing.

19. Curatescape was built using Omeka, the standards-based, open-source digital archival tool that is widely used by cultural and historical institutions. Learn more about Omeka at http://omeka.org/. Projects nationwide use Curatescape. For a current listing, see: http://curatescape .org/projects/. The first Curatescape project was Cleveland Historical, and it still serves as an excellent example of the range of stories and presentation methods Curatescape projects can deploy. http://clevelandhistorical.org. See also: Mark Tebeau's white paper, "Strategies for Mobile Interpretive Projects," available at http://mobilehistorical.curatescape.org/.

20. Maureen McConnell and Honee Hess, "A Controversy Timeline," *Journal of Museum Education* 23, no. 3 (1998): 4–6.

21. Debbie Ann Doyle, "Historians Protest New Enola Gay Exhibit," *Perspectives on History,* December 2003, https://www.historians.org/publications-and-directories/perspectives-on-his tory/december-2003/historians-protest-new-enola-gay-exhibit.

22. The National Parks have developed a series of case studies to show what civic engagement looks like in diverse contexts. See: https://www.nps.gov/civic/casestudies/index.html. See also Monica Post, "Fearless Evaluation: Webinar for the National Park Service," March 6–8, 2012, https://www.nps.gov/hfc/services/interp/interpPlanning/FearlessEvaluationManual.pdf.

RESOURCES AND SUGGESTED ACTIVITIES

Interpreting Material Culture Objects

Choose a common object in today's society to analyze. Material culture scholar Karen Harvey has developed a beginner's approach to this analysis, which includes three steps. The first step is to develop a physical description of the object. If at all possible, get into the same room as one of the objects and, if it is small enough, hold it in your hands. Choosing an object that you can physically interact with is key for beginners. The description should include "what the object is made of, how it was made and (of course) when; production methods and manufacture, materials, size, weight, design, style, decoration and date." The second step is to "place the object in historical context, primarily by referring to other evidence. Here we can explore who owned this (or similar) objects, when, and what they were used for." In this step, the focus is on how the object was used and by whom during a particular time period. In the final step, an even broader view is taken to begin exploring what the object meant in that time period. Placing the object into its "socio-cultural context" enables a deeper understanding of the significance of the object in people's lives.[1] This method could be applied to the Polk Sanitary milk caps discussed in this chapter: the first step would detail what the object was and how it was made; the second step would explore how this milk cap sealed glass bottles and to whom this finished product was distributed; the final step would include the discussion of how this item became significant for the Indianapolis African American community living under segregation. A fourth and final step in this exercise would be to write an interpretive text label for the object, using the guidelines discussed in this chapter. To begin the process of thinking about material culture, the short video "Twenty Questions to Ask an Object," provides a useful starting point: http://www.theasa.net/caucus_material/item/twenty_years_twenty_questions_to_ask_an_object_the_video/.

Reviewing an Exhibition

Visiting an exhibition with a critical lens is one of the best ways to practice what you have learned about the history and best practices in exhibition design. Select a museum or historical site that you would like to visit. Make sure you do plenty of research before you go to ensure that you have a strong grasp of the subject first.

It is important that you understand the intended purpose of the exhibition and the intended audience, as well as the institutional context in which the exhibition was produced. Is this a large museum with a large staff and an adequate budget to carry out an elaborate design and extensive research and pre-exhibition planning with many experts carrying out individual aspects of the planning and installation? Or is this a small museum with a few staff handling most aspects of the design, research, and installation working within rigid budget constraints? These two extremes will certainly result in different exhibitions. Contact the curator if possible or another high-level employee or director who can answer these questions. Any review of an exhibition should take these matters into consideration if the review is to be fair.

When writing your review, you should first offer an overview of the exhibition theme, subject matter, content, and form, keeping an eye out for factual accuracy, quality of design and display, tone, and use of space, sounds, lighting, and color. Are there any experimental techniques used that affect your experience? Does the exhibition contribute to larger scholarly conversations on the topic? *The Public Historian* recommends that reviewers keep in mind the following questions: What can you do in the exhibit that you cannot do in traditional history presentations? Is the curator enhancing public knowledge and debate on the subject area covered? What might other professionals learn from this effort?

Reviews for professional journals are typically between 1,000 and 1,250 words in length, which is the equivalent of four to five double-spaced pages. Reviews also contain information in the heading that will identify the museum, the exhibition title, the name of the curator and/or historical consultant, the sponsor if there is one, the date of the exhibition, and any other information that would help identify and give credit to those who were responsible for the exhibition. Here are some sample headings for your exhibition reviews:

The Museum of American Political Life. University of Hartford. Edmund B. Sullivan, director and curator; Christine Scriabine, museum historian.

A City Comes of Age: Chicago in the 1890s. Robert Goler, curator; Susan Hirsch, exhibit historian; Sam Bass Warner Jr., consulting historian. Chicago Historical Society, October 25, 1990–July 15, 1991.

Illustrations should be included whenever possible. It is a good idea to ask the museum/institution if they have stock photos of the exhibition they would like you to use to accompany your review. If they do not, make sure you ask permission before taking photographs on your own, and it is usually best practice to take photos without a flash. *The Public Historian* and most other history-specific journals use *The Chicago Manual of Style* for footnotes, spelling, punctuation, and overall format.

Fort Snelling—Which Stories Are Told?

The Minnesota Historical Society operates Fort Snelling, a site on the river in St. Paul that they promote as "a great place to learn about military history from before the Civil War through World War II, fur trade history, slavery in Minnesota, the US-Dakota War of 1862 and much more."[2] A group of public history students at the University of Minnesota became interested in making the traditionally patriotic site part of the Guantanamo Memory Project, which seeks to build public awareness of the history of Guantanamo Bay.[3] The students found an effective parallel to Guantanamo in the US government's use of Fort Snelling during the US-Dakota War of 1862.[4] During this conflict, a number of Dakota men were accused of killing US civilians. Three hundred and three men were sentenced to death, but Abraham Lincoln reduced that number to thirty-nine, and one of those was released. The remaining thirty-eight prisoners were hanged simultaneously on the day after Christmas in 1862. Their punishment remains the largest mass execution in US history.

After the hangings, the US government relocated 1,600 Dakota men, women, and children who had surrendered to authorities to Fort Snelling, where they spent the winter of 1862–1863. The Dakota reported daily abuse at the hands of the fort soldiers and civilians alike. When measles entered the area, as many as 300 Dakota died. In May 1863, those who survived the winter were relocated to Crow Creek Sioux Reservation.

Currently, the site provides information about the Dakota on a tab on their website. If users click on the tab, they will find no reference to the US-Dakota War. They can find a description of the war in 1862 if they visit the timeline on the site. Inside the fort, six textual panels make reference to the Dakota. Public history students annotated the panels with information about the 1862 conflict, the mass execution, references to the Dakota "concentration camp," and comments about Guantanamo Bay. Their changes disturbed the visitors to the point that the site removed them. In response, the students replaced the annotations with more open-ended questions.[5]

Questions for Discussion:

1. Is Fort Snelling an appropriate site for the Guantanamo Public Memory Project?
2. How should the site interpret the winter of 1862–1863?
3. Should the site use the term "internment camp" or "concentration camp" in its interpretation of that period?

Notes

1. Karen Harvey, *History and Material Culture: A Student's Guide to Approaching Alternative Sources* (New York: Routledge, 2009), 1–23.
2. http://www.historicfortsnelling.org.
3. http://gitmomemory.org.
4. http://www.historicfortsnelling.org/history/us-dakota-war.
5. Rose Miron, "Sacrificing Comfort for Complexity: Presenting Difficult Narratives in Public History," *Public History Commons*, April 24, 2014, http://publichistorycommons.org/sacrificing-comfort-for-complexity.

RESOURCES FOR FURTHER STUDY

Ames, Kenneth. *Death in the Dining Room & Other Tales of Victorian Culture*. Philadelphia: Temple University Press, 1995.

Bennett, Tony. *The Birth of the Museum: History, Theory, Politics*. London: Routledge, 1995.

Cohen, Daniel J. and Roy Rosenzweig. *Digital History: A Guide to Gathering, Preserving, and Presenting the Past on the Web*. Philadelphia: University of Pennsylvania Press, 2005.

Diamond, Judy. *Practical Evaluation Guide: Tools for Museums and Other Informal Education Settings*. Walnut Creek, CA: AltaMira Press, 1999.

Gordon, Tammy. *Private History in Public: Exhibitions and the Settings of Everyday Life*. Lanham, MD: AltaMira Press, 2010.

Hayward, J. and R. Loomis. "Looking Back at Front-End Studies." *Visitor Studies: Theory, Research and Practice* 5 (1993): 261–265.

Hood, Adrienne. "Material Culture: The Object." In *History Beyond the Text: A Student's Guide to Approaching Alternative Sources*. Edited by Sarah Barber and Corinna Peniston Bird. London and New York: Routledge Press, 2009.

Leon, Warren and Roy Rosenzweig, Eds. *History Museums in the United States: A Critical Assessment*. Chicago: University of Illinois Press, 1989.

National Park Service. "We Provide Interpretive Media and Services to National Parks," available at https://www.nps.gov/hfc/ and "Exhibits and Museums," available at https://www.nps.gov/hfc/products/exhibits/.

Screven, C. "Formative Evaluation: Conceptions and Misconceptions." *Visitor Studies: Theory, Research and Practice* 1 (1988): 73–82.

Taylor, Samuel, Ed. *Try It! Improving Exhibits through Formative Evaluation*. Washington, DC: Association for Science and Technology Centers, 1991.

Wallace, Michael. *Mickey Mouse History and Other Essays on American Memory*. Philadelphia: Temple University Press, 1996.

CHAPTER 6

Engaging Audiences

KEY TERMS	
interpretive techniques	recreations
interpretation	historical context
first-, second-, and third-person interpretation	civic engagement
	mission statements
living history	International Coalition of Sites of Conscience
open-air museum	
relevance	difficult encounters
anarchist tags	discomfort zone
fingerprinting	visitor identification
authenticity	

SOME VISITORS COME TO public history venues in a virtuous vacation mode, proud that they have made the choice to spend some of their leisure time engaged in a cultural activity. They may arrive in multigenerational groups, willing to read a few labels and examine some artifacts, but also hoping there will be benches for the grandparents, hands-on activities for the kids, and possibly some authentic local ale, old-fashioned ice cream, or hand-pulled taffy to buy. Other visitors pour out of school buses, teachers and students alike excited to be out of the classroom for the day. Still others are local residents who want to learn more about the place where they live or who may have brought some out-of-town guests with them. Some visitors may arrive with lots of background knowledge, already interested in the history, while others may have chosen the site because it has a good restaurant or pretty views and know nothing about the place or its significance. For the most part, visitors want to be thoroughly entertained and somewhat educated. If some of the goals of public history are to spark curiosity in public audiences about history and its connection to their lives, to increase awareness of a historical topic and why it matters today, and to create opportunities for furthering the public's understanding of historical thinking as a useful skill beyond the academic realm, public historians must employ a wide range of engagement strategies, some controversial, none perfect.

Engaging Audiences through Interpretation

Public history venues often seek to transport visitors back in time through a variety of **interpretive techniques**. Having the opportunity and the responsibility to provide accurate and thorough content, they must deliver it in a way that attracts visitors and interests participants who come as free-choice learners, ready and willing to pay attention or not that interested. As they have grappled with the competing expectations of education and entertainment, public historians have developed a number of methods to engage their audiences. While the interpretative methods vary considerably, all good historical **interpretation** creates connections between visitors and historic sites.[1]

Third-Person Interpretation

The most common interpretive technique uses **third-person interpreters**, the knowledgeable staff members and volunteers who provide information to visitors and speak and write in the third person. Third-person interpreters do not play the role of a historical character; rather, they retain their own identities and speak to audiences about the past as themselves. A guide at Drayton Hall, near Charleston, South Carolina, might tell visitors about the grand country estate the Draytons built in the eighteenth century and the enslaved laborers who were forced to do the work, using third-person interpretation, saying something like, "The Draytons wanted to recreate the feeling of an English country estate here in North America," and "Enslaved men and women accessed the different floors of the house using this very narrow staircase." Because the guide is not pretending to be a particular historical figure from the site, who can only speak from his or her individual point of view, this kind of interpretation allows guides to help visitors see a site from a wide variety of perspectives. A single guide can help visitors better understand both what life was like at Drayton Hall for the wealthy white families who owned and lived at the estate and for the enslaved men, women, and children who worked and lived there as well. A third-person interpreter can also include discussion of the site's entire history, from its founding to the present day.

Third-person interpretation does not require the physical presence of an interpreter. Audio guides can use third-person interpretation to help visitors navigate an exhibition or a historic site, or take a personalized tour of a historic house in the language of their choice. The content of audio guides can be targeted to different groups of visitors: with headphones, children can listen to one script and adults to another, but they can move through the site together. Public historians can use audio guides to make their sites accessible to a wider audience, accommodating the needs of visitors who may have low vision or mobility issues that prevent them from visiting upper floors of historic buildings. Conveniently, the pause button allows listeners to move at their own pace.

Second-Person Interpretation

In recent years, some historic sites and museums have begun to employ a new method of audience engagement, **second-person interpretation**, in which visitors themselves play a part in the story being told. At many sites, visitors try their hands at historic activities—like rolling hoops or churning butter—to experience physically some small aspect of what life would have been like in the past. Second-person interpretation can also be used to frame a person's entire visit to a historic site or museum. The United States Holocaust Memorial Museum in Washington, DC, gives each visitor an identity card of a person to follow while going through the museum. Near the end of the experience, visitors learn the fate of the person they had been assigned.[2] Other sites have developed more immersive second-person experiences, where visitors are put in situations that attempt to replicate historic events. This sustained second-person experience presents challenges for public historians and visitors alike, as you will see in the case studies in the following chapter.

First-Person Interpretation

In an attempt to engage their audiences, some public history sites make a commitment to **first-person interpreters**, those dedicated workers who research historical figures, put on the clothes they might have worn, and speak to the visitors as if they actually lived in a different time period. A first-person interpreter can deliver narratives and answer questions from their character's point of view and engage with emotions as they speak about what they "actually" experienced. The first-person approach can be effective if even one interpreter at a site takes on the challenge, but first-person interpretation becomes an all-encompassing effort when sites employ a technique called **living history**. Here visitors "go back in time," strolling quaint streets and conversing with numerous costumed staff members and volunteers who make crafts or grow heritage crops. Living history sites are popular destinations for families. Skansen, located in Stockholm, Sweden, was the world's first **open-air museum** (another term for the living history museum that is spread out over a large area representing a historical town or village). Still in operation today, it inspired Colonial Williamsburg, the most well-known living history museum in the United States. Both sites invite guests to experience aspects of a different era and engage in second-person interpretive activities, without exposing them to many of the inconveniences of the past. This approach has often been immensely popular with the public; Williamsburg is currently the largest living history museum in the world, and 100 million people have visited since its first building opened in 1932.[3] Rather than engaging in a completely immersive first-person experience, sites can include both first-person and third-person interpreters so that visitors can easily ask questions that fall outside the time period or perspective of a first-person interpreter, including not only questions of historical interest but also where to find the bathrooms.

Having some employees who can answer questions that are outside the scope of knowledge of the characters first-person interpreters play can be useful as a way to bridge the disconnect between the rules of the living-history approach that mandate interpreters stay in character, speaking in long-lost accents while twenty-first century visitors ask questions and snap pictures with their phones. Questions from guests can lead to interesting and sometimes problematic exchanges with first-person interpreters who are bound by their role to stay within a very specific time period. In her web series "Ask a Slave," actress Azie Mira Dungey recounts some of the interactions she had with visitors when she portrayed Caroline Branham, Martha Washington's enslaved housemaid, at Mt. Vernon during Barack Obama's first term as president.[4] As public historian Amy Tyson writes, the "Ask a Slave" series is satire and "good comedy—but its larger message isn't funny." Most tourists who came to Mt. Vernon knew little about slavery and were often "reveling in the glory of the past" and not wanting to grapple with the reality of slavery at Mt. Vernon or more broadly in the history of the United States. Sometimes, when a guest was interested in discussing slavery, Dungey's first-person role as Branham limited her ability to share her knowledge. As Dungey recounted, "some people would want to know what I thought about Africans selling each other into slavery, and I'd just say, 'I wouldn't know about that sir, I'm a Virginian.'" Dungey acknowledged that these limitations could be convenient, noting that "I didn't even want to get into that," because they gave her a reason not to engage in one more difficult conversation that day about slavery. Playing the role of a historical figure from the past takes an extraordinary amount of emotional energy that can lead to employee burnout at historic sites. The emotional toll on first-person interpreters must be taken into account by the site administrators and boards as they consider salaries and work schedules.[5]

The Problem of Relevance

If public historians are going to engage audiences, first we need an audience to engage. Research on public participation at traditional venues like cultural events, museums, and historic sites all point to some disturbing trends. In general, the population that visits cultural events and institutions does not reflect the diversity of the American nation and is growing older. The National Park Service recognizes the obvious gap between the overall population and the demographics of park visitors, as a 2010 study of surveys taken at National Parks that summer "showed that an overwhelming majority of visitors, often as high as 90% or more, are white."[6] Add to this concern the reality that most public history sites are very small and run by mostly volunteer staffs on meager budgets. What can be done to engage visitors, attract new and returning audiences, and improve the **relevance** of our programs and interpretations for diverse audiences? Two recent publications have discussed this problem and pointed the way toward solutions.

The *Imperiled Promise* of History in the National Park Service

In 2011, a group comprised primarily of public historians produced *Imperiled Promise: The State of History in the National Park Service*, a comprehensive study of the role of history in the National Park Service. *Imperiled Promise* praised the way some National Park Service (NPS) sites incorporated history in meaningful and innovative ways, including Manzanar National Historic Site, for example, which was highlighted for being "a leading light in effective community engagement," and Shenandoah National Park, which had made "itself the subject of public interpretation" so that visitors could understand how the National Park Service had itself "shap[ed] the history of the southern Appalachian Region" in which the park is located. On the whole, however, the authors concluded that NPS needed to expand their understanding and application of history at many of their sites in order to more fully interpret the past and engage a more diverse audience. One key recommendation the authors made was that NPS sites needed to "[e]xpand interpretive frames beyond existing physical resources," in order to more fully recognize "the imperfect alignment between extant physical remains and the important legacies of the past." Here the authors recognized that National Park Service sites sometimes left out stories that were critical to the history of the site but that may no longer be "well represented among the physical resources." Continuing in this vein, the authors also encouraged the National Park Service to link their sites with the important stories that connect them to the wider world of places, events, and ideas, "either in the immediate, physical sense or in a narrative or thematic sense."[7] The ability of the National Park Service to develop these more complex and interconnected stories, however, is significantly weakened because the efforts of historians and interpreters in the National Park Service have been separated from each other so that historians are not able to use their skills to benefit the work of interpreters who engage with audiences in the National Parks. Historians are tasked instead with work related to preservation and stewardship, not the kind of endeavors that translate into history education. The National Parks are one of the most visible places on the American landscape where audiences have the opportunity to engage with sites and stories from the past. Unfortunately, the structure of the National Park Service and its too often limited commitment to history make it difficult for audiences to be engaged in meaningful ways at many of their sites.

Anarchist's Guide to Historic House Museums

Problems of visitor engagement have reached such a serious state that some believe they will require something of a revolution to solve. Franklin D. Vagnone and Deborah Ryan published the *Anarchist's Guide to Historic House Museums: "A Ground-Breaking Manifesto"* in 2016. Appropriate for a manifesto, the book's cover comes already looking worn and slightly dirty with what appears to be a greasy fingerprint on the back cover, all designed to evoke the type of book a revolutionary character might keep constantly by her side. The table of contents for the *Anarchist's Guide* has an image of a lit bomb at the top of the page, as does each chapter header, as if to indicate that time is running out for historic sites to become relevant in their communities. While some of the *Guide*'s ideas are new, historic sites have experimented with many of them in recent years. The guide's revolutionary nature is in being the first publication to bring many of these approaches together in one place and also by pushing further than current practice with some of their suggestions.

The *Guide* paints a bleak picture of the current state of historic sites and house museums. In a section on neighborhood engagement, the authors lament that historic house museums, which they refer to as HHMs, "ignore their neighbors. House staff make very little effort to learn about local residents or businesses or discover their interests. . . . We often hear that neighbors who walk or drive by HHMs on a regular basis never knew they are open to the public, never knew they are museums, and never feel invited."[8] While this language might alienate employees at HHMs who *have* engaged with their communities, the *Guide* does go on to offer detailed suggestions for how historic sites can overcome this isolation and better connect with their neighbors, certainly an important goal for sites seeking to engage a wider potential audience that does not already include these groups. The *Guide* also challenges sites to share more than their history, suggesting that they consider becoming meeting places, if appropriate, for dogs and their owners (in something like an informal dog park), a place for food trucks to sell their offerings, and a host of art exhibitions.

The *Guide* is also committed to increasing opportunities for visitor participation. The authors developed "**anarchist tags**," paper luggage tags that can be affixed by a string where the visitor chooses at a historic site. Before depositing the tag, the visitor responds to a prompt, including "I liked" or "I didn't like," and then lodges the tag in an appropriate place. A potentially far more radical approach, dubbed **fingerprinting**, allows guests "to individualize their experiences and leave a mark." Fingerprinting includes allowing photography, providing opportunities for guests to use rooms at a historic site as they would have been used in the past, and even allowing guests to "write on the house itself," as they do at the Yellow House in the Heidelberg Project in Detroit, Michigan. Few historic house museums might undertake that final suggestion, which has been described elsewhere as a "wacky public art project," but the publication of the *Anarchist's Guide* reflects the critical need for historic sites and houses to think creatively and deeply about engaging audiences.[9]

Telling New Stories

One of the problems facing smaller institutions is that many of them have had little ability to update their offerings since the time of their founding. Historic sites in the United States were often saved because of their associations with the elite. A flurry of sites opened, for example, in the 1970s as part of bicentennial celebrations because of their association with the founding of the country, without long-term plans for funding and interpretation beyond the original "great events of history" model.[10] This interpretative approach discourages attendance over time both because it is a static story (once you have visited and heard the story, there is no need to return) and because it does not engage directly with the lived experiences of the vast majority of visitors who do not see themselves reflected in it.

How can historic sites and house museums solve the problems of sites that were founded based on outdated assumptions about what is historically important, whose interpretive strategies and narratives are static, and whose sites are understaffed and underfunded? One answer lies in telling new stories: returning to those core skills of the historian and doing new research that complicates the narrative and illuminates the lives of women and children, the servants or enslaved people who lived or worked at the site, and others who may have interacted with the family in different ways. One study of historic sites that interpreted the lives of domestic servants after 1865 found "that visitor interest in the servants' work is due to their ability to relate to these duties in their own lives. Comments such as, 'People can relate better to servants/working class than to wealthy,' were common responses in the survey."[11] With limited funding, sites might partner with local colleges and universities, especially those with faculty and students interested in public history, to do research and develop new interpretive stories.

Authenticity

While audiences want to be entertained and engaged at public history sites, they also seek **authenticity**—a real and meaningful connection to the past. Although authenticity is difficult to define, we know it when we see it. Historic sites and house museums have at their core the unmistakable advantage that their visitors stand in a place where history happened—where someone from the past lived, where a battle was fought, where important political decisions or daily labor took place. Visitors who come to historic sites and house museums expect to see interpretive exhibits in authentic settings, and these venues have opportunities to use their buildings and locations as interpretive tools. These sites have an increased responsibility to provide authentic experiences, or to be transparent when they cannot. When the original cannot be found, a recreation might serve a useful purpose, but while most audiences will gamely walk through a reconstructed log cabin, they will in the end shun an exhibition or program that does not have authenticity at its foundation.

Historic sites have erected questionable **recreations** since the early years of historical interpretation. In 1934, the National Park Service built a "replica" of George Washington's birthplace in Wakefield, Virginia, on a spot where his adopted grandson thought the home had existed. There were no photographs of the house since the original had burned in 1780, and no one knew what materials to use. Virginian Josephine Wheelwright Rust spearheaded the effort to recreate the building; when it was finished, it was discovered that the replica was on the wrong site and that it bore a suspicious resemblance to Mrs. Rust's childhood home. Despite charges of inauthenticity from the beginning, the National Park Service conducted tours of Wakefield as Washington's birthplace until 1992.[12] We can contrast the Wakefield site, which has been dubbed "Fakefield," to George Washington's farm at Mt. Vernon. After extensive research there, staff members recreated his sixteen-sided barn and stocked it with heritage breeds of farm animals. In the surrounding fields, they demonstrate Washington's advanced agricultural techniques. While the barn is a replica of the original, the farm is authentic in its look and practices.

Authenticity has been a challenging goal for some public history sites, especially those that have difficult stories to tell. Many times such sites have much more information, for example, about the slave owner than about the enslaved. Unfortunately, some sites have used the lack of readily available information to stay away from these more difficult topics. While sites need to maintain authenticity, the absence of authentic artifacts does not absolve a site from interpreting controversial histories. One effective way to handle difficult issues for a site that lacks significant resources is by introducing **historical context** to help visitors understand what life was like for a significant percentage of people in the past and what was likely true for the specific people who are being interpreted at a public history site. One site that has done this well is McLeod Plantation in Charleston, South Carolina, which was opened in 2015 to tell a diverse history so that "all of their stories—black and white, enslaved and free—are given their due" and seen as "essential to understanding Charleston's complex past." One text panel in the owner's house at McLeod tells the story of an enslaved woman, Isabella Pinckney, who was enslaved by the McLeod family. In telling her story, the text twice takes a wider view to explain the historic context, introducing it both times with the word "common":

Isabella Pinckney was the daughter of an unknown white planter and enslaved mother—a common outcome of often forced relationships between owners and enslaved women. According to family tradition, Isabella was an adult when she and her son David were given to William Wallace McLeod for Isabella to serve as a "companion," or nanny, to William's young daughter, Annie. Selling, giving people away, or threatening these actions, was common and done with little regard for the disruption it caused. How do you think Isabella may have felt when she and her child were given to a new family?[13]

The word "common" signals to visitors that they are engaging with information that will help them understand the site-specific materials being discussed. By using historical context, sites can help visitors understand the meaning and significance of these events. While historic sites have often wanted to focus only on those specific stories that relate to their site and about which they have a great deal of primary source material to draw from, when visitors do not know much about a historic experience like slavery, such site-specific information may lack the very kind of meaning that sites hope to impart.

Civic Engagement

Audience engagement seeks to pull the audience into the historical content; **civic engagement** encourages audiences to use that content in the wider world. When public historians practice civic engagement by linking events of the past to today's issues such as environmental concerns, human rights, racism, or violent conflicts, they push or even transgress the boundaries of traditional public history. Current events have historical dimensions, and there are times when asking the public to solve today's problems becomes the primary goal of a public history project. Many public history institutions have a **mission statement** that includes engaging audiences in conversations about the present. The mission statement of the Tenement Museum in New York City reads:

> The Tenement Museum preserves and interprets the history of immigration through the personal experiences of the generations of newcomers who settled in and built lives on Manhattan's Lower East Side, America's iconic immigrant neighborhood; forges emotional connections between visitors and immigrants past and present; and enhances appreciation for the profound role immigration has played and continues to play in shaping America's evolving national identity.

The Tenement Museum is one of the founding members of the **International Coalition of Sites of Conscience**, a movement begun in 1999 to engage historic sites "in programs that stimulate dialogue on pressing social issues."[14] One of the key programs developed by the Tenement Museum to promote dialogue on current-day issues is its Kitchen Conversations. This program gives visitors the opportunity, after taking a tour at the Tenement Museum, to engage in a conversation, led by a facilitator, that links the immigration stories told at the museum with issues around immigration today. In part, this program began in response to comments Tenement Museum employees heard guests make that negatively compared today's immigrants to those they were learning about who had immigrated a century earlier.

The Kitchen Conversations enable visitors to understand the experiences of today's immigrants through the lens of those who came before them and to become more informed about the issue of immigration today. The Tenement Museum makes explicit the ways in which a site can "use the past," returning to the categories of historical inquiry introduced in chapter 1, to help make sense of the present. Civic engagement begins by putting the public at the center of interpretive, educational, and management planning.

Taking Audience Engagement to the Streets

Engagement strategies are not confined to museums, historic sites, or other formal places of memory. Sometimes public historians bring their engagement to the public. Interpretation can move outside the museum, away from the historic site, and engage the public where they work, study, and live. One of those strategies is the mobile museum. Similar to a food truck, mobile museums can bring historical interpretation to communities instead of asking communities to come to the museums. The Philadelphia Public History Truck, for example, was created by Temple University public history graduate student Erin Bernard as a creative alternative to the traditional thesis. The history truck partners with grassroots organizations from Philadelphia neighborhoods to explore and tell their own histories through objects, art, and archival research. All interpretive projects are created in collaboration with the people who live in the communities and neighborhoods represented, and the results are displayed in neighborhood spaces, making it truly a community interpretive exhibition.[15]

Engagement through Technology

There is no doubt that advances in technology have changed the way the public takes in knowledge, transforming audience expectations. Social media has conditioned young and old to expect an active role in their informal learning experiences. In fact, it seems that most people have become experts in curating, interpreting, and presenting their lives to the public through social media. Since many people take significant amounts of their free time to shape and maintain their own digital presence, being a passive consumer of information is no longer the norm. Newspapers, for example, have been shaped by social media—most allow comments on news stories as a way of allowing the public to engage with the news, even if that engagement is often ill-informed—and social media has quickly overtaken traditional news outlets as the public's primary method of accessing the news. According to the Pew Research Center, in 2016, 62 percent of US adults access news through social media.[16] Nina Simon wrote in her book *Participatory Museum*, "As more people enjoy and become accustomed to participatory learning and entertainment experiences, they want to do more than just 'attend' cultural events and institutions." Museums understand this demand and attempt to create opportunities for visitor participation via technology. However, sometimes the user experience falls short of the expectations of the museum organizers. Simon recalls a visit to a Chicago museum that invited guests to record their responses on camera at the end of an exhibit. Instead of delivering thoughtful analyses, visitors mumbled in front of the lens; teens posed for selfies. Simon notes: "This is not the participatory museum experience of my dreams. But I don't blame the participants. I blame the design. . . . Whether the goal is to promote dialogue or creative expression, shared learning or co-creative work, the design process starts with a simple question: which tool or technique will produce the desired participatory experience?"[17]

The Limits of Audience Participation

What, if any, should be the limits of public historians' efforts to give the public a voice? When scholars gathered in 2006 as a part of the advance planning for the NPS Centennial in 2016, Patricia Nelson Limerick, professor of history and environmental studies at the University of Colorado, related a story about the limits of public involvement and the need to maintain historical accuracy. Limerick spoke about her attendance at a 150th anniversary commemoration of the Whitman massacre, the 1847 murder of thirteen white missionaries in the Northwest Territory. Marcus and Narcissa Whitman had settled near what is now the town of Walla Walla, Washington. Even though Marcus Whitman was a physician, he was unable to stop the rapid spread of measles through the population of American Indians, and he and his wife, blamed for the deaths of over 200 Native people, were murdered, along with eleven other missionaries. Their deaths are often portrayed as a climax of misunderstandings between missionary settlers and Native peoples in an era of rapid expansion of white settlements west and displacement and catastrophic death rates among American Indians from disease. Because of the complicated relationship between settlers, missionaries, and American Indians, descendants from these different groups have very different perspectives on the story of the Whitmans. Limerick explained the nature of the event organized to remember them:

> I was at an event commemorating the 150th Anniversary of the Whitman Massacre and there were many different interpretations offered by different people as to what the Whitmans had done to get themselves killed. One person was saying very insistently that they had purposely and intelligently and thoughtfully introduced disease to Indian people which I really can't see as tenable. We all had to be respectful because we'd all said, "Oh, well, there's different types of views." That first man who was making that argument caused me to write the limerick, which I shall recite:
>
> > A swirl of diverse points of view
> > mushes history into a stew
> > facts now are fiction
> > earning much malediction
> > leaving liars with nothing to do.[18]

Balancing respect for public involvement with the need to maintain a level of academic integrity can be difficult, especially when the public historian intends to respect persons whose lives were affected by history and to implement best practices in terms of maintaining a sense of democratic representation and social justice.

In many cases, the central narrative does demand revision. The pushback against updating or correcting the misdeeds or exclusive histories of the past requires as much care as any other aspect of public history. It also requires a commitment to standards, as well as an understanding of politics. Sometimes public history education includes the explicit education of our political leaders. Michael Kammen, professor of American history and culture at Cornell University, as well as a member of the National Park Service Advisory Board, said near the conclusion of the board's 2006 meeting:

> When there was debate in Congress and especially in the Senate over renaming what was once called Custer Battlefield National Monument, senators from Wyoming, Montana, intermountain states were receiving very strong pressure from interest groups who did not want the name changed. They made remarks like, "Why can't they leave history the way it was written? Don't they understand that the historical facts are known and were established?" And so when we talk about the public, at least when I talk about the public and the lay public, it does not just include ordinary citizens who come to these sites but members of Congress share this failure to understand that our perceptions of what happened at these places, and the significance of what happened at these places, changes over time.

Engaging diverse publics in conversations about the past, particularly past events when the public represents the descendants of diverse points of view, requires dedication to the best standards of historical thinking on one hand and an ability to listen to and give room for multiple ways of framing the meaning of history in the lives of the public today on the other hand. In Oregon, children are taught in school about the Whitmans as leaders who led families across the Blue Mountains and into the Willamette Valley where the majority of Oregon's population now resides. This story may be celebratory as the beginning of the state's history, or it may be a memorial to the loss of freedom, loss of life, and loss of many traditional ways for Native Americans. Even though tempers and feelings can run very high when the public comes together to discuss how they relate to the past, there is a line that should be drawn between diverse historical narratives and conflicting views on history and legend, myth, and, as Limerick said, lies. Historical education is at the core of participatory democracies and at the core of civic virtues. Since the stakes are so very high, the work involved will never be dull, and will never be a solitary venture.

Engaging Audiences through Difficult Encounters

Historic sites have traditionally attracted public audiences with information and exhibits that evoked positive emotions: feelings of pride and patriotism, appreciation of fine craftsmanship or a picturesque vista, and moments of amusement when modern guests marvel at chamber pots and corsets. But attitudes toward history sites have shifted. Colonial Williamsburg in particular came under criticism early on for its pristine byways, perfectly manicured gardens, and its frequent paint jobs.[19] Historians pointed out that no actual colonial town could have been so meticulously maintained. Streets would have been littered with horse manure; the smells, sounds, and nuisances of everyday life in an eighteenth-century town would not have been so neat and tidy. Today, peeling clapboards and worn shingles indicate a degree of historical authenticity in the physical fabric of the town. But public historians need to ensure that they are not whitewashing anything other than their historical buildings; history was literally and metaphorically messier than some living history sites and house museums would lead visitors to believe. As those interviewed for *The Presence of the Past* revealed, Americans trust museums' educational process. With these levels of trust and that breadth of influence, public history sites have an obligation to deliver complex narratives, even if they challenge visitors' understanding of the past. This approach could lead to more productive audience engagement.

Museum studies show that many adult museum visitors actually learn more when they experience **difficult encounters** at a public history site.[20] Telling a more complete story about American history may also increase interest from groups whose histories have too often been ignored. Traditionally, museums and historic sites have been reluctant to present audiences with ambiguous narratives, debatable ethical issues, or even straightforward facts that might have disturbed them. Many progressive public historians feel strongly, however, that this is a core component of their work. At many sites across the country, public historians have worked in recent years to transform displays and interpretation to address difficult topics. Increasingly, sites ask visitors to enter what public historian Carl Weinberg calls a **discomfort zone** and to stay there.[21] In addition, members of the public whose ancestors' stories have all too often been excluded from museums and historic sites have added their voices, seeking change as well. While difficult encounters differ widely in subject matter and format of delivery, they all seek to prompt visitors to reflect deeply on the meaning of past events and their relevance in today's world.

Difficult Encounter: New or Surprising Information

A difficult encounter can come in the form of surprising information. In eighteenth-century Williamsburg, half of the population was of African descent, and most of the black inhabitants were enslaved. The majority of twentieth-century visitors to Colonial Williamsburg would have had no notion of these statistics because for fifty-seven years all of the first-person interpreters were white. Black men had portrayed coachmen at the site for decades, and one black woman had interacted with visitors in one of the historic kitchens in the early years, but visitors came away with a completely inaccurate understanding of the racial makeup of the pre-Revolutionary Virginia town.[22] In 1979, the Colonial Williamsburg Foundation hired six African Americans to depict enslaved people. Although the percentages were considerably off, the presence of the new interpreters forced visitors to confront the fact that African Americans had inhabited the colonial capital and that most of them had been enslaved. Depending on their prior knowledge, this information may have challenged their expectations that a visit to Williamsburg would provide a narrative that was designed, in the words of Colonial Williamsburg's mission statement, to interpret "the origins of the idea of America, conceived decades before the American Revolution."[23] Visitors had to contend with the notion that our nation's founders promoted liberty while they profited from the labor of people who were not free. In his discussion of difficult encounters, the sociologist Roger Simon highlights moments like this where sites ask visitors to process "multiple, conflicting perspectives of historical events resulting in narratives whose conclusions remain complicated and uncertain."[24] Simon notes that during these periods of ambiguity, visitors can become angry, frustrated, or just refuse to interact with the presentation any further. When slavery entered their previously uncomplicated narrative of Colonial Williamsburg, many guests responded predictably. Some became visibly upset; one white visitor complained about the presence of black interpreters in a letter to the editor of a local newspaper.[25] Others challenged the first rule of living history museums by asking black interpreters questions that they found impossible to answer in character; eighteenth-century slaves could not have known what slavery was like in the other colonies or the economics of the Atlantic triangle trade. It is impossible to know how many guests simply refused to interact with the black interpreters or how many potential guests decided not to visit Williamsburg after slavery entered the presentation.

The observations of historian Andrew Schocket, in a study of Revolutionary-era sites, suggest that white audiences may continue to avoid this kind of difficult encounter today at the same time that such interpretive content speaks meaningfully to those whose histories are finally being recognized and included. In 2003, the Liberty Bell Center opened on Independence Mall in Philadelphia, embedded in an interpretive context that challenged visitors to remember that this symbol meant very different things to white and black Americans throughout the nation's history. After much public pressure and controversy, the National Park Service also greatly increased its interpretation of the nation's first White House, also located on Independence Mall, where George Washington lived alongside men and women he enslaved. Schocket observed, "when tourist buses disgorge their charges across the street, white American groups stride briskly through the first white house installation, stopping to look for a moment or two, having been distracted by the audio or video, and move on to get in line to see the Liberty Bell. Black people of all ages linger, raptly watching, often standing through the entire loop [that depicts the experience of enslaved people on the site] in front of one screen and before strolling to another. Sometimes they absorb silently, sometimes families discuss what they see."[26] Museums and historic sites must engage in significant work to identify who their visitors are and to set clear goals when tackling difficult subjects. Visitor studies show that regardless of how brilliant our interpretive strategies may be, or how compellingly the interpretive narrative interacts with the historic site or objects on display, visitors are in a free-choice learning environment, and they will engage differently based on their own previous knowledge and their own identities.[27] All interpretive and engagement strategies should be accompanied by evaluation, but this is especially important when dealing with difficult encounters.

Difficult Encounter: Systemic Injustice or Violence

A second form of a difficult encounter takes place when visitors are confronted with a narrative of systemic injustice or even violence. Colonial Williamsburg created this type of difficult encounter in 1994 when their African American interpretations and presentations department staged Publick Times, a forty-five-minute recreation of a slave auction. Black actors were placed on auction blocks and were bid on by white actors, with the exception of one black actor who portrayed a free black man trying to buy his enslaved wife. Nell

Irvin Painter, the Princeton historian who has written extensively on the history of race, noted that in the slave auction restaging, visitors were forced to see the truth at the heart of slavery—that through the system of slavery, people were turned into economic units and that those transactions were not hidden away but were the public activity of America's upstanding citizens, a fact that the event's title underscored.[28] As they watched the auction, visitors were reminded that the human being as an economic unit provided the historical foundation for one of the most successful economies in the history of the world; the labor of unpaid African Americans enriched the rest of the nation, both Northerners and Southerners. While they might have come to Williamsburg expecting to don a tri-corn hat and have their picture taken in the stocks, guests who witnessed Publick Times confronted a sobering truth about their own nation. Instead of simply celebrating America's beginnings, visitors wrestled with a more complicated and troubling origin story.

Difficult Encounter: Visitor Identification

A third type of difficult encounter uses a psychological finding: visitors who witness depictions of violence can identify with the victims, perpetrators, bystanders, and/or rescuers.[29] The United States Holocaust Memorial Museum in Washington, DC, has developed a strategy of visitor engagement that uses themed question cards as a tool to encourage visitors to look for one or more of these roles throughout the permanent exhibition. Of particular interest is the role of the bystander. Until very recently, the bystander has been interpreted as a passive individual, witnessing events as they unfold, but not taking an active role. After conducting extensive research, recording oral histories, and collecting new material for a temporary exhibition titled *Some Were Neighbors*, which we will discuss later in this chapter, the educational specialists developed an interpretive strategy that encourages visitors to think in more complex ways about the many roles that people played during the Holocaust. The "question cards" visitors receive before they enter the permanent exhibition encourage the public to think of all actors in history as having agency and holding themselves accountable for the small decisions they make every day in the face of prejudice, intolerance, hatred, and/or violence.[30] In this way visitors can identify with individuals with whom they might share something in common, but they are also encouraged to view the exhibition analytically, through the eyes of one of the roles they were given randomly before entering the exhibition, and they are encouraged to discuss what they find with others in their group and to compare what they see with visitors who were given different roles.

The slave auction at Colonial Williamsburg also confronted its participants with **visitor identification**. The event must have reminded some visitors of the history of their own ancestors, including sellers, buyers, bystanders, and the enslaved. On the day of the auction, some guests might have empathized with a character who was their same age or held a similar position in life. The separation of families proved particularly wrenching for visitors. Some spectators wept as enslaved children were sold away from their parents.[31] Still others might have been shamed that they, like the antebellum slaveholders, actually enjoyed the spectacle. They might have counted themselves lucky to have visited the site on such an unusual day, appreciated the event, and felt anxious guilt for even participating as an observer (bystander). Although the auction was intended to illuminate the history of African Americans, the Virginia chapter of the NAACP protested the reenactment, as did many individual African Americans. A *New York Times* reporter recounted that an African American maintenance worker at Williamsburg told him prior to the event: "'Blacks around here don't want to be reminded,' said the man, who refused to give his name because he said he feared 'retribution' by Williamsburg officials. 'It bothers people. People think it's very insensitive to dig it all up again.'"[32] Some critics would agree with this anonymous commentator. David Marriott, a professor at the University of California, Santa Cruz, questions the endless reenactment of African Americans' brutal past. If today's young people of color are continually confronted by depictions of violence and injustice against people who look like them, they internalize the psychology of victimhood.[33] The slave auction might have educated white visitors, but it could have added to the burden of the history of slavery for black visitors. Christy S. Coleman, Williamsburg's African American department director who herself played a slave on the auction block, defended the program in the *New York Times*: "I recognize that this is a very, very sensitive and emotional issue. But it is also very real history, and it distresses me, personally and professionally, that there are those who would have us hide this or keep it under the rug." Although most visitors who were present are not likely to forget their witness of a slave auction, this encounter proved too difficult for the museum to repeat. They have not staged another since 1994.

Difficult Encounters Online

Public historians who attempt to engage audiences online may face the most difficult task because their content competes with so many digital distractions. Websites that deliver difficult knowledge face even more challenges. It is hard to manage the visitor experience when members of your audience can leave the site at any time to check e-mail, place a bid on a vintage item, or check what's trending. The United States Holocaust Memorial Museum (USHMM) faced these hurdles as they developed a companion online component of *Some Were Neighbors*, a temporary exhibit that deals with the difficult subject of Hitler's collaborators among the civilian German populace.[34] Edward Linenthal chronicles the debates that museum professionals and Holocaust survivors engaged in as they developed the physical USHMM in the 1980s in *Preserving Memory: The Struggle to Create America's Holocaust Museum*.[35] The museum, situated just off the national mall in Washington, DC, had no collection of artifacts and set out to interpret events that had not occurred in the United States. Elie Wiesel, a survivor, wanted the museum to serve as "an initiatory center. Here the sacred mystery that was the Holocaust would stamp itself on individual psyches, and visitors would, ideally, emerge with renewed appreciation of the mystery."[36] Stuart Silver suggested a chronological story designed to "transform self-awareness . . . to bring about the realization that everyday ordinary human beings can become both victims and victimizers."[37] The online exhibit *Some Were Neighbors* advances both of these objectives into the digital age, creating difficult encounters that would be impossible in a physical museum setting. The site maintains its status as a Site of Conscience by its refusal to surrender the overall interpretation even as it engages audiences visually and invites their interaction.

When a visitor first opens the site, quotations of different sizes and colors float across the screen:

"And this was done by young people, whom we knew." —SURVIVOR

"The neighbors waited like vultures for us to leave our apartment." —SURVIVOR

The movement and visual variety of the sentences themselves catch the viewer's attention, and the content prepares them for the rest of the exhibit. The words briefly hover in layers then disappear.

After about a minute new quotations stop appearing and viewers see a montage of seven static images: a photograph of unsmiling people looking out an industrial window; a color portrait of a twenty-first-century man; a crisp black-and-white photograph of people boarding a train; a page from a sketchbook depicting a mill house in the middle of a heart accented by flowers; a sepia print of a nun giving the Hitler salute; a black-and-white snapshot of a girl and her doll; a handmade paper Star of David with "Swing 42" fashioned in colored pencil. These opening images have been carefully chosen. Viewers with knowledge of the Holocaust will recognize some aspects of them, but together they don't immediately tell a comprehensible story. No element is particularly disturbing; they look as if they have fallen from a scrapbook. The items sit brightly lit over a background of darkly ghosted images—identification papers, more photographs, letters, documents with official stamps.

On the left-hand side of the page, organizers have provided this copy: *"Millions of ordinary people witnessed the crimes of the Holocaust—in the countryside and city squares, in stores and schools, in homes and workplaces. Across Europe, the Nazis found countless willing helpers who collaborated or were complicit in their crimes. What motives and pressures led so many individuals to abandon their fellow human beings? Why did others make the choice to help?"* Here the creators of the site insert unequivocal language: "complicit," "abandon their fellow human beings," the repeated use of "crimes." The site passes judgment on the Nazis' willing helpers; it does not invite them to contribute. It does not open the door for Holocaust deniers.

The seven central images lie inert until the visitor takes the initiative and passes a cursor over them. Only then does the viewer discover that they are labeled: *Neighbors, Workers, Teenagers, Teachers, Religious Leaders, Friends,* and *Policemen.* For each group, the visitor discovers a description that leaves little room for interpretation. For example, under *Policemen,* the copy reads in part, "Whether acting out of conviction or simply following orders, these policemen played a role in the persecution and murder of millions." There is no question about the argument of the site's organizers. If visitors click on the accompanying link labelled "Explore," they make a commitment to engage on the website's terms.

If a visitor clicks on "Explore" in the *Neighbors* category, they see stacks of images that stretch beyond the boundaries of the page. Some color images have video links, others are documents, but most are photographs. On the top of the first stack sits a black-and-white image of an apartment building courtyard filled with people and their belongings. On the opposite side of the courtyard, a couple leans out of a second-story window to get a better view. The public historians have entitled this image "Watching Neighbors." By placing it on the top of the first stack, the organizers brilliantly pull the visitor into the difficult encounter: in the foreground of the photo sit two china cups on a window ledge. Viewers find themselves in a building in Amsterdam in 1943, having just finished their tea, witnessing the deportation. They ponder the question that the public historians ask in the introduction to the image: "Why did so many people betray their personal loyalty to neighbors, classmates, co-workers or friends?" They wonder what they would have done.

If a visitor clicks on the image, it almost fills the page, and seven buttons appear on the left, allowing a user to zoom in on parts of the image, see a map of Amsterdam, summon identifying labels for the various groups in the photo, or share the image on social media. The public historians are unrelenting in their interpretation: these Dutch Jews are headed for Westerbork, "a way station to the Auschwitz killing center."

The video on top of the next stack is the oral testimony of a Lithuanian woman who was told as a child that Jews needed Christian blood for their holiday rituals. In another image, organizers move the viewer to different areas of an image, effectively animating a still photo in a technique known as the Ken Burns effect. This guided examination encourages viewers to explore the amused faces in a crowd surrounding a Jewish man forced to cut the beard of a fellow Jew in violation of Jewish law. In a clip from the Shoah Project a survivor recalls that the Christian woman who harbored him and his sister constantly berated them for putting her family in danger. In another Shoah interview, a survivor remembers that as he and his family were waiting to be deported, a German woman stepped from the crowd and embraced his mother: "If more people had done something like that, things may have changed," he says. The site incorporates material culture in digital form. Viewers see a purse a child knitted in a concentration camp, a school child's autograph album, a shovel used in digging mass graves, an axe blade from a Croatian detention facility overseen by a priest. The selection of documents, objects, and witness testimony provides an unrelenting yet complex testament to these events.

After reviewing the items in the seven categories, viewers are invited to reflect on the exhibit. Six images appear, and viewers are able to comment on them at length and to see the comments other visitors have left. One photo shows three SS officials and their ten female assistants laughing and posing on a bridge. One of the officers is playing an accordion. In the comment section, one visitor demonstrates the effectiveness of the exhibit: "As a twenty-three-year-old gay man, this picture haunts me. It shows that those who commit unspeakable evil are not the shadowy, monstrous figures that we imagine. They were people like me. People who laugh and take silly pictures and have otherwise normal lives, except for the fact that they had a helping hand into the murder of millions."[38]

The exhibition had its origins as a brick and mortar installation at the US Holocaust Memorial Museum in Washington, DC. Critics acknowledged its power there, but it may be even more effective as an online exhibit.[39] Viewers click through its images and video clips the way they might view a friend's Facebook page. They select the items that intrigue them, and they are invited to interact and comment. That extra step reveals the story behind the benign image. This octogenarian stole a Jewish person's house. That smiling girl was a murderer. Those faces are not in a museum case, but are on the visitor's desktop, or on their phone, or in their lap. They have invited them into their social space, just as they would a neighbor. There is an advantage in engaging audiences in the discovery of personal stories of betrayal in the online exhibition as opposed to the physical exhibition at the USHMM. One may experience what can sometimes be intense emotional responses to the oral histories and difficult stories presented in private, without the distraction of being observed by other visitors. When this site was demonstrated to a workshop of future teachers in a training workshop sponsored by the USHMM, students were able to browse the site at their own pace and listen to a variety of oral history testimony in relative privacy using headphones and sitting at individual computer stations. Some students were overcome with emotion and were unable to communicate their feelings immediately afterward. The intensity of being confronted with the very personal, neighborly forms of betrayal and victimization creates an emotional response that may require more time and more personal space to absorb. An online format allows users to revisit this space at their own pace, and in a setting that can allow them to respond in a less guarded, private manner.

The online exhibit *Some Were Neighbors* combines many of the best practices of audience engagement: the engineering of a difficult encounter, the effective use of technology, the analysis of authentic sources from the past, and learner choice. It also invites visitors to solve a problem: how does a society protect "the other" in times of threat, encouraging a consideration of civic engagement. Even though no public historian is present to guide the user, the guiding principles of public history make this experience highly effective and accessible.

Creative Uses of the Past

Artists have been successfully engaging audiences through their interpretations of history for centuries. Think of *The Iliad*, or *Chushingura* (a mid-eighteenth-century puppet scenario and kabuki play based on the real story of forty-seven loyal samurai), Shakespeare's history plays, hide paintings by the native peoples of the American plains, and ballads that recounted tragic deaths a community wanted to remember. Today, artists continue to mine specific stories and broader themes from history to create their art. In some cases, their work stands alone and visitors encounter it without accompanying materials to provide historical context. Sometimes public historians work with artists to develop an artistic component to a larger public history project, building a layered experience for audiences. Their work, whether undertaken alone or in partnership with historical institutions, can serve as models for public historians who are not afraid to take some risks to engage the public.

Duke Riley made a literal splash in 2009 when he staged a twenty-first-century *naumachia*, a Roman-style naval battle like the ones ancient Romans had engineered in the Coliseum. *Those About to Die Salute You* took its name from the Latin *"Moritori te selutant,"* the last words prisoners had delivered to Emperor Claudius in 52 AD before they battled to the death on the manufactured sea. Riley partnered with the Queens Museum of Art to create his interactive spectacle that attracted thousands. A few years earlier he had built a submarine based on "The Turtle," a Revolutionary-era vehicle the Americans had launched unsuccessfully against the British in the Battle of Brooklyn. Riley navigated his one-man, egg-shaped craft around New York Harbor for some time before being arrested. In 2016, he returned to the waterfront, this time with permission, to stage *Fly by Night*, an event held at dusk over the course of several weeks. Riley trained 2,000 homing pigeons to follow commands he delivered through signal flags, then he attached LED lights to them and guided them through the night sky. *The Guardian* reported that there were 45,000 people on the waiting list to sit on the waterfront and watch the event. Riley's motivation for this work was not simply a beautiful "avian ballet." He wanted to expose audiences to the time-honored exercise of "pigeon fancying" and at the same time highlight their lost connection to the life of New York as a port city. Riley told *The Guardian* reporter: "There is so much information that is not written down. People give credibility to what is written in books. But what is important to me, might be so buried in history that it gets lost."[40]

Kara Walker began her career using silhouette, a technique that was historical in itself. She took the tropes of the Old South (moonlight and magnolias, plantation houses, trees heavy with Spanish moss) and created life-size installations of stark black-on-white tableaus that seem quaint at first glance. When viewers take a second look, however, they discover tails on some of the human figures, additional legs under the hoop skirts, depictions of sexual acts and organs, everyday household objects transformed into weapons and torture devices. Although she is a modern artist, Walker adopted the older practice of giving her works long and involved titles, calling one of her earliest installations "Gone: An Historical Romance of a Civil War as It Occurred Between the Dusky Thighs of One Young Negress and Her Heart" (1994). Walker went on to create even larger pieces, including "A Subtlety, or the Marvelous Sugar Baby an Homage to the unpaid and overworked Artisans who have refined our Sweet tastes from the cane fields to the Kitchens of the New World on the Occasion of the demolition of the Domino Sugar Refining Plant" (2014), a massive sphinx with the head of a "mammy" installed in a warehouse. Walker's medium for this piece: white processed sugar.[41]

As we write this book, Lin-Manuel Miranda's *Hamilton* is the hottest ticket on Broadway. Seats are sold out for months. When artists attract media attention, critical analysis, and a waiting list of thousands, they have tapped into the public's hunger to connect to the past. Works of art often provide an emotional dimension to an interpretation of history that might be lacking in a traditional exhibit based on argument and evidence. Artists have much to teach us about what makes audiences care about a subject.

Notes

1. An important early work on interpretation is Freeman Tilden's *Interpreting Our Heritage*, 4th edition (1957; repr., Chapel Hill: University of North Carolina Press, 2008). See also interpreter David Larsen's thoughts on the meaning and potential of interpretation, "Interview with David Larsen," from the collection of Mather Training Center, National Park Service, Harpers Ferry, WV, available at: https://www.youtube.com/watch?v=TgEOa118j-o.
2. The Holocaust Museum's identity cards can be seen here: https://www.ushmm.org/remember/id-cards.
3. "That the Future May Learn from the Past: A Center for History and Citizenship," Colonial Williamsburg Foundation, http://www.history.org/foundation/mission.cfm and "The History of Colonial Williamsburg," http://www.history.org/Foundation/cwhistory.cfm.
4. http://www.askaslave.com/.
5. Amy Tyson and Azie Mira Dungey, "'Ask a Slave' and Interpreting Race on Public History's Front Line: Interview with Azie Mira Dungey, *The Public Historian* 36, no. 1 (February 2014): 36–60, quotations on 38, 49, 53. See also: Amy Tyson, *The Wages of History: Emotional Labor on Public History's Front Lines* (Amherst: University of Massachusetts Press, 2013).

6. Nina Simon, *The Participatory Museum* (Santa Cruz, CA: Museum 2.0, 2010), http://www.participatorymuseum.org/read/; Betty Farrell, and Maria Medvedeva, *Demographic Transformation and the Future of Museums* (Washington, DC: American Association of Museums Press, 2010), http://www.aam-us.org/docs/center-for-the-future-of-museums/demotrans aam2010.pdf; National Endowment for the Arts, "2008 Survey of Public Participation in the Arts," Research Report #49, 2009, https://www.arts.gov/sites/default/files/2008-SPPA.pdf; Rebecca Stanfield McCown, Daniel Laven, Robert Manning, and Nora Mitchell, "Engaging New and Diverse Audiences in the National Parks: An Exploratory Study of Current Knowledge and Learning Needs," *The George Wright Forum* 29, no. 2 (2012): 272–284, quotation from 273, http://www.georgewright.org/292stanfield_mccown.pdf.

7. Anne Mitchell Whisnant, Marla R. Miller, Gary B. Nash, and David Thelen, *Imperiled Promise: The State of History in the National Park Service*, 27, 35–42, 55–56. Available at: http://www.oah.org/site/assets/documents/Imperiled_Promise.pdf.

8. Franklin D. Vagnone and Deborah E. Ryan, *Anarchist's Guide to Historic House Museums: "A Ground-Breaking Manifesto"* (Walnut Creek, CA: Left Coast Press, 2016), 55.

9. Tina Susman, "Detroit Resident Finally Feels at Home Next to Wacky Public Art Project," *Los Angeles Times*, March 19, 2015.

10. Jennifer Pustz's survey of historic houses interpreting the period after 1865, which garnered 358 responses, found that 27.7 percent of these museums opened in the period 1970–1979, with "the most frequently cited year being 1976 (thirteen opened that year)." 56.3 percent of the house museums in Pustz's survey opened after 1970. Jennifer Pustz, *Voices from the Back Stairs: Interpreting Servants' Lives at Historic House Museums* (Dekalb: Northern Illinois University Press, 2009), 42.

11. Pustz, *Voices from the Back Stairs*, 54–55.

12. Michael Kammen, Review of "Here, George Washington Was Born: Memory, Material Culture and the Public History of a National Monument," *The Public Historian* 31, no. 3 (Summer 2009): 96–98.

13. "Close Quarters at McLeod Plantation," Text Panel, McLeod Plantation, Charleston, SC, June 2015.

14. International Coalition of Sites of Conscience, "Founders," http://www.sitesofconscience.org/founders/.

15. For more information on the Philadelphia Public History Truck, see: https://phillyhistory truck.wordpress.com.

16. Jeffrey Gottfried and Elisa Shearer, "News Use Across Social Media Platforms 2016," *Pew Research Center*, May 26, 2016, http://www.journalism.org/2016/05/26/news-use-across-so cial-media-platforms-2016/.

17. Nina Simon, *The Participatory Museum*, available at: http://www.participatorymuseum.org/chapter1/.

18. Rolf Diamant, Laura J. Feller, and David L. Larsen, eds., "Scholars Forum: The National Park Service and Civic Reflection: A Summary Report," Conservation and Stewardship Publication no. 13, 2006, http://www.nps.gov/civic/newsevents/Scholars%20Report_12_13_2006print.pdf.

19. See Anders Greenspan, *Creating Colonial Williamsburg, The Restoration of Virginia's 18th Century Colonial Capital*, 2nd ed. (Chapel Hill: University of North Carolina Press, 2009).

20. Scott Magelssen, "'This Is a Drama. You Are Characters': The Tourist as Fugitive Slave in Conner Prairie's 'Follow the North Star,'" *Theatre Topics* 16, no. 1 (March 2006): 19–34. For a more detailed discussion of difficult encounters, see Roger Simon, "A Shock to Thought:

Curatorial Judgment and the Public Exhibition of 'Difficult Knowledge,'" *Memory Studies* 4, no. 4 (October 2011): 432–449.

21. Carl. R. Weinberg, "The Discomfort Zone: Reenacting Slavery at Conner Prairie," *OAH Magazine of History* 23, no. 2 (April 2009): 62–64.

22. Ywone Edwards-Ingram, "Before 1979: African American Coachmen, Visibility and Representation at Colonial Williamsburg," *The Public Historian* 36, no. 1 (February 2014): 9–35.

23. "Colonial Williamsburg Foundation: Mission," http://www.history.org/foundation/mission.cfm.

24. Visitors thought they knew what they were getting into, but the museum presents "multiple, conflicting perspectives of historical events resulting in narratives whose conclusions remain complicated and uncertain," from Roger Simon, "A Shock to Thought," 433.

25. James Oliver Horton, "Slavery in American History: An Uncomfortable National Dialogue" in *Slavery and Public History: The Tough Stuff of American Memory*, James Oliver Horton and Lois E. Horton, eds. (Chapel Hill: University of North Carolina Press, 2009), 50.

26. Andrew Schocket, *Fighting Over the Founders: How We Remember the American Revolution* (New York: New York University Press, 2015), 90–97.

27. John Falk and Lynn Dierking, *Learning from Museums: Visitor Experiences and the Making of Meaning* (Walnut Creek, CA: AltaMira Press, 2000).

28. Horton, "Slavery in American History," 51.

29. Simon, "A Shock to Thought," 433.

30. "During Your Visit: Using the Question Cards," *USHMM*, https://www.ushmm.org/information/visit-the-museum/group-reservations/resources/during/question-cards. The question cards are available for download, "Student Question Cards," *USHMM*, https://www.ushmm.org/m/pdfs/20070416-using-question-cards.pdf.

31. Horton, "Slavery in American History," 50.

32. Michael Janofsky, "Mock Auction of Slaves: Education or Outrage?" *New York Times*, October 8, 1994. http://www.nytimes.com/1994/10/08/us/mock-auction-of-slaves-education-or-outrage.html.

33. See David S. Marriott, *On Black Men* (New York: Columbia University Press, 2000).

34. *Some Were Neighbors*, http://somewereneighbors.ushmm.org.

35. Edward T. Linenthal, *Preserving Memory: The Struggle to Create America's Holocaust Museum* (New York: Columbia University Press, 1995).

36. Linenthal, *Preserving Memory*, 122.

37. Linenthal, *Preserving Memory*, 132.

38. *Some Were Neighbors*, http://somewereneighbors.ushmm.org/#/reflection/465.

39. Edward Rotstein, "Bystanders, Not So Innocent: 'Some Were Neighbors,' at U.S. Holocaust Memorial Museum," *New York Times*, April 25, 2013, http://www.nytimes.com/2013/04/26/arts/design/some-were-neighbors-at-us-holocaust-memorial-museum.html?pagewanted=all&_r=0.

40. Amana Fontanella-Khan, "Duke Riley: The Pigeon Fancier Whose 'Avian Ballet' Enchanted New York," *The Guardian*, June 28, 2016, https://www.theguardian.com/artanddesign/2016/jun/28/duke-riley-pigeons-avian-ballet-new-york. Explore more of Riley's work at http://www.dukeriley.info/.

41. Explore more of Walker's work at http://www.theartstory.org/artist-walker-kara-artworks.htm.

RESOURCES AND SUGGESTED ACTIVITIES

Plan a Pop-Up Museum on Campus or in Your Community

Pop-up museums can be elaborate and formal, or extremely simple and basic. They can be prepared by professionals to pop-up quite literally overnight for a short-term display at a site or in a public space, or created by and for the public as a participatory event.

The Santa Cruz Museum of Art and History defines the pop-up museum as a temporary exhibit created by the public themselves. As organizers, you would select a theme and a venue and then invite people—other students, the public, or students from your own class—to bring an object related to the topic to share with one another. After your guests arrive, you will explain the principles of how to create an object label and what it should contain (see chapter 5). Each participant writes their own label to accompany their object. The results can be put on display in ordinary or unexpected places. You might enjoy the display only for a class period, leave it in the classroom for others to see throughout the day or week, secure it in a display cabinet on campus, or find room in the library or student union where the display can be exhibited, or some more unusual space on campus or in the community. The exhibition is not meant to be permanent, and the experience of creating the exhibition through collaboration and participatory involvement is more the point of the exercise than the exhibition itself. For more ideas, visit: *Pop Up Museum* at http://popupmuseum.org. If you visit the site, you can select "How To" to find a free downloadable toolkit for organizing a pop-up museum event.

Explore the Ways Community, History, and Art Intersect

Artists who embrace historical themes often engage the community in their work. Look for artists who work with historical institutions, old buildings, and experients (community experts who have gained knowledge through their own lived experiences) to not only create art but to make a difference in a community. Here are some examples to start your investigation:

Visionary Voices is an interdisciplinary project that tells the untold story of people in Pennsylvania fighting for the civil rights of people with intellectual disabilities. One component of the multilayered project is a play, *A Fierce Kind of Love*, based on interviews with leaders of the intellectual disability rights movement, including self-advocates, family members, and government officials. The cast of the interactive production is made up of professional actors and aspiring performers with intellectual disabilities. David Bradley, the director, told the *Philadelphia Inquirer*, "What hit us was, to tell this story of the expansion of rights and the goal of an inclusive society, we needed a cast that embodied that."

Temple University's Institute on Disabilities conducted the interviews and commissioned playwright Suli Holum with support from the Pew Center for Arts and Heritage. Running concurrently with the play, which premiered in April 2016, were storytelling workshops, a photo/audio exhibit, and an academic symposium. Every aspect of the production took its audience into consideration. Every performance included ASL interpretation, real-time captioning, ample wheelchair and companion seating, sensory seating, sensory-friendly guides to the performance and the venue, and audio descriptions. As ticket holders purchase their tickets, they receive an illustrated booklet about what to expect during the performance, including advance notice that cast members interact with members of the audience, enter from a number of doorways, sometimes burst into song, and roll pieces of the set around the performance area. This information makes the theater experience more welcoming to audience members with autism or intellectual disabilities, allowing them to take in more of the play's content and experience the emotions the creators hope to evoke. The efforts to make the production as accessible as possible ties in seamlessly with the historical content, demonstrating that because of civil rights activism for and by people with disabilities, things do change. *A Fierce Kind of Love* continues to be produced in Pennsylvania, and there are plans to produce the work in other venues across the country. *Visionary Voices* interviews and archives are accessible on the project's website, http://www.temple.edu/instituteondisabilities/voices/afkol/.

Theaster Gates delivered a TED talk in March 2015 about his work using historic preservation as a tool for community development in Chicago. The son of a roofer and a potter himself, he began by working with his abilities to make something out of nothing. He started with one abandoned building on his own block, converting it to The Archive House. He then converted two more to The Listening House and Black Cinema House. For each project, he engaged the surrounding community, creating spaces for neighbors to explore their own past. He constantly asked, "How do you talk about tough ideas without separating people from that content?" and through art presented in his various venues, he invited people outside the neighborhood to come in to rediscover an area they had once considered unsalvageable. See his TED talk here: https://www.ted.com/talks/theaster_gates_how_to_revive_a_neighborhood_with_imagination_beauty_and_art?language=en.

In *Places with a Past* in Charleston, South Carolina, 1991, many artists participated in installations all over this historic city. Joyce Scott hung strands of beads and an entire charred tree from columns in a park. Liz Magor photographed Civil War reenactors in nineteenth-century style and hung the images in the house of a Civil War widow. Ann Hamilton piled 14,000 tons of used blue work shirts and pants in a vacant garage. The shirts each sported an embroidered name tag over the pocket. Antony Gormley suspended mannequins from the ceiling of an abandoned jail, their heads embedded in the plaster, hanging like human stalactites. Although the installations were temporary, you can read about the pieces in Mary Jane Jacob's 1992 book *Places with A Past*, http://www.brooklynrail.org/2013/07/criticspage/places-with-a-pastnew-site-specific-art-in-charleston-belongs-to-its-place-and-time and http://www.nytimes.com/1991/05/27/arts/review-art-visual-arts-join-spoleto-festival-usa.html?pagewanted=all.

Difficult Images

Erased Lynching

Modern digital technology allows artists to manipulate historic documents in ways that can provoke difficult encounters for viewers. Ken Gonzales-Day found photographs of lynchings that took place in California. He embarked on a research project to contextualize the images and discovered that between 1850 and 1935 mob violence took the lives of over 800 people. Throughout the American west, Mexican men were killed in the highest numbers. Chinese, American Indians, and African Americans were also targets.[1]

The perpetrators often captured their victims on film. They kept these pictures in personal photo albums and sent them through the US mail as postcards. Collectors can still purchase them at flea markets today. In examining the photographs decades after they were produced, Gonzales-Day noted that the body of the victim held the central position and, as a result, demanded the attention of the modern-day viewer. Aware of the dangers of saturating the culture with images of victimized bodies of color, Gonzales-Day used photo software to remove the bodies from the images. He obscured the nooses and other instruments of torture as well. In his installations, viewers see groups of whites, mostly men, clustered together, pointing at a void, often smiling.[2] Two of his images are available online at http://www.kengonzalesday.com/projects/erasedlynching/01.htm.

1. How do modern viewers read these images? What does our understanding of them tell us about our expectations of lynching photography?
2. Does the removal of the images of the victims make you look at the crowd in a different way? Does it do justice to the victims?
3. Should artists manipulate historical images in order to create difficult encounters?

Photographs Depicting the Pain and Suffering of Others

When Alfredo Jaar returned from a trip to document the human suffering that the world seemed to be ignoring during the Rwandan Genocide, he was overwhelmed with grief and angry that this human tragedy had been brushed aside, forgotten, or willfully dismissed. In response, he did not display the thousands of photographs he took. Instead, he displayed them in boxes and asked visitors to the exhibition to think about our responsibility when it comes to witnessing the suffering of others in photographs.

Whether depicting war, genocide, lynching, or any other acts of violence, is it ever ethical to show these images? What are the unintended consequences? When we observe the photograph of an individual who is about to die, and we know they have been killed, in what ways are we complicit in our observation, knowing the outcome? Do we reenact the violence in our collective gaze? Study the ways in which Alfredo Jaar chose to raise awareness of the suffering he witnessed in Rwanda that avoided the ethical problems he found in sharing photographs of the violent deaths he witnessed.

Jaar Rwanda Project: "Let There Be Light," http://imaginarymuseum.org/MHV/PZI mhv/JaarRwandaProject.html.

Alfredo Jaar, *Protest: Art in the Twenty-First Century*, Season 4 (2007), http://www.pbs.org/art21/artists/alfredo-jaar.

See also: Susan Sontag, *Regarding the Pain of Others* (New York: Picador, 2004); and *On Photography* (New York: Picador, 2001 [1973]).

Photographs Originally Taken as Propaganda

During the Second World War, the War Relocation Authority hired photographers, some of whom were quite famous, to document what they wanted to portray as the compassionate treatment of Japanese Americans relocated from their homes for their own protection. The photographers depicted Japanese Americans living an American life inside of a "Relocation Center." People look happy and content. When these photographs are used today to illustrate the wartime experiences and traumas suffered by Japanese Americans, they must be accompanied by a discussion. Why does everyone look so happy if things were so bad? Are there other pictures or images available that were not created for propaganda purposes that could be used instead? For more information on the War Relocation Authority's photography program, see:

Lane Ryo Hirabayashi, "Government Photography of the WRA Camps and Resettlement," *Densho Encyclopedia*, http://encyclopedia.densho.org/Government_photography_of_the_WRA_Camps_and_Resettlement/.

To explore photos of Manzanar, visit: https://www.nps.gov/manz/learn/photosmultimedia/photogallery.htm.

Difficult Encounters, Courageous Conversations

Host a Courageous Conversation of Your Own

What would be a difficult encounter for your class, for your campus, for your community to discuss or confront at a public site or in a local history museum or historic house?[3] What would such an encounter look like? How might you use strategies or approaches you have learned about in this book or in other case studies to facilitate a conversation. You might try it out either in a mock setting using your classroom as the venue, or you might initiate a conversation with a broader audience. Some call these experimental conversations "Courageous Conversations." There may be no other events associated with the conversations, or it may become a regular event hosted by your college or university. Either way, how do the principles of public history better prepare you to carry out a productive and respectful conversation on a difficult subject that represents multiple points of view? Issues may involve underrepresentation of minorities and women on campus or at historic sites or in the area's monuments and statues, conflicts over place names or glorification of individuals with controversial or immoral pasts, or the struggles of undocumented immigrant students and their families, poverty in the community, or problems of privilege in a gentrified community.

Notes

1. Ken Gonzales-Day, *Lynching in the West: 1850–1935* (Durham: Duke University Press, 2006).
2. Leigh Raiford, "Photography and the Practices of Critical Black Memory," *History and Theory, Theme Issue* 48 (December 2009): 127.
3. To experience a family having a courageous conversation about the legacies of slavery in the United States with many implications for public history, see the documentary film *Traces of the Trade: A Story from the Deep North*, http://www.tracesofthetrade.org/.

RESOURCES FOR FURTHER STUDY

Arnold de-Simine, Silke. *Mediating Memory in the Museum: Trauma, Empathy, Nostalgia.* England: Palgrave Macmillan, 2013.

Beer, V. "Great Expectations: Do Museums Know What Visitors Are Doing?" *Curator* 30, no. 3 (1987): 206–215.

Brink, Peter. "Heritage Tourism in the USA: Grassroots Efforts to Combine Preservation and Tourism," *APT Bulletin* 29, no. 3–4 (1998): 59–63.

Carnes, Mark C. *Minds on Fire: How Role-Immersion Games Transform College.* Cambridge: Harvard University Press, 2014.

Diamond, Judy. *Practical Evaluation Guide: Tools for Museums and Other Informal Education Settings.* Walnut Creek, CA: AltaMira Press, 1999.

Handler, Richard and Eric Gable. *The New History in an Old Museum: Creating the Past at Colonial Williamsburg.* Durham, NC: Duke University Press, 1997.

Hayward, J. and R. Loomis. "Looking Back at Front-End Studies." *Visitor Studies: Theory, Research and Practice* 5 (1993): 261–265.

Friedman, Max Paul, and Padraic Kenney, Eds. *Partisan Histories: The Past in Contemporary Global Politics.* New York: Palgrave Macmillan, 2005.

Horwitz, Tony. *Confederates in the Attic: Dispatches from the Unfinished Civil War.* New York: Pantheon Books, 1998.

Kammen, Michael G. *Mystic Chords of Memory: The Transformation of Tradition in American Culture.* New York: Knopf, 1991.

Kelman, Ari. *A Misplaced Massacre: Struggling Over the Memory of Sand Creek.* Cambridge: Harvard University Press, 2013.

Linenthal, Edward and Tom Engelhardt, Eds. *History Wars: The Enola Gay and Other Battles for the American Past.* New York: Holt Paperbacks, 1996.

Loewen, James. *Lies Across America: What Our Historic Sites Get Wrong.* New York: New Press, 1999.

Lowenthal, David. *The Past Is a Foreign Country.* Cambridge: Cambridge University Press, 1985.

National Endowment for the Arts. "2008 Survey of Public Participation in the Arts," Research Report #49, 2009. https://www.arts.gov/sites/default/files/2008-SPPA.pdf.

Meringolo, Denise. *Museums, Monuments, and National Parks: Toward a New Genealogy of Public History.* Amherst: University of Massachusetts Press, 2012.

Peers, Laura. *Interpreting Ourselves: Interpreting Native Histories at Historic Reconstructions.* Lanham, MD: AltaMira Press, 2007.

Rose, Julia. *Interpreting Difficult History at Museums and Historic Sites.* Lanham, MD: Rowman & Littlefield, 2016.

Rothman, Hal. *Devil's Bargains: Tourism in the Twentieth-Century American West.* Lawrence, KS: University Press of Kansas, 1998.

Screven, C. "Formative Evaluation: Conceptions and Misconceptions." *Visitor Studies: Theory, Research and Practice* 1 (1988): 73–82.

Shaffer, Marguerite. *See America First: Tourism and National Identity, 1880–1940.* Washington, DC: Smithsonian, 2001.

Taylor, Samuel, Ed. *Try It! Improving Exhibits through Formative Evaluation.* Washington, DC: Association for Science and Technology Centers, 1991.

Trouillot, Michel-Rolph. *Silencing the Past: Power and the Production of History,* 20th Anniversary Edition, 2nd Revised Edition. Boston: Beacon Press, 2015.

Wallace, Mike. "Visiting the Past." In *Mickey Mouse History and Other Essays on American Memory.* Philadelphia: Temple University Press, 1996.

Williams, Paul. *Memorial Museums: The Global Rush to Commemorate Atrocities.* Oxford, UK: Bloomsbury Academic, 2008.

CHAPTER 7

Engaging Audiences
Case Studies from the Field

A S WE HAVE ARGUED throughout these chapters, public historians must be responsive to their audiences, must interpret an inclusive history, and must constantly reflect on their practice. The three case studies in this chapter illustrate some of the risks and rewards inherent in innovative efforts to engage audiences. Two come from traditional public history sites: Conner Prairie Interactive History Park, a reconstructed set of historic sites, including an 1836 village and an early nineteenth-century American Indian trading camp, located outside of Indianapolis, Indiana; and Manzanar National Historic Site, one of the Japanese American confinement sites from World War II, located in central California. The third case study is of a remembrance of the 100th anniversary of the Battle of the Somme that took place outside of the walls of any cultural institution and brought history to the streets and people throughout the United Kingdom in 2016.

Conner Prairie Interactive History Park

Conner Prairie interprets a homestead in Indiana where emigrants of European stock settled on land near Native peoples. The site is also located in an area where the Underground Railroad operated. Public historians there work with a historic home, relocated historic buildings, a local American Indian community, and a rich trove of possible historical contexts to interpret. They embarked on a series of investigative efforts to determine their visitors' experiences and expectations, and as a result developed several innovative strategies to engage the public. In the process, they did not shy away from engineering difficult encounters.

Conner Prairie began, as many public history sites do, with a house—the William Conner Homestead. Conner, an early white settler, was not a prominent national figure, but he built one of the first brick buildings in Indiana, traded extensively with local Native peoples, and ran a successful farm. The Eli Lilly corporation bought the property in the twentieth century, grew experimental crops on it for pharmaceuticals, opened the house and grounds as a house museum, and then turned the operation over to Earlham College.[1] In 1974, Earlham acquired additional buildings and created Prairietown where first-person interpreters told the story of European pioneers on the Indiana frontier in the year 1836.[2]

The site grew to include an 1886 farm, now interpreted as part of Conner Prairie's exploration of Morgan's Raiders in its Civil War Journey, but it took more than thirty years for the college to interpret the American Indian experience at the site, a somewhat surprising delay considering that Conner's first wife, Mekinges, had been Lenape. (Conner Prairie may not have wanted to highlight the fact that Mekinges had left Conner in 1818, taking their six children with her.[3]) In 1993 Michael Pace, a descendant of Mekinges and a former assistant chief of the Delaware Tribe of Indians, organized a celebration of Native culture at Conner Prairie, which grew into the 1816 Lenape Indian Camp or Lenapehoking, now a permanent installation. John Herbst, a former president of Conner Prairie, acknowledged the importance of the Indian camp in a 2014 newspaper article: "Until we built the trading post, there was a discarding of the Native American part of the story. Everything started with the building of the brick home for Conner's second wife."[4] The interpretation of the Lenape experience forced visitors to acknowledge that the Europeans had settled land that belonged to Native peoples. The museum asked Pace to join the staff in 2001, and he remains there as the only Native first-person interpreter.[5] Like many Native interpreters at historic sites, Pace interprets both the story of the nineteenth-century Lenape and serves as a witness to Native survivance today.

In 2002, the directors of Conner Prairie embarked on a **visitor study**, which is an intentional reflective exercise to study their visitors' experience. They transparently describe the research process on their website: "We recorded guest visits, transcribed the research data, and analyzed those transcriptions for clues to how guests and interpreters interacted." Their investigation led to a change based on visitors' feedback: "It turned out, we were doing all the talking. They were doing all the listening. We operated from scripts that were delivered to anyone—and everyone—who dropped by to listen. It was a one-sided conversation that led to a less-engaged guest, and a less-than-inspiring experience."[6] Their findings led them to develop a new approach to audience engagement, the Opening Doors Initiative, in which they call themselves "ambassadors to the past," "active engagers—not stage actors"—who encourage guests to participate in immersive experiences tailored to their interests.[7]

The current Conner Prairie website encourages free-choice learning by breaking down activities according to the audience: *families, little ones, kids only, teens,* and *adults*; every verb encourages visitor participation: *Design, Create, Invent,* and *Connect.* Instead of retaining the label of outdoor history museum, Conner Prairie defines itself as an "interactive history park." While they emphasize history content, they also promote their science and arts activities and acknowledge the underlying reason most visitors come to the park: their home page states, "There's a place where interactive experiences are intertwined with life-long memories. Where families grow . . . closer together and discover they have acres of common ground. We call it Conner Prairie. Here, science, art and nature are living—and playing—on the edge of history. Millions of great questions. 12 incredible months of the year."[8] The prominence of this statement in their promotional materials demonstrates that the history park did in fact listen to its visitors, reflect on its practices, and come to the conclusion that most people, many of whom came repeatedly throughout the year, visited Conner Prairie to make "lifelong memories" during a fun day with their families.[9] Acquiring history knowledge served as a vehicle for discovering "acres of common ground" with loved ones. Conner Prairie's 1859 Balloon Voyage, Hearthside Suppers, and Prairie Pursuits prove popular because they can bring families together to participate in wholesome activities that take place away from screens.

This aspect of the Opening Doors Initiative emphasizes comfort. The focus on individualized experiences assures visitors that they will be able to find an activity just for them, that their visit will meet their expectations. Conner Prairie pushes guests a bit outside of their comfort zone when they encourage them to ask questions of the first-person interpreters instead of simply receiving historical information as a given. Although they can encounter a variety of first-person interpreters who speak to them as if they, too, live in the early nineteenth century, visitors are rarely outside the range of a Conner Prairie employee, easily identified by a bright-blue shirt, who can answer any questions that fall outside the first-person interpreters' frame of reference.

In an additional step, Conner Prairie invites guests to participate as historical actors, incorporating second-person opportunities into their museum programming. Some of this interpretation is conventional by living history standards. Visitors can select a card at the beginning of the experience that will assign them to roles from 1836, such as merchant or craftsman or even a criminal, and guide them through activities during their visit. On the *1863 Civil War Journey*, young visitors join the muster line, just as they have for generations at Lexington and Concord. Children dress in Union uniforms and help the officers strategize a battle plan. On a more sophisticated level, teenagers and adults can sign up for workshops where they practice blacksmithing and tan deer hides, learning the finer points of "fleshing, wet scraping, staking and smoking."[10] In more challenging recent programs, Conner Prairie also invited visitors to sit on a jury in a trial of Seneca Indians or to spend two working days and nights on a Victorian farm.[11] These activities are definitely targeted to deliver a customized experience, and educational theory has demonstrated that whenever you ask adults or near-adults to learn a new skill, you push them to the point where real learning can occur.

Follow the North Star: Participating in a Difficult Encounter at Conner Prairie

In its most **sustained second-person encounter**, Conner Prairie offers *Follow the North Star*, a program about the Underground Railroad. In this night-time reservation-only activity, the site encourages visitors to confront unsettling material and challenges them to fully immerse themselves in an unpredictable learning experience. Here public historians employ second-person interpretation, inviting visitors to take on the personae of historical figures and engage in historical activities as if they had actually lived in an earlier era. Aimed at teenagers and adults (you must be twelve or older to participate), the program has won critical acclaim in the museum field for the risks it takes, but has also garnered criticism.

An African American staff member, Michelle Evans, developed the program in 1999 in consultation with black leaders in Indianapolis. In this ninety-minute experience, participants come to Conner Prairie in the spring or fall to play the part of fugitive slaves on the Underground Railroad. They begin by watching a short introductory video and listening to a Conner Prairie volunteer explain some of the elements of the experience. The video sets the scene: the year is 1836, and participants will be playing fugitive slaves who had been brought to Indiana by their owner, Joshua Taylor. But because Indiana in law is a free state, Taylor needs to sell his enslaved workforce. At the conclusion of the video, participants receive a few pieces of information about what to expect during the evening. Although the experience will be intense, participants are emphatically told that the actors will never touch or hurt them in any way (and participants are asked to return the favor). They learn that they will meet several people and groups of people and that they are to interact with all of them. Each participant is also given a thin piece of white cloth to tie around his forehead if the experience becomes too intense and he wants to move from a participant to a spectator role.

Ushered out into the night, visitors take a short tram-ride and are dropped off in a wooded area where the slaveholder, Joshua Taylor, awaits. Unknown to participants, there is also among them a Conner Prairie employee disguised as a guest who will help if necessary. The experience begins with what is arguably the most intense scene as Taylor takes his enslaved workers to be sold. The slave traders immediately sort the group into men—who they

Photograph 7.1. *Follow the North Star* program. Courtesy of Conner Prairie.

call "bucks"—and women—"breeders." Lined up by gender, the traders speak individually to each person in the group, seeking to find information about what kind of work they do, their age, and how many children they have. These encounters are designed to degrade as the traders yell at, challenge, and humiliate the participants. One of the clearest lessons from this first encounter is that participants must not look white people in the eye, a violation of the racial codes of the 1830s. Everyone looks down, standing as still as possible, hoping to escape the notice of the aggressive traders. Sometimes a white interpreter will force participants to kneel on the ground. As they move through the landscape, they will be ordered to perform nonsensical manual labor like moving wood from one pile to another, all the while being berated by white interpreters. Some will be instructed to order their fellow runaways to perform tasks. This opening scene ends with the white traders fading away as the enslaved men and women become fugitives. As the evening continues, sympathetic Quakers welcome the runaways into their home and free blacks offer them guidance, but a poor white man from South Carolina tries to capture them.[12] They hear from the experience of a free African American woman and, at the end of the journey, meet a person who has "sight" to enable her to know the fate of each person in the group—some of whom make it to freedom while others do not. Walking away from this final scene, the Conner Prairie employee reveals her identity to the group and leads everyone inside for a facilitated discussion, and juice and cookies, as participants resume their twenty-first-century identities.

The final element of *Follow the North Star* is a **debriefing session** led by a Conner Prairie facilitator. Participants are given space to reflect on what they experienced and how they felt during the program. Facilitators are trained to make a wider historical connection by introducing participants to the vexing problem of modern-day slavery in the

Photograph 7.2. *Follow the North Star* program. Courtesy of Conner Prairie.

United States and around the globe. Missing from the discussion is the more immediate legacy of African slavery in North America.

The power of *Follow the North Star* comes from Conner Prairie's insistence that participants enter a discomfort zone rooted in historical reality. The Underground Railroad is often portrayed as a feel-good example of interracial cooperation and friendship, and guest experiences director Evans could certainly have worked up an Underground Railroad program under that premise, inviting participants to hide under a stairwell until the heroic Quakers came to the rescue. But *Follow the North Star* tells a fuller and more complicated story. Not all white northerners were abolitionists: some whites try to recapture the runaways and send them back to the South, motivated not entirely by racism but definitely by money. Even whites who opposed slavery were not necessarily integrationists: one white couple helps the group but encourages them to return to Africa with the Colonization Society. The inclusion of these ambivalent characters adds a layer of historical complexity that another Underground Railroad program might evade.

Follow the North Star has attracted a great deal of attention in the museum world. Carl R. Weinberg, the editor of the Organization of American Historians' *Magazine of History*, went through the program and wrote about his experience in the spring of 2009, declaring that he and the other visitors became "central actors in a drama, taking on a whole new identity." He felt himself getting angrier and angrier during the encounters, fully pulled into the experience even though he is a professional historian taught to look at historical

Photograph 7.3.   *Follow the North Star* program. Courtesy of Conner Prairie.

content from a critical stance. Afterward, he interviewed a history professor who applauds the program, calling it "edgy," and African American public historians, some who say it goes too far and some who say it does not go far enough.

Scott Magelssen, a professor of theater who studies participatory performance in many non-theater venues, also applauds the program for its pedagogy: "An experience like 'Follow the North Star' can quickly show how difficult it would have been to deviate even the slightest bit from behavioral expectations imposed on enslaved individuals, much less revolt."[13] But at the same time, he sees some tension in the racial dynamics of the program: "The idea of the (nonblack) tourist body performing the historical and, in this case, explicitly 'racial' body is particularly knotty."[14] Others might argue that whites in Indiana in particular could benefit from this difficult encounter. In his book *Sundown Towns*, James Loewen exposes dozens of Indiana communities that required blacks to leave the city limits at night during the mid-twentieth century.[15] In the 1920s, the Ku Klux Klan counted 400,000 members in Indiana, then considered the epicenter of the resurgent Klan, and Klan members controlled the Indiana state legislature.[16] As recently as 1996, six hundred Klan members and supporters rallied in New Castle, Indiana, and in 2014, the Klan distributed recruiting leaflets in Winchester, Indiana, a town that was 96 percent white, according to the 2010 census.[17]

On the night that Magelssen participated in the program, a number of middle-aged white people were giggling and talking back to the interpreters; the museum staff realized that the evening had been ruined for the other guests and allowed them to go through the program again free of charge. The white visitors' behavior reveals the limits of second-person interpretation: guests cannot act in a way runaways would not have acted or take charge of the situation and change the outcome of the journey. The museum staff member in every group makes sure that the group comes to decisions that follow the plan of the overall historical scenario. That precaution might make the program more structured, but no less powerful. Magelssen acknowledges that the giggling group's misbehavior might have provided more evidence of the program's impact; they might have been reacting to their discomfort by exhibiting "less sensitive **self-comforting tactics**," he suggests.[18] Or they may have reacted as Roger Simon predicted when he warned that some visitors experience a "narrowing" of understanding when they face a difficult encounter.[19] They refuse to take in new information or see the past from a new perspective. This type of second-person interpretation of difficult knowledge does not work for everyone, but a number of people who saw Prairietown simply as a homespun history theme park now have a new appreciation of the historical actors who operated in Indiana. Others who have criticized *Follow the North Star* ask whether it is appropriate for such a program to exist at all because of the trauma it may inflict on children of color, a strain of commentary that also accompanied Colonial Williamsburg's 1994 Slave Auction.[20]

Manzanar National Historic Site

Manzanar National Historic Site engages audiences in a variety of innovative ways in the story of the wartime forced removal and incarceration of 120,000 Japanese Americans. Manzanar became a National Historic Site in 1992 when Congress passed enabling legislation recognizing the significance of Manzanar as a place of national importance. Manzanar was the first "relocation center" to be operated by the War Relocation Authority, and became the first confinement site to achieve the status of National Historic Site administered by the National Park Service (NPS). Over the course of more than two decades, efforts to preserve and interpret Manzanar's history and to establish NPS stewardship over the site involved strong public support, particularly from Japanese Americans who were incarcerated at one of the ten War Relocation Authority camps, or one of the other wartime sites of confinement, and their families.

Interpretation and public engagement at Manzanar follows both typical and innovative strategies, some of which predate NPS stewardship over the site. The annual Manzanar **pilgrimage** started formally in 1969 when 150 Japanese Americans, students, activists, and religious leaders organized the first annual pilgrimage to the site. At that time, the site was not formally protected and only the guard shacks at the historical entrance, the recreation hall that now houses the interpretive museum and gift shop, and the cemetery were left standing and obviously visible. The pilgrimage became a focus point for community engagement to educate future generations of Japanese Americans about their history, to demand formal recognition and preservation of this historic site, and to advocate for continued **public memory** of the civil rights abuses that took place during World War II in the hope that something like this will never happen again.

Throughout the rest of the year, visitors can stop on their way from Southern California up the scenic 395 state highway that stretches along the eastern Sierra Nevada mountains to Mammoth Lakes or Reno for a rest and to browse the interpretive center, watch the brief introductory film, and explore the reconstructed barracks and the interpretive mess hall to glimpse what life might have been like for Japanese Americans during the war. A reconstructed basketball court gives visitors a non-text-based, noncognitive way of interacting with history. As visitors pause between the barracks that demonstrate what it was like to arrive at Manzanar in the first weeks of their incarceration, and the barracks containing the furniture made by incarcerees from scrap lumber and furnished over time from mail-order catalogues, along with an interpretation of conflicts that came one and two years into their confinement over the "loyalty questionnaire" and the draft, families can pick up a basketball and shoot some hoops. The reactions visitors have to the basketball court could not be replicated with another interpretive display. Visitors drop their roles as learners, and take on the role of being there, of being transported back in time and taking on the role of one of 10,000 incarcerated Japanese Americans at Manzanar. What must it have been like to be in the camp, as a young person, as a parent, and be faced with the uncertain reality of being locked up without due process, having committed no crime, for the unknown duration of the war? How important must it have been to have diversions like basketball to ease the boredom and take one's mind off one's own uncertain, precarious future?

The reconstructed basketball court is just one way that visitors can move from consumers of history (sometimes literally by purchasing items at the gift shop) to taking on the role of an incarcerated Japanese American, as they consider more deeply what it must have been like and the many difficult decisions individuals had to make as they confronted their own loss of freedom. The court was created as a part of a **public archaeology** program initiated by Jeff Burton, head of cultural resources and archaeology at Manzanar. He directs the

Photograph 7.4.   Reconstructed basketball court, Manzanar National Historic Site. Photo by Cherstin M. Lyon.

project with the assistance of the educational outreach and interpretive specialists at Manzanar, as well as other NPS personnel who manage cultural resources, the historic orchards, and maintenance. Through their efforts, the public can participate in projects designed to uncover, conserve, and restore historic features at Manzanar.

Archaeological projects at Manzanar began as a close partnership with Japanese Americans who have a first-hand knowledge of the site. Oral history interviews, family photos, and information gathered from Japanese American volunteers have helped NPS archaeologists plan projects that include more information than official records may contain. For example, during her 2006 interview about memories of "camp," Madelon Arai Yamamoto mentioned a family pond. No one ever followed up to see if there were any physical traces of it. The Arai family had lived in block 33 of Manzanar, but if the pond still existed, it was hidden under years of plant growth and debris.

In 2010, Jeff Burton reached out to Mrs. Yamamoto to see if she would be interested in helping him locate the pond for a Japanese film crew. With her assistance and using archaeology techniques, they found the buried pond. With the help of NPS staff and volunteers, they uncovered it, cleaned it out, and eventually restored it to working order. In recent years, it has been refilled with water for the annual pilgrimage to show the public the significance of having a space of cool, refreshing beauty in a harsh, dry place like Manzanar. Volunteers, including former incarcerees, family members of those who were sent to Manzanar, university students, and the general public, have been given many opportunities to contribute to projects uncovering rock gardens and ponds, digging out basements, re-creating a basketball court, reconstructing a fire department building to house and protect the historic fire engine, and realigning and painting the military style rock-lined driveways and walkways in the administration block. Excavation and restoration of the Arai pond remains special among these activities because it was found through oral history and a member of the family was able to participate in the dig.

Photograph 7.5. Arai family in front of pond. Photo by Toshi Yoshizaki, c. 1944, courtesy Madelon Reiko Arai Yamamoto.

Other public archaeology projects may be slightly less glamorous. The land upon which Manzanar as a wartime incarceration camp was built was used after the war for cattle grazing, informal camping for locals, and as a storage yard for the county before the site was eventually transferred to the Department of the Interior to be preserved and interpreted by the National Park Service. Much of the site is overgrown with sagebrush, weeds, dirt, and flood debris. The majority of the labor needed at the site is to remove the overgrowth that obscures the historic features. Recently crews have also begun working to restore the rock alignments and uncover features in the administration blocks. The military style of the painted rocks that lined the perimeter of roads through the administration area stands in sharp contrast with the gardens Japanese Americans created to beautify their living areas.

Mary Farrell, retired National Forest archaeologist, coauthor of *Confinement and Ethnicity*, and long-time volunteer at Manzanar, wrote for the *Densho Encyclopedia* entry on archaeology at various sites of confinement:

For those who were incarcerated, the physical traces uncovered and recorded during archaeological projects have sparked memories and stories of daily life inside the camps. For other participants, finding a child's toy or fragment of porcelain forges a poignant connection to

Photograph 7.6. Excavation of the Arai pond. Photo by Jeff Burton, courtesy Manzanar National Historic Site, National Park Service.

Photograph 7.7. Arai pond restored, shown here without water for the purposes of long-term preservation. The pond is refilled with water during the annual pilgrimage for interpretive purposes. Photo by Jeff Burton, courtesy Manzanar National Historic Site, National Park Service.

the people who lived there, while the often harsh weather and dusty conditions force an appreciation for the hardships faced by the incarcerated Japanese Americans.[21]

After volunteering for a project and attending the annual pilgrimage where Japanese Americans, community members, university students, representatives from the Council on American-Islamic Relations (CAIR) from Los Angeles, and local residents of the Owens

Photograph 7.8.   Volunteers paint military-style rocks on the Administration Block, Manzanar National Historic Site, March 31, 2015. Photo by Cherstin M. Lyon.

Photograph 7.9.   Volunteers uncover features at the Administration Block, Manzanar National Historic Site, March 29, 2016. Photo by Cherstin M. Lyon.

Photograph 7.10. "Watashi wa Manzanar" (translation "I am Manzanar") was the theme of the 2015 Manzanar pilgrimage. Photo by Mario Gershom Reyes.

Valley come together to remember the wartime incarceration of Japanese Americans, one volunteer commented that he had certainly not walked a mile in their shoes (referring to those who were confined at Manzanar), but he had at least walked a hundred yards. When he labored in the hot, dry climate, fighting the fierce winds, cold overnight temperatures, and punishing sun to uncover historical features, sleeping out in a local campground, and trying to keep sand out of his food during lunch breaks, he caught a glimpse of what it was like to live in this environment at the same time that he was able to connect with the past by contributing to a meaningful restoration project. The results are the deepest and most meaningful forms of engagement that transform people's understanding and relationship with the past.

Everyone does not have the time or the physical ability to participate in a public archaeology project, but most people can participate in the annual pilgrimage to Manzanar. The annual pilgrimage is still an important part of Manzanar's public programming, and while it is supported by NPS staff, it remains an event organized by the public through the Manzanar Committee, formed in 1970 with the goal of preserving the site and educating the public. The theme of the 2015 pilgrimage was "I am Manzanar"—"Watashi wa Manzanar." The pilgrimage has grown and expanded since 1969 to include a diverse public, all of whom were encouraged to claim that they are Manzanar.

Individuals and groups from many backgrounds, including Japanese Americans who were incarcerated during the war and their families, as well as Muslim Americans, most visibly groups from the Council on American-Islamic Relations of Los Angeles, students from all backgrounds, Owens Valley residents, and visitors from across California, the United States, and internationally, attend the pilgrimage annually to remember the civil rights abuses of the past and to commit to sharing and preserving the memory of this historical period so that this may never happen again.

We're Here Because We're Here: Remembering the Battle of the Somme

On the morning of July 1, 2016, volunteers took the idea of bringing history to the public to an extreme with *We're Here Because We're Here*, an art installation designed to memorialize the 100th anniversary of the beginning of the Battle of the Somme.[22] Throughout the United Kingdom, 1,140 men dressed in World War I uniforms appeared unexpectedly in public spaces. They gathered in train stations, rode public transportation, walked on city streets, and sat down on park benches in groups and alone.

The volunteers did not speak but used hand signals to organize each other: grouping together, spreading out, moving to another location. At certain points, they would sing the WWI song created by soldiers themselves, "We're Here Because We're Here." This song, which was used as the title for the public art installation, was sung by soldiers during the war. It represents the futility of a war in which tens of thousands of soldiers died in single offensives, millions dying overall, to gain victory over small stretches of land. Soldiers wondered why they were there in the trenches and responded with this haunting song. They were there simply because they were there.[23] On the 100th anniversary, volunteers dressed in World War I uniforms, stood in public spaces, and moved about using public transit

Photograph 7.11.   *We're Here Because We're Here*, July 1, 2016, Manchester, England, with permission from 14–18 NOW. Photo by Joel Chester-Fildes.

Photograph 7.12. *We're Here Because We're Here*, July 1, 2016, Newcastle, England, with permission from 14–18 NOW. Photo by Topher McGrillis.

with no other purpose than to be present as a public reminder of those who died on that day in history. When people approached them, they remained silent and offered only a card explaining that they represented one of the 19,240 soldiers who had died 100 years earlier on the first day of the Battle of the Somme. This battle lasted until November 1916 and ultimately claimed more than 1 million lives. In the image above, the same one that is on the cover of this book, you can see a woman reading the card given to her by this volunteer who was representing just one of those who died. The cards gave the WWI soldier's name, his age when he died, his role during the war, and his service unit. The simplicity of this exchange between volunteers who represented the dead and the public who wanted to understand why so many men were dressed in period uniforms not doing anything other than being present on that day was emotionally moving for the public and the volunteers alike.

The Centenary Art Commission, 14-18 NOW, had commissioned this extraordinary work of art as part of a larger effort to connect the public with the First World War. *We're Here Because We're Here* brought the memorial experience directly to the streets. This project was conceived and created by award-winning artist Jeremy Deller in collaboration with Rufus Norris, director of the National Theatre. The men who played the roles of WWI soldiers killed during the first day of battle were not actors but volunteers from many different backgrounds, recruited to participate in the largest **participatory public arts project** ever staged in the United Kingdom. They gathered in theaters across the United Kingdom to rehearse leading up to their performance, supported by hundreds of volunteers and a network of supporting theaters. The men who volunteered ranged in age from sixteen to fifty-two, a realistic depiction of the ages of men who fought for Britain during the war. Each was assigned an identity that corresponded with a man who had died from the region in which they performed. Despite the large numbers of people involved, the project remained top secret until July 1, 2016.[24]

Creator Jeremy Deller, Director Rufus Norris, 14-18 NOW Director Jenny Waldman, and Associate Lead Director Emily Lim gathered for a public discussion of the concept, planning, and implementation of the installation at the National Theatre on July 11, 2016. During the discussion, volunteers who had depicted soldiers reported that they were moved by their experiences. They in turn inspired the public to respond in ways that were unique because they appeared unexpectedly in the places where the public was going about their daily lives. Peter, playing George Edward Morris—a rifleman in the 9th Battalion / London Regiment (Queen Victoria's Rifles) who died on July 1, 1916, at the age of twenty—commented that as a science teacher, he felt that the experience was incredibly accessible for people like himself who were not actors. He was positioned in Waterloo Station and found the experience to be extremely emotional. During the weeks of preparations leading up to their performance, Peter said, "it started off quite light hearted," but "once we started giving cards to members of the public, and demanding a response from them by our presence, it really hit home what we were doing and it was incredibly moving." After participating, the experience led him to find out more about his own grandfather's experience in the war and the Battle of the Somme. Another volunteer said that when he was playing his role outside of Euston Station, he caught the gaze of a woman across the street who had already started to break down into tears. When she

Photograph 7.13. *We're Here Because We're Here*, July 1, 2016, Southampton, England, with permission from 14–18 NOW. Photo by Luke MacGregor.

Photograph 7.14.   *We're Here Because We're Here*, July 1, 2016, London, England, with permission from 14–18 NOW.

approached him, he handed her his card, she nodded, crying a bit more, and walked away. The experience, he said, caught him by surprise because he had not anticipated that level of emotional response from the public, but as he reflected, he said, "being in public and putting a public face to these men who a lot of us knew nothing about" led to many volunteers having similar experiences throughout the day.

The purpose of the performance was, as Jeremy Deller said, to bring the war memorial experience to the people, to create an intervention in the lives of the public that would give them pause. But he said he was not expecting the response they received. They had prepared for the instances where a child might run up and try to take a hat, or other mischief, but the reverence with which they were approached and the respect given the volunteers surprised them. "It was amazing," Deller said, and he placed it in context. The anniversary of the beginning of the Battle of the Somme came two weeks after the United Kingdom voted by a very narrow margin to leave the European Union, and the fallout had created what Deller called two of the worst weeks in public life in the United Kingdom as people made it clear that they "would sacrifice their country for themselves." Then the public was confronted with "men who were willing to sacrifice their lives for their country." He said, before the event he had written, "I wanted to make children cry . . . but we seemed to make a lot of adults cry."[25]

Reflection on These Case Studies

All three case studies presented here have a similar goal—engaging the public directly in important historical topics in less traditional ways. No single approach is right for all historical topics or for every situation. *Follow the North Star* has raised ethical questions about whether it is appropriate for all audiences. Not every member of the public is in a position to work on a public archaeology project, and not every site is prepared to host such an event. Participatory public arts projects such as *We're Here Because We're Here* are fleeting one-day events that may or may not have lasting effects on public awareness or attract new audiences to public history sites in a way that is sustained. As public historians battle the increasing sophistication of their audiences in terms of their over-familiarity with new technologies rendering unimpressive what may have had a high impact just a few years ago, and the public's continued reluctance to read complicated text, innovative engagement strategies will certainly continue to push the boundaries of what the public expects when it comes to historical interpretation.

Notes

1. Aili McGill, "Defining Museum Theater at Conner Prairie," in Scott Magelssen and Rhona Justice-Malloy, eds. *Enacting History* (Tuscaloosa: University of Alabama Press, 2011), 89.
2. Gaea Leinhardt, and Karen Knutson, eds. *Listening in on Museum Conversations* (New York: AltaMira, 2004), 43–44.
3. Alysa Landry, "Getting It Right: Lenape Man Changing Indiana's Views on Native History," Indian Country Today Media Network, August 8, 2014, http://indiancountrytoday medianetwork.com/2014/08/08/getting-it-right-lenape-man-changing-indianas-views -native-history-156296.
4. Landry.
5. Landry.
6. Conner Prairie, "Our Mission at Work," http://www.connerprairie.org/About-Conner-Prai rie/Driven-by-Our-Mission/Our-Mission-at-Work. These surveys were conducted when the site was operated by Earlham College.
7. Conner Prairie, "Opening Doors to Provide Families with Acres and Acres of Common Ground," http://www.connerprairie.org/About-Conner-Prairie/Driven-by-Our-Mission/ Our-Mission-at-Work#Opening-Doors.
8. Conner Prairie, "Acres and Acres of Interactive Awesomeness," http://www.connerprairie.org.
9. Leinhardt and Knutson, 43.
10. For more information about suggested activities at Conner Prairie, see their "Fun Guide" flipbook online at: http://www.connerprairie.org/flipbook/fun-guide/files/assets/basic-html/ page-1.html.
11. Scott Magelssen, "'This Is a Drama. You Are Characters': The Tourist as Fugitive Slave in Conner Prairie's 'Follow the North Star,'" *Theatre Topics* 16, no. 1 (March 2006): 19–34.
12. See the description of the experience in Carl R. Weinberg, "The Discomfort Zone: Reenacting Slavery at Conner Prairie," *OAH Magazine of History* 23, no 2 (April 2009): 62–64.
13. Magelssen, "This Is a Drama," 26.

14. Magelssen, "This Is a Drama," 20.
15. James W. Loewen, *Sundown Towns: A Hidden Dimension of American Racism* (New York: The New Press, 2005).
16. Richard K. Tucker, *The Dragon and the Cross: The Rise and Fall of the Ku Klux Klan in Middle America* (Hamden, CT: Archon Books, 1991).
17. Seth Slabaugh, "Klan Leaflets Left Around Indiana City," October 10, 2014, *The Star Press* http://www.indystar.com/story/news/2014/10/10/ku-klux-klan-winchester-indiana-recruit ing/17028771/.
18. Magelssen, "This Is a Drama," 28.
19. Roger Simon, "A Shock to Thought: Curatorial Judgment and the Public Exhibition of 'Difficult Knowledge,'" *Memory Studies* 4, no. 4 (October 2011): 434.
20. Olivia Lewis, "Conner Prairie Slavery Re-Enactment Draws Criticism," *Indianapolis Star*, August 7, 2016. Embedded in this article is a three-minute clip that features some of the more difficult moments experienced by audiences during *Follow the North Star*, http://www.indystar.com/story/news/2016/08/06/conner-prairie-slavery-re-enactment-draws-crit icism/82987036/.
21. Mary Farrell, "Archaeology," *Densho Encyclopedia*, http://encyclopedia.densho.org/Archae ology%20of%20the%20Japanese%20American%20incarceration/.
22. The installation's title, *We're Here Because We're Here*, is taken from one of the most popular WWI era songs. See Steven Brocklehurst, "Far Far from Ypres: Soldiers' Songs Shine Light on WW1 Attitudes," *BBC Scotland News*, January 17, 2014, http://www.bbc.com/news/uk-scotland-25653122.
23. Brocklehurst, "Far Far from Ypres," *BBC Scotland News*, January 17, 2014, http://www.bbc .com/news/uk-scotland-25653122.
24. "Soldiers," 14-18 NOW: WWI Centenary Art Commissions, https://becausewearehere .co.uk/we-are-here-soldiers/. See also, "Lives of the First World War," https://livesofthefirst worldwar.org.
25. "Meet the Creators Behind 'We're Here Because We're Here,'" Jeremy Deller, Rufus Norris, Jenny Waldman, and Emily Lim, National Theater on July 11, 2016, Available at: https://youtu.be/yJEy5Y3JFCU.

RESOURCES AND SUGGESTED ACTIVITIES

What are the innovative engagement strategies in your own area? How do they compare with the case studies provided here? What strategies feel overly intrusive? Which make you want to learn more? Become a participant in an activity in your area and reflect on your experience using the participant observer strategy for gathering information firsthand.

Participant Observer

Participate in a public history event or visit a site or museum that uses any type of engagement strategy. Participate in the activity and take notes of your experience. The idea behind participant observation is that what people say and what people do are often at odds. In public history terms, the intentions of an engagement strategy may not match the experiences of participants. Using all that you know about the theories of public history, strategies for engaging audiences, and your own personal preferences and noncognitive reactions, become a participant in any type of public history event/exhibition/experience and take notes about that experience. You should take notes on three different levels.

1. What happened? What was the experience/event like, where was it located, what was the topic/purpose, and, based on your observations, what was the intended outcome? What were the interpretive and engagement strategies? First, third, or second person? Did the approach favor a banking model or problem-posing model of education? Or was the event meant to be educational, celebratory, or merely entertaining?
2. What was your experience? Did you enjoy it or find it interesting, boring, off-putting, exciting, engaging? Did you feel comfortable, nervous, intrigued? Would you recommend it to your friends and family? Is there anyone you would not recommend it to and why?
3. What principles of public history did you see or not see in this experience? Did you see the incorporation of diverse points of view? Were you able to see history through their eyes or understand the complex questions of historic interpretation such as change over time or the relevance of history to your own life? Was there any evidence of community involvement, shared authority, or civic engagement? Were there silences in the narrative or blind spots erasing parts of the story? What did you see that worked well from a public history theoretical or practical perspective? What recommendations would you make based on your own experience and what you have learned about public history so far that might make the experience for the public more satisfying?

RESOURCES FOR FURTHER STUDY

Budreau, Lisa M. *Bodies of War: World War I and the Politics of Commemoration in America, 1919-1933*. New York: New York University Press, 2010.

Burton, Jeffery, and Mary Farrell. *A Place of Beauty and Serenity: Excavation and Restoration of the Arai Family Fish Pond, Manzanar National Historic Site*. National Park Service, US Department of the Interior, 2014.

du Lac, J. Freedom. "Slavery Is a Tough Role, Hard Sell at Colonial Williamsburg." *The Washington Post*, March 8, 2013. http://www.washingtonpost.com/local/slavery-is-a-tough-role-hard-sell -at-colonial-williamsburg/2013/03/08/d78fa88a-8664-11e2-a80b-3edc779b676f_story.html.

Dubrow, Gail Lee. "Claiming Public Space for Women's History in Boston: A Proposal for Preservation, Public Art, and Public Historical Interpretation." *Frontiers: A Journal of Women Studies* 13, no. 1 (1992): 111–48. doi:10.2307/3346948.

"Guidelines for Teaching About the Holocaust." The United States Holocaust Memorial Museum, n.d. http://www.ushmm.org/educators/teaching-about-the-holocaust/general-teach ing-guidelines.

Hughes, Catherine. *Museum Theatre: Communicating with Visitors through Drama*. Portsmouth, NH: Heinemann Drama, 1998.

Hurley, Andrew, ed. "Taking It to the Streets: Public History in the City." In *Beyond Preservation: Using Public History to Revitalize Inner Cities*, 32–54. Philadelphia: Temple University Press, 2010.

Magelssen, Scott. *Enacting History*. Tuscaloosa: University of Alabama Press, 2011.

———. *Simming: Participatory Performance and the Making of Meaning*. Ann Arbor: University of Michigan, 2014.

Merriman, Nick. *Public Archaeology*. London: Routledge, 2004.

Miron, Rose. "Sacrificing Comfort for Complexity: Presenting Difficult Narratives in Public History." *Public History Commons*, April 24, 2014.

Okamura, Katsuyuki, and Akira Matsuda. *New Perspectives in Global Public Archaeology*. New York: Springer, 2011.

Peers, Laura. *Playing Ourselves: Interpreting Native Histories at Historic Reconstructions*. Lanham, MD: AltaMira Press, 2007.

Purcell, Sarah J. "Commemoration, Public Art, and the Changing Meaning of the Bunker Hill Monument." *The Public Historian* 25, no. 2 (2003): 55–71.

Simon, Nina and Jon Moscone, *The Art of Relevance*. Museum 2.0, 2016. Available at: http://www .artofrelevance.org.

Simon, Roger I. "A Shock to Thought: Curatorial Judgment and the Public Exhibition of 'Difficult Knowledge.'" *Memory Studies* 4, no. 4 (2011): 432–449.

Thorpe, Angela. "Rethinking Diversity: Who Does History Belong To?" *Public History Commons*, January 8, 2015.

CHAPTER 8

Putting Public History to Work in Your World

Would you show up if your town was having a hearing about whether to remove Confederate monuments from the community's public spaces? Would you respond to a call from a local museum to evaluate an exhibit under development? Would you contribute financially to the preservation of a local historic site? Would you volunteer to provide tours at a historic house museum?

WHEN WE FIRST CONCEIVED this book, we thought about the students who have taken our public history courses at California State University, San Bernardino; the University of Baltimore; the University of Wisconsin at Whitewater; and Indiana University-Purdue University at Indianapolis. Those students come from diverse backgrounds and go on to pursue careers in an equally diverse number of professions. A few of them do graduate work in public history and secure careers in the field. But the vast majority of our students do not. We came to this project because of our strong belief, honed in countless conversations over the years with our students, that public history should matter to all of us. History is a constructed interpretation about the past that we use as individuals, communities, and nations to understand the world. Public history is the lens through which millions of people come to know those histories. The buildings that are preserved, the objects that make their way into museum collections, the documents that are archived—all of these are crucial raw materials that enable us to tell stories in public history venues that include all of us and point the way to a more just and democratic future. We want to instill in our students the belief that these activities matter and that they should engage actively in their own communities.

For some of you, a study of public history may develop into a career. We recommend that you begin to think about your options by using the National Council on Public History's *The Public History Navigator: How to Choose and Thrive in a Graduate Public History Program*, a rich resource for exploring next steps.[1] Whether you are interested in pursuing a career in public history or not, we also encourage you to consider a public history internship. There are most likely local historical societies, historic house museums, and historic sites that would be eager to develop an internship with you. There are also several internships at nationally known public history sites that draw college-aged interns from all across the country.[2] Others of you will go on to teach history or social studies in a K–12 educational setting or pursue doctoral degrees in history on the path toward becoming a professor of history at a college or university. We encourage you to use the insights gained from this book to think about how you might provide opportunities for your students to visit public history sites on field trips and ways you can teach your students to become historians in and out of the classroom. Most of you will pursue careers outside of historical work. Yet the lessons of this book—the ways that people use the past to make sense of the present, how historians work like detectives to uncover evidence and to make an argument—should be applicable in a wide range of careers. We hope that all of you will take from this experience a deeper appreciation of the field of public history and a commitment to preserving and sharing the past.

Becoming a Public Historian

Developing a career is rarely a straight path that involves only coursework and degrees. Most working professionals will tell you that they got to where they are in life through hard work, being in the right place at the right time, learning how to adapt one set of skills to a new challenge, and taking advantage of extra opportunities to gain experience—often without pay or course credit. Below we have invited a few students to share with you their journeys from classroom to employment as public historians.[3] Their experiences were all different, but each took advantage of opportunities to professionalize early and gained hands-on experience while still in school. Read together, these three students give valuable tips about how they made the transition from learning about public history to finding internships and additional professional training, which for two included graduate degrees, to finding jobs. We would encourage you to interview people who are employed in what you might consider to be your dream job and ask questions not only about which degrees they earned, but about the other things that led them to where they are today.

Michelle Garcia-Ortiz, El Pueblo Historical Monument

My name is Michelle D. Garcia-Ortiz, and I am a certified administrative service worker II for the City of Los Angeles at El Pueblo Historical Monument in the History and Special Events Division. I oversee four museums, help manage social media marketing, design and run our educational public outreach programming, coordinate with our partners and friends groups to organize and host special events, supervise our volunteers and interns, curate exhibits, and perform accounting and administrative work for our gift shop and my departments.

My career really started at school because without the guidance, wisdom, and support of my professors and fellow classmates, I would not be where I am today. I was an above average student who loved history and had no plan beyond that. The only thing I knew was that I didn't want to be a teacher, but that I wanted to educate outside the classroom. I had some in-depth talks with my professors, and they started pushing me toward internships. I also switched my major to public and oral history and graduated with a BA degree in public

Photograph 8.1. Michelle Garcia-Ortiz posing with "Smokey the Bear" at an event at the El Pueblo Historical Monument in Los Angeles, California.

and oral history in 2012. Internships helped me figure out what type of public history suited me best. Some were things I thought were my dream jobs, but then ended up being tedious and boring. Others, I liked, and then finally, I found one that I loved. That internship was with the Getty Multicultural Foundation, and it changed my life. That internship is the reason I have my job today.

The Getty Multicultural Internship is a paid summer internship where they give grant money to arts organizations in Los Angeles County so that they can hire interns. I was hired as a public outreach intern. When the internship first started, I was given a lot of administrative tasks and not a lot of projects, which was disheartening because I saw interns from other departments with heavy workloads and major projects, but I worked hard and kept my eyes and ears open and soon enough an opportunity presented itself. My supervisor mentioned in passing that he wanted a website designed for a new museum that was opening, and I volunteered. Now let me be clear that I had no idea how to design a website. I had not done it before or since, and I was honest and upfront about it, but I was able to sell my supervisor on the idea because of the skills I did possess. I told him I was a historian, which meant I was a great writer and researcher. He gave me the project, and that website stayed up for the next two years.

My supervisor liked my initiative so much that he mentioned that he was debating whether or not the museum should offer a curriculum guide for students and teachers. He asked if I had any ideas or suggestions. That is how I ended up writing a book. When the internship was over my supervisor loved my hard work and professionalism so much that he wanted to hire me to work in the history and public outreach department full time, but he could not due to financial and bureaucratic reasons. He and another supervisor strongly recommended that I apply to work in the museums located on site. I applied and was hired one month later.

Working in the museums instead of getting the job I wanted was not a setback—it was a steppingstone to get where I wanted to be. I worked hard as a museum guide, and I didn't just do my job, I strived to be exemplary at it. I received a lot of visitor compliments not only from the public, but from city employees who would stop by, and my bosses began to take notice. Sometime later there were some shifts in management, and I decided to approach them and let them know that I had some great ideas to improve visitor numbers and to generate more public outreach programming. I offered to work projects on a volunteer basis, and gradually, the management team gave me more responsibility. One day my boss asked me what my degree was and what my long-term goals were. When I told her, she was astonished. I realized I had made a huge mistake and wasted a lot of time because I had not advertised that I had major skills as a public historian that made me a great resource for this organization. From that point on, she started giving me public history projects, until a year later, when my dream job opened up and was offered to me. Now I manage the museums at which I used to work as a docent.

The public history field is extremely competitive in Southern California, especially if you do not have a graduate degree. After an education, the most important thing you can have is a great network. Even after you get a job, you have to continue to diversify and cultivate your network. People in your network hire you, they partner with you on special projects, they volunteer or advertise your events, and they are sounding boards for ideas. I always say don't be bitter when you think people are hiring their friends or people they know, simply make them a part of your network and become someone they know and want to hire.

Start attending events in the community and learn to market yourself. Do not be intimidated by the fact that you are just starting out; you have random skills that could be of great use to an organization. Perhaps you have a knack for hanging paintings. Maybe you really understand Adobe software and can design newsletters and posters. Perhaps you used to be a film major, so you can edit oral history videos; or perhaps you used to be a waitress, and you know the best way to dress tables for special events.

Last, be patient and be flexible. Really think about what your long-term goals are and what you are willing to do to achieve them. Sometimes that can mean relocation. Other times it can mean working at a job that is still in the field, but not quite where you want to be. The point is no one is going to hand you the job of your dreams just because you have a diploma. You have to work for it, you have to compete for it, you need to network, and you have to continue to learn and develop your own unique set of skills. The opportunities are there if you are willing to dedicate yourself to your goals.

Renee Slider, Cultural Resource Specialist, Wyoming Territorial Prison State Historic Site

When I transferred from Chaffey Community College and began my academic career as a historian in training at California State University, San Bernardino (CSUSB), I chose

Photograph 8.2.   Renee Slider at the Wyoming Territorial Prison State Historic Site in Laramie, Wyoming.

public and oral history as my focus. The first class I took that spring was a class on archives. This class solidified my love for everything museums and archives. The summer after my first quarter at CSUSB, I was given the opportunity to intern and help accession a collection through Pechanga Cultural Resources. Never one to say no, I accepted and thus began my two-year internship with Pechanga, where I branched out with outstanding experiences in the museum world. I curated an exhibit at the Temecula Historical Society, served as an education specialist for the Pechanga Mobile Museum, and also played a role in the design of the CSUSB Robert A. Fullerton Museum of Art (RAFMA) – Pechanga exhibit, *Temeeku*. I also assisted on several key projects that are now becoming a part of the Pechanga Cultural Resources Documentary Series.

My original intention was to just get a BA degree, start my career, and be done with school, but my professors encouraged me to consider graduate school. I applied for the

McNair Scholar program and was accepted. The McNair Scholar program helped me with the application process for graduate school and provided me with an opportunity to do a research project over the summer. I combined my research with my internship at Pechanga, where I researched the Luiseño waterways. Through the McNair program, I attended two conferences where I presented my research and established contacts with different history graduate programs. After applying to ten graduate programs and getting accepted to six, I ultimately chose the University of Wyoming (UWYO). I moved to Laramie, Wyoming, in the fall of 2012 and spent the next two years in the land of cowboys and snowstorms.

As a student at UWYO, I became a graduate intern at the American Heritage Center and became employed as a seasonal tour guide at the Wyoming Territorial Prison State Historic Site. It was through these two opportunities and the experience I developed through my undergraduate internships and research that I was hired as the full-time, permanent cultural resource specialist at the Wyoming Territorial Prison State Historic Site. As the cultural resource specialist, my job encompasses education, volunteer programing, archives/ collections, and the internship program. I really do encourage all history students, not just those interested in public history, to explore an internship in the fields that interest you. It was through my internships, in combination with my coursework both as an undergraduate student and graduate student, that I gained both the experience and knowledge that I needed to move forward. I can testify that there is not a day that goes by where I do not use a skill or tool that I learned in the classroom or through my internships.

Hope Glenn, Independent Transcriptionist

In 2009, I enrolled at CSUSB and chose public and oral history as the focus for my BA in History. I took many history classes but also several classes focused on archives, museums, and other aspects of public history. These classes gave me hands-on experience and provided a forum for learning and discussing the many different practices, opportunities, approaches, and even debates involved in public history work. The faculty of the history department was always ready to give advice for class and career planning, as well as opportunities to learn outside of the classroom, including internships.

The two internships I completed during my CSUSB schooling greatly increased the amount of hands-on practice I had and exposed me to a wide variety of public history work. My career goals focus on archives, and I learned a lot by interning at the A. K. Smiley Public Library in Redlands, where there is an amazing museum and archives—the Lincoln Memorial Shrine and the Heritage Room. My experiences there were unforgettable. I learned and practiced archival skills such as arrangement and description, transcription, paging, cataloging, research, and article writing. I also got to work with many wonderful artifacts and documents. I'm not at all embarrassed to admit that I nearly cried when they handed me a box of over fifty letters from one American Civil War soldier on my first day. That soldier's name was William H. Fairfield, and I had the privilege of getting to know him through these letters, which he sent home to his wife during the war. It was an emotional, insightful, and incredibly rewarding experience.

My second internship was at CSUSB's John M. Pfau Library, in the special collections room. Under the direction of the special collections librarian, I gained experience in a

Photograph 8.3.   Hope Glenn, Student Archivist, Oregon State University's Special Collections Library.

variety of tasks, such as exhibit design, inventory, audio and video transcription, research, and writing, and much more. I also worked on the Latino Baseball History Project, which I had also worked on in the oral history class at CSUSB. This internship gave me experience in an academic special collections setting, which came in handy when I later applied for a similar position at Oregon State University's Special Collections Library.

The combination of my classes and internships gave me knowledge and experience that I continue to use today. Before my husband and I moved to Oregon, we visited the archives at Oregon State University (OSU), and I immediately said, "I want to work there." A year later, after finishing my schooling at CSUSB, I brought my resume back to OSU and was hired as a student archivist at Special Collections and Resource Archives (SCARC). I have been working there for almost two years now, and I have been given many tasks that mirror what I learned and experienced during my time at CSUSB. When someone asks me to arrange and describe a collection, edit metadata, transcribe an oral history interview, or do research for a patron or a project, as well as many other tasks I've been given, it feels great to say, "Yes, I can do that. I've done it before." Having my degree and internships on my resume also made getting the position easy. SCARC is an amazing place with more than enough documents, rare books, and artifacts to fulfill any history nerd. I feel grateful to work there every day. Working in archives where history can be seen and touched is extremely rewarding to me, and my courses in combination with my internship experiences made this possible.

Postscript to Hope's story: Hope worked on her MLIS degree through San Jose State while working as a student archivist. She graduated with her degree in 2015 and is now working for herself as a transcriptionist. She plans to return to archive work, but for now is enjoying the freedom of her own transcription business.

Engaging with History in Your Communities

There are many ways to get involved with history outside of the classroom in your own community. Most public history relies heavily on the civic engagement of the public and volunteers. Historical societies are always looking for volunteers. The Wayne County Historical Society of Ohio, for example, lists the following as examples of the types of work that their volunteers do (emphasis added):

> Our *Tour Guides* (docents) go through a complete training process with periodic updates and special interest workshops. Members of the various *Acquisitions Committees* work with artifacts, displays and research. *Building and Grounds* volunteers help clean permanent exhibits, work on the grounds to repair and maintain historical society buildings and sometimes assist in the dismantling of buildings on other sites for rebuilding on our campus. Volunteers are also needed for *Special Events*, acting as hosts, manning the information booth or assisting with children's activities. Or, for those with an organizational bent, there's the *Board of Trustees* and an opportunity to help direct the future direction of the Wayne County Historical Society.[4]

Visit the website of any historical society, and you will likely find a call for volunteers to get involved and to be a part of local history in your community.

Photograph 8.4. Elizabeth M. Nix speaks at the Maryland Confederate Soldiers and Sailors Monument as part of the special commission appointed by the mayor which voted in 2016 to employ contextual signage and art. Photo by Audrey Hayes.

Local government often is involved with history through various commissions related to history and historic preservation. Sometimes all you need is to be a resident of the city and have an interest and some training in history to volunteer to become a part of one of these commissions or committees. Even if becoming a member of a local committee or commission would require too much of a time commitment, or if opportunities to become involved formally are not readily available, watch for events hosted by the city or take a tour of your own city's neighborhoods sponsored by a historic neighborhood association or preservation group. Attend a community event celebrating a cultural tradition or holiday. And watch for public announcements of city planning meetings regarding historic designations or plans to demolish a historic structure. Your informed participation makes a difference.

Notes

1. *The Public History Navigator: How to Choose and Thrive in a Graduate Public History Program* is available at: http://ncph.org/wp-content/uploads/The-Public-History-Navigator-2015-Web.pdf.
2. A few of these internship programs are at Mount Vernon, http://www.mountvernon.org/the-estate-gardens/historic-trades/internships/; Plimoth Plantation, https://www.plimoth.org/learn/internships; and the Smithsonian's National Museum of American History, http://americanhistory.si.edu/getinvolved/internship.
3. These essays were originally written by the students for publication in the CSUSB Department of History Newsletters. Professor Thomas E. Long, current coordinator for public and oral history, and Cherstin M. Lyon, contributing faculty to the program, wanted to give alumni the opportunity to give their advice to students just getting started in their academic careers. Each essay is reprinted here with permission from each of the three authors.
4. Wayne County Historical Society, http://waynehistoricalohio.org/get-involved/volunteer/.

RESOURCES AND SUGGESTED ACTIVITIES

Getty Multicultural Internships

The Getty Foundation created the Multicultural Undergraduate Internship program in 1993 to provide substantive, full-time work opportunities for undergraduate students from groups underrepresented in careers related to museums and visual arts with the aim of encouraging greater diversity in these professions. The program provides funding for internships at cultural organizations across Los Angeles, including at the Getty Center and the Getty Villa. The foundation's support enables organizations to host students in full-time, paid internships for ten weeks during the summer. To be eligible, students must be from one of the target groups, must be a current student, live in Los Angeles County, and be a US citizen. For more information, visit: http://www.getty.edu/foundation/initiatives/current/mui/. Check in your local area to see what kind of internships may be available to you.

McNair Scholars Program

The McNair Scholars Program is a federal program offered at more than one hundred and fifty institutions throughout the United States. It is funded through the Department of Education and is designed to prepare undergraduate students for doctoral study. They support student research and other scholarly activities, waive application fees for graduate school, and offer other types of financial support. To be eligible, students must be either first-generation college students with a demonstrated financial need or be members of a group that is traditionally underrepresented in graduate programs. All students must have strong academic potential. The goal of the McNair Scholars Program is to increase graduate degrees among students from underrepresented populations. For more information, visit: http://mcnairscholars.com

Career Path Interview

Find an individual working in a job that you might consider to be your "dream" job, or after learning more about public history, interview a person who works in a field that you knew nothing about before you started exploring public history. What is their job, what are their "official" responsibilities, and what do they do that is not in their job description? What formal training was required to get the job? What degree(s) did they complete, where, and when? What other preparations did they pursue along the way, both while they were in school and after, to develop their professional skills and to create opportunities for advancement? What about their career trajectory did they expect, and what did they not expect? What surprises or twists and turns did they experience and why? What do they love about their work? What would they change if they could? What do they want to do next or what are their goals moving forward personally or professionally? What advice do they have for anyone who might like to pursue a career doing what they do?

Jobs, Internships, Fellowships, and Volunteer Research

There are many websites that help connect those who are looking for work and some that also post opportunities for internships, fellowships, and other professional opportunities. Use several to investigate a path that you might like to take moving forward. What types of jobs are being advertised now? What qualifications, what kind of experience do they require?

Professional Meetings

Attend a professional meeting that relates to your desired field of study and your desired career path. This may be as simple as attending a meeting held regionally, or it could involve applying for travel money from your department, university, or student association to attend a national conference. The National Council on Public History annual meetings are very friendly to students and always host first-time attendees' receptions; there is usually a speed-networking session for soon-to-graduate students and young professionals, and typically you can sign up to be paired with a professional mentor for the conference. Similarly, the American Association for State and Local History (AASLH) annual meeting welcomes graduate students and provides opportunities to hear from and meet with many potential employers in the field. Think about proposing a poster about one of your projects for a professional meeting once you are further along in your program. Phi Alpha Theta, the national history honors society, hosts biennial conferences nationally, but smaller regional conferences are also available that are geared specifically toward students as presenters. Practice presenting your research in a professional setting or just attend to see what a professional conference is like. Look for other regional professional organizations that bring teachers, preservationists, archivists, librarians, historic preservationists, or museum professionals together. Ask a professor for suggestions and browse the internet for ideas.

RESOURCES FOR FURTHER STUDY

AASLH Jobs and Career Resources: http://about.aaslh.org/jobs/.

"About the Field," *National Council on Public History*, http://ncph.org/what-is-public-history/about-the-field/.

"Careers in Public History," *American Historical Association*, https://www.historians.org/jobs-and-professional-development/career-resources/careers-in-public-history.

Doyle, Debbie Ann. "Practical Advice on Getting a Public History Job," *Perspectives on History*, April 2006, https://www.historians.org/publications-and-directories/perspectives-on-history/april-2006/practical-advice-on-getting-a-public-history-job.

H-Net Job Guide, *Humanities and Social Sciences Online*, https://www.h-net.org/jobs/home.php.

Iacovetta, Franca and Molly Ladd-Taylor, Eds. *Becoming a Historian*. Canadian Historical Association, Canadian Committee on Women's History, AHA Committee on Women Historians, and American Historical Association, http://www.chashcacommittees-comitesa.ca/becoming%20a%20historian/pdfs/becomingahistorian.pdf.

Koenigsknecht, Theresa, Michelle Antenesse, Kristen Baldwin Deathridge, Jamie Gray, Jenny Kalvaitis, and Angela Sirna. *The Public History Navigator: How to Choose and Thrive in a Public History Graduate Program*. National Council on Public History, 2015, http://ncph.org/wp-content/uploads/The-Public-History-Navigator-2015-Web.pdf.

PreserveNet: http://preservenet.cornell.edu/employ/ncpe.php.

"Resources for Students," *National Council on Public History*, http://ncph.org/publications-resources/students/.

Student Conservation Association: https://www.thesca.org/serve.

USAJOBS, https://www.usajobs.gov.

Index

engagement, 120; engaging, 36, 113–118, 121–125, 127–131, 142, 147; shared authority, 10–11, 35–36
audio guide, 97–98, 114
Auschwitz, 129
authenticity, 76, 92, 113, 119, 123

Bachelet, Michelle, 84
Balderrama, Francisco, 72–73
Ballard, Martha, 31, 63
Baltimore '68 Project, 13, 33–37, 47–48, 73
Baltimore City College High School, 38
Baltimore, Maryland, 13, 28, 33–48
Baltimore School for the Arts, 38
Baltimore Sun, 44, 94
banking model of education, 1, 7, 160
Bartlett, Sarah, 96
Bascom, Marion, 44
Battle of Brooklyn, 130
Baylin, Lee, 44
Baylor University, 61
Beauty Behind Barbed Wire: The Arts of the Japanese in Our Relocation Camps, 70
Becker, Carl, 59
Belmont Report, 33, 40
Belote, Theodore, 64
beneficence, 33, 40–41
Bernard, Erin, 121
best practices, ix, 11, 36, 41–42, 109, 122, 130
Bethune-Cookman College, 65
Bethune, Mary McLeod, 65
big idea, 83, 90–93, 95–98
Birt, Robert, 47
Black Cinema House, 135
Blue Mountains, 123
Boston College, 40
Bradley, David, 134
Branham, Caroline, 116
British Museum, 61
Brown, Michael, 46
built environment, 57, 59, 76
Bunch, Lonnie, 100
Burton, Jeff, 148–149, *151*

Caballero, Cesar, 72–73
cabinets of curiosity, 57, 60
CAIR, *see* Council on American-Islamic Relations
California Council for the Promotion of History, 16
California State University, San Bernardino, California (CSUSB), 72–74, 168–170, 172
Cape Town, South Africa, 100
case label, 95–96
cause and effect, 21, 23–24, 33, 92–93, 95
CBPR, *see* community-based participatory research
Centenary Art Commission, 14–18 NOW, 154–158
Center for Digital + Public History, Cleveland State University, 102
Central Park, New York City, 18
Chaffey Community College, 166
Chamber of Art and Curiosities, Austria, 61
change and continuity, 21, 23, 33, 92, 95
Chester-Fildes, Joel, *154*
The Chicago Manual of Style, 110
Chile, 84–89
Chinese Americans, 8, 136
The Chinese Laundryman: A Study in Social Isolation, 8
Chushingura, 130
civic engagement, 11, 106, 113, 120–121, 130, 160, 170
Civil War, 22, 63–65, 110, 131, 135, 142–143, 168
Cleveland Historical, 102
Cleveland State University, 102
Cohen, Art, 44
Coleman, Christy S., 127
collaboration, 2–3, 10–13, 35, 38
collections, 17, 31, 57, 60–64, 71, 99, 102, 163, 168–170
collections management plan, 79–80
Colonial Williamsburg, 115, 117, 123–126; Slave Auction (1994), 147
Columbia, 98
community-based collecting, 72–74, 76–78

Frances Willard House, 98
free-choice learning, 1, 9, 125, 142
Freedom of Information Act (FOIA), 57, 62
Freire, Paulo, 7–9
Frisch, Michael, 10, 35
front-end evaluation, 83, 106
funder list, 83, 96
funerary objects, 69

Gaines, Barbara, 45
Gans, Herbert, 60
Gans-Huxtable debate, 57, 60
Garcia, Angie, *74*
Garcia-Ortiz, Michelle, 164–166
Garner, Eric, 46
Gates, Theaster, 135
La geometria de la conciencia (*The Geometry of Conscience*), 87
George C. and Hazel H. Reeder Heritage Foundation, *58*
Getty Center, Getty Villa, 173
Getty Multicultural Internship, 165, 173
Giordano, J.M., 47
Glenn, Hope, 168–170
Gonzales-Day, Ken, 136
Gormley, Antony, 135
Gray, Freddie, 34, 37, 46
Greenfield Village, 98
group label, 83, 95–96
Grundtvig, Nikolaj Frederik Severin, 9; folk school, 9
Guantanamo Bay, 110–111
Guantanamo Bay Memory Project, 110
The Guardian, 130

Hall, Radclyffe, 66
Hamilton, 131
Hamilton, Ann, 135
Hanebrink, Sandy, *6*
Hardrick, Herbert, 45
Harris, Paulo Gregory, 47
Harvey, Karen, 109
Hayden, Dolores, 60
Hayes, Audrey, *28, 171*

Hawkins, John R., 65
Heart Mountain Interpretive Center, 72
Heart Mountain Wyoming Foundation, 71
Heidelberg Project, 118
Henry Ford Museum, 99
Herbst, John, 142
Heye, George Gustav, 68
Hirabayashi, Lane Ryo, 137
historic house museums (HHM), 117–118, 163
historical categories of inquiry, 21, 23, 93
historical context, 2, 8, 27, 109, 113, 119–120, 130, 141
historical method, 1, 2, 23, 40
historical thinking, 21, 23, 26, 29, 31, 33, 46, 47, 92, 113, 123
historiography, 21, 23
history as a practice, 21–23
Historypin, 17, 102
Hoarding: Buried Alive, 58
Holocaust, 83, 126–128
Holum, Suli, 135
Hopi, 69
human subjects, 33, 40, 41
Huxtable, Ada Louise, 60

The Iliad, 130
immersive second-person experience, 115
Imperiled Promise: The State of the National Park Service, 116–117
Independence Hall (recreation), Dearborn, Michigan, 98
Independence Mall, Philadelphia, 125
Indiana University-Purdue University at Indianapolis, 165
informal learning 9, 121
informed consent, 33, 40, 41, 42, 53, 78
Ingoma Foundation, 47
Institute for the Public Understanding of the Past, 16
Institute of Disabilities, Temple University, 135
Institutional Review Board (IRB), 33, 40, 52
International Afro-American Museum of Detroit (Charles H. Wright Museum of African American History), 65

About the Authors

Cherstin M. Lyon is an associate professor of History at California State University, San Bernardino, where she currently serves as coordinator of the MA program in social science and globalization and contributes to the public and oral history program. Lyon studies the history of citizenship and the law from the late nineteenth century through the present. Her first book, *Prisons and Patriots: Japanese American Wartime Citizenship, Civil Disobedience, and Historical Memory*, was published by Temple University Press in 2011. Her next book, *On the Borders of Citizenship*, includes case studies that explore the diversity of quasi-, non-, and limited citizenship in the United States with chapters on Chinese immigrants, American Samoa, Japanese Americans, US-Mexico borderlands, and Native Americans. She regularly works with students and community partners to research immigrant histories, historic preservation, and public outreach in the inland region of Southern California.

Elizabeth M. Nix is an associate professor at the University of Baltimore where she teaches public history. An American Studies graduate of Yale University, Nix received her PhD in American Studies from Boston University. She was part of the steering committee for *Baltimore '68*, which won the American Association of State and Local History's Award of Merit and WOW Award in 2009 and which was the co-winner of the National Council on Public History's Outstanding Project Award in that same year. With project organizers, Nix coedited an anthology entitled *Baltimore '68: Riots and Rebirth in an American City* (Temple University Press, 2011). Her work and interviews have appeared in *The Public Historian*, *The History Teacher*, *Slate*, *Time Magazine*, *New York Times*, *CNN*, and *NPR*.

Rebecca K. Shrum is an assistant professor of History and assistant director of the Public History Program at Indiana University-Purdue University Indianapolis (IUPUI) where she works with both graduate and undergraduate students studying public history. Shrum was previously an Assistant Professor and Director of the Undergraduate Program in Public History at the University of Wisconsin at Whitewater. She received her PhD in 2007 from the University of South Carolina. Her research interests include early American history, material culture and identity, and historic site interpretation. Shrum's published work includes: "Selling Mr. Coffee: Design, Gender, and the Branding of a Kitchen Appliance," published by *Winterthur Portfolio* and *In the Looking Glass: Mirrors and Identity in Early America* (forthcoming in 2017 from Johns Hopkins University Press). Shrum is currently working on a project that explores the interpretation of race and gender at historic sites. Along with local partners, she also directs the IUPUI Public History Program's Curatescape project, Discover Indiana, available at http://www.discoverin.org/. Follow her on Twitter @material_world.